Anne Elizabeth Elbrecht

Telling the Story
The Armenian Genocide in *The New York Times* and *Missionary Herald* 1914-1918

with a foreword by Dickran Kouymjian

Gomidas Institute
London

Published by Taderon Press by special arrangement with the Gomidas Institute.

© 2012 Anne Elizabeth Elbrecht. All Rights Reserved.

ISBN 978-1-903656-36-5

Gomidas Institute
42 Blythe Rd
London W14 0HA
England
Email: *info@gomidas.org*
Web: *www@gomidas.org*

*Dedicated to the Memory of
Richard Allan Elbrecht
1933 - 2008*

Give to the Departed Eternal Rest; Let Light Perpetual Shine upon Them.

Acknowledgements

I owe a great debt to Professor Emeritus Joseph A. Pitti of California State University Sacramento whose devotion to his students is well known. Professor Pitti took the time to read my lengthy manuscript and offered helpful critique which improved the text significantly. Any errors are, however, my own responsibility.

I also want to thank Professor Emeritus Dickran Kouymjian of California State University, Fresno, a devoted friend in times of personal loss, whose interest in this manuscript led me to Mr. Ara Sarafian of the Gomidas Institute. I am most grateful to the Gomidas Institute for publishing this work.

I must also express my appreciation of the help given me by my late husband Richard. He not only encouraged me to learn about the Armenian Genocide, but also willingly endured numerous visits to modern Turkey to see where some of the events described in this work occurred. His photographs of some of the remaining Armenian monuments in Turkey are now available on the web site of the Armenian Studies Program at California State University, Fresno. This work is dedicated to his memory.

Table of Contents

Foreward by Dr. Kouymjian	vii
Preface by Author	xi
Historical Map	xiii
1. Introduction	1
2. The Year 1914	34
3. The Year 1914 1915	48
4. The Year 1914 1916	101
5. The Year 1914 1917	157
6. The Year 1914 1918	189
7. Conclusion	224
Bibliography	227

Forward

A study devoted to the intelligent and detailed exploration of primary sources of a historical event, one in which those sources are not only carefully examined but skillfully compared and contrasted, is always a pleasure to behold. Anne Elbrecht has succeeded wonderfully in this exercise. She has chronicled on almost a daily basis news accounts regarding the Armenian Genocide as reported by the *New York Times* during the five calendar years of World War One, 1914-1918. This work also presents the monthly reporting of the *Missionary Herald*, written by members of a particular but important segment of American Protestant missionary society for their colleagues at home and in the field, as well as their families and church members. The incisive contrast and comparison of style and content, of attitude and involvement, of the events presented to us by the author is fascinating.

In the early 1980's the late Richard Kloian (1937-2010) published a book titled *The Armenian Genocide: News Accounts from the American Press (1915-1922)*. Until this compilation, the quantity of contemporary reports on the Genocide was only known to specialist scholars who painstakingly looked through bound volumes and later microfilm editions of journals. At about the same time as Richard Kloian was meticulously locating and photographing those *Times* articles, I met with the late Andrew "Andy" Shahinian (1919-2005) of New Jersey, a great collector of the paintings of Hovhannes Aivazovsky and of American Impressionists. Andy Shahinian showed me a large scrapped book he had acquired of American newspaper clippings on the Armenian massacres of 1895-6 ordered by Ottoman Sultan Abdul Hamid II. I suggested to Richard Kloian that he contact Andy Shahinian and publish the newspaper reports of those massacres as well. I do not know if Richard Kloian contacted him, but in the 2005 edition of Kloian's work, he added a section on the earlier massacres.

While reading Anne Elbrecht's manuscript, my thoughts also went back even farther when thinking about all the work involved in sifting out the Armenian material from the individual missionary reports in successive issues of the *Missionary Herald*. I had been introduced to that material much earlier through a librarian at the American University of Beirut named Yusuf; his last name has long since eluded me. One day at the AUB Library, Yusuf brought out a set of binders containing paste-ups of photocopies of all articles from the *Herald* on Armenians and the Armenian missions with several devoted to other oriental churches. It was entirely Yusuf's work. His idea was like Andrew Shahinian's: to publish this raw material as a primary source reference easily exploited by scholars.

For years it remained in my imagination as an important "to do." Of course, Anne Elbrecht had no way of knowing this, and as with the *Times*, she went through issue after issue of the *Herald* photocopying the articles relating to Armenians.

These reminiscences from the past invoked by *Telling the Story* are laid out here to illustrate once again that the study of the Armenian Genocide has moved into a stage beyond the gathering and inventory of data and archives. It is now possible to exploit these records, retelling in analytical terms the story and the history they contain, refining a series of discrete incidents into a coherent whole. In the book to hand, two totally different but very consistent sources are evenly exposed in parallel accounts generated by and for Americans far removed from these catastrophic events.

Other scholars have used the information in both *The New York Times* and the *Missionary Herald* to inform studies of the Genocide, but for the first time an analysis of the evolution of the reports of the journalists and the missionaries is presented as the subject of inquiry. Year by year, the text shows the optimism in the face of adversity, a position pitted against the more realistic pessimism toward the fate of the Armenians in the pages of New York's preeminent newspaper.

This year-by-year and place-by-place examination is performed by a researcher completely at home with the subject and its geography: Anne Elbrecht knows well each town and village where the violence inflicted on Armenians was enacted. For two decades she and her husband Richard (1933-2008), photographer and lawyer like herself, made regular trips to Turkey and historic Armenia to carefully photograph what was left of the architectural heritage of Armenians on their abandoned homeland. Over the years they mounted numerous exhibits of the extraordinary photographs at university conferences and churches throughout California. These are now available on a special page "Churches of Historic Armenia: A Legacy to the World" on the website of the Armenian Studies Program at California State University, Fresno (http://armenianstudies2.csufresno.edu/research/

churches/index.shtml). It is this intimacy with the land and the landscape of what was once Armenia that projects an authenticity and authority to her research and writing in a limpid prose of great clarity.

Perhaps most remarkable is the unflinching position that Anne Elbrecht takes toward the reporting of the *Times* and the *Herald*, often underlining the extreme caution of the missionary publication toward its readers. For example: "During most of 1915, the *Times* informed its readership in vivid prose about Armenian affairs on a regular basis. As 1915 drew to a close, the *Herald* recognized that it needed to provide more informative reporting, so that the [American] Board's supporters would be as familiar with the conditions facing the deportees in its Near Eastern mission field as the *Times'* readers were." Throughout there are bits of information that many of us have long forgotten: the precocious use of the term "holocaust" by the *Times* to describe the massacres of Sultan Abdul Hamid in the mid-1890s or reports that Ottoman officials compelled locals in the same period to tell reporters that the inhumane slaughter was the work of Kurds rather than Turkish forces.

Despite the lucid evaluation of the reporting from these two contemporary sources, Anne Elbrecht's *Telling the Story* offers a detailed year by year, month by month, at times day by day unfolding of this first major assault against humanity. One finds this same day by day account in the memoirs of Armenian intellectuals who survived arrest and exile, some recently translated into English: Yervant Odian (1869-1926) *Accursed Years: My Exile and Return from Der Zor, 1914-1919*, London: Gomidas Institute, 2009; Grigoris Balakian (1876-1934), *Armenian Golgotha, A Memoir of the Armenian Genocide, 1915-1918*, New York: Alfred A. Knopf, 2009; Aram Andonian (1875-1952), *Exile, Trauma and Death. On the Road to Chankiri with Komitas Vartabed*, London: Gomidas Institute, 2010. But these individual accounts redeem some of the horrors they describe because in the end these authors escaped or survived. The moral rectitude and gripping collective narrative of Anne Elbrecht's *Telling the Story* offers little relief to the suffering of the Armenians or the duplicity of Ottoman authorities and, unfortunately, the indifference and often political cynicism of the governments of the Allied Powers.

Dickran Kouymjian
Paris, April 2011

Preface

This work stemmed from a vacation in Turkey where my late husband and I visited a one thousand-year-old Armenian church on a small island in historic Armenia, now eastern Turkey. Taken by the beauty of an exterior decorated with reliefs depicting Biblical figures, the church represented a people and culture about which my husband and I knew very little. We had stumbled on to one of the few current reminders of Armenian civilization that had existed in Turkey for millennia before the Armenian Genocide of 1915.

Vaguely aware of the Armenian Genocide of 1915, I wanted to know more about these people, who they had been, how they had lived, and what had happened to them, but I did not know Armenian and found the prospect of learning it daunting. Then, while perusing a card catalog in the California State Library in Sacramento, I stumbled on an account in English of an American missionary who had served in the Ottoman Empire in 1900. I quickly located other missionary accounts and realized that the writings of American missionaries, particularly those who served under the American Board of Commissioners for Foreign Missions (the Board), the missionary arm of the Congregational Church, provided a means to access the information I was seeking. By looking at the content of their monthly publication, the *Missionary Herald* (the *Herald*), I could read the Board's reports of events in Turkey during 1914-1918 and learn about the experiences of Armenian people during an era that encompassed both the First World War and the genocide of Ottoman Armenians. Somewhat skeptical about relying solely on a missionary publication, I also chose to review *The New York Times* (the *Times*), the preeminent American newspaper, to see how that newspaper treated the same events. My review of those two publications for those years resulted in this work.[1]

My overall purpose was to examine the ways two American publications reported the facts about the experiences of Ottoman Armenians during the

---

1. This book was originally written as a Master of Arts Thesis in History at California State University, Sacramento (2008).

war years of 1914-1918, and about the relief efforts launched to save them from annihilation.

The book begins with an introductory review of Ottoman history pertaining to Armenians and the American missionary movement. The introduction provides the context for the textual material of the chapters that follow. Five chapters, one for each year of the war, and a conclusion, make up the rest of the work.

I have limited the scope of the work to events occurring within the Ottoman Empire and the adjacent Caucasus. I have ignored for the most part events in Persia (Iran) and Syria, because most of the missionaries to Persia and Syria were not Board missionaries, but were supported by other mission boards. When news reports about the part of Persia adjoining the Ottoman Empire included information relevant to Ottoman Armenians, I have included them. (The material pertaining to Syria largely relates to the deportations of Armenians who were sent to the Syrian desert.) I have also ignored some peripheral issues that the records address, such as the question of alleged German complicity in the planning and implementation of the Genocide.

For the most part, I have analyzed the source documents without seeking further sources to validate their accuracy. I have, however, relied on my own knowledge of the subject matter resulting from reading secondary sources to evaluate the accuracy of some of the news reporting presented in the two publications.

Throughout my work, I have tried to use the place names used by the documents at the time of their writing. For example, I have used the term "Near East" rather than the current term the "Middle East," because both the publications use the now outdated term "Near East." For place names such as towns or villages, I have followed the same pattern, using the contemporary name followed by the current name in parenthesis after first mention. For example, Istanbul is always referred to as Constantinople in the missionary and newspaper articles reviewed. Similarly, Trabzon is called Trebizond, and Merzifon is designated as Marsovan. I have used several terms to designate the Ottoman Empire, including Turkey, the Empire, and the Ottomans. I have also used the words "relief worker," "missionary," and "relief staff" interchangeably.

To help organize the material, I subdivided the months of each year after the year 1914 into four parts of three months each. For example, January-

March, April-June, July-September, and October-December. While this division makes my work more understandable, it also points out the timing issues when comparing the reporting by a daily newspaper with that of a monthly journal. For example, a January edition of the *Times* might include events that happened in January, but the *Herald*'s reporting of the same event might not be published until its May issue, or later.

As the Introduction explains, I have not addressed the issue of the authenticity of the genocide of Armenians that took place during the war years. Based on a variety of sources, including historian Jay Winter, and genocide scholar Samantha Power, there is no doubt that the elimination of the Armenian population of the Ottoman Empire was planned and carried out by the Ottoman government to create a unitary Turkic state stretching from Constantinople to Central Asia. It is my hope that this work will help readers to better understand the events that befell Armenians in Turkey during the war years of 1914-1918.

Historical Map Showing Location of United States Consular
and Missionary Personnel in Ottoman Turkey, 1915-1917*

* Map based on Joseph Greene, *Leavening the Levant*, Boston: The Pilgrim Press, 1916, p. 2.

HISTORIC ARMENIA IN OTTOMAN TURKE[Y]
also showing United States consu[lates]

THE RUSSIAN EMPIRE AND PERSIA CIRCA 1914*
centers and missionary stations

Chapter 1

INTRODUCTION

By the end of the First World War, the Armenian population of Asiatic Turkey and the Caucasus had been nearly annihilated. During the war, over one million Armenians had been killed, the vast majority of them victims of Turkey's genocidal scheme to create a unified Turkish state in the lands of the Ottoman Empire. Those Armenians who had somehow survived lived largely in subhuman conditions, without the means to feed, clothe, warm, or shelter themselves. Scattered throughout the Russian Caucasus, northern Mesopotamia, and numerous towns and cities of the Ottoman Empire, the surviving Armenians were trying desperately to hold on to life until some relief could rescue them.

Since about one thousand years before Christ, Armenians, an Indo-European people, had lived in the highlands between the Black, Mediterranean, and Caspian Seas.[1] Known for the scorching heat of its summers and the biting cold of its winters, their lands were nevertheless fertile enough for agriculture, at which Armenians excelled. Toward the end of the first millennium, Armenians also began to occupy the land located in the northeast corner of the Mediterranean Sea called Cilicia.

Although at times Armenians were self-governing, their location astride international crossroads – "at the confluence of warring imperialist tribes" – guaranteed that their history would include repeated invasions, forced emigration, destruction, and slaughter.[2] After each devastation, they would somehow renew themselves, only to be ravaged again.[3]

Despite these depredations, and the potential for assimilation by the conquering peoples, they maintained their identity as a people separate from those surrounding them.[4] Part of Armenians' sense of difference stemmed from their conversion to Christianity in about 301 C. E. by an evangelist named Gregory, after which Armenians were called "Gregorians."[5] While the distinction of being Christian was a source of communal pride, it set them apart from their pagan neighbors and later from the various Muslim groups that invaded Armenia.[6]

Among the invaders moving into Armenia were Turkic, nomadic peoples whose origins in the steppes of Central Asia remain shrouded in mystery.

Their abandonment of paganism and embrace of Islam provided these nomadic tribes with a way of life and an understanding of men's relations with God and each other.[7] Pushing westward into the lands of what is now Iran, Iraq, and Turkey, the Seljuk Turks confronted the Byzantine Army, and inflicted a decisive defeat at the famous battle of Manzikert (Malazgirt) in western Armenia in 1071.[8] The Seljuk victories in turn opened the way for further Turkic penetration into Asia Minor and guaranteed that Armenians would be living within an Empire in which they would be a religious minority relegated to a subordinate social status.[9]

It was left to another Turkic tribe, the Ottomans, to continue to overcome the Byzantine hegemony in Asia Minor and to gradually extend their control into Europe.[10] At a slow but steady pace, the Ottomans expanded their conquests, gradually encircling the Byzantine capital, Constantinople. The city finally fell to the Ottomans under the leadership of Sultan Mehmet in 1453.[11] After a day of looting,[12] Mehmet set about restoring order and beginning the reconstruction of the city.[13]

Mehmet projected himself as the heir of a dynasty linked to previous rulers of a great Islamic past, a sovereign in whose person Turkic, Islamic and Byzantine traditions were unified, and whose Empire must therefore embody a rule of law based on the secular and religious precepts of Islam.[14] Accordingly, Mehmet developed "codes" that covered all aspects of government and society in a manner that previous Islamic rulers had never attempted or accomplished.[15]

The conquest of Constantinople and the consolidation of Ottoman power raised the question of the way the subject peoples of the Ottoman Empire, including the non-Muslim minorities, should be governed. About twenty-five percent of the population was Christian, of which Armenians were a majority.[16] Because they were conquered peoples, the non-Muslim minorities, called the *dhimmi*, could never be granted the privileges accruing to first-class citizens of the Empire. But as believers of one the other monotheistic faiths, they could live unmolested with the rights to property ownership, livelihood, and freedom of worship, as long as they accepted Islam's political authority over them.[17]

According to tradition, Mehmet established the *millet* system, the "term commonly used to describe the institutional framework governing relations between the Ottoman state and its large and varied non-Muslim population."[18] This system of organization allegedly established self-governing *millets* in which minorities, Greeks, Armenians, and Jews, preserved their own laws and practices under the leadership of a religious head, who was responsible in turn to the Sublime Porte[19] for the administration and good behavior of his people.[20] The non-Muslims also had to pay a special tax, the *jizya,* or poll tax, from which Muslims were exempt.[21] The state granted considerable autonomy to the heads of the *millets*, particularly in matters of religious observance, education, and personal status (birth, marriage, death, and inheritance). In addition to this autonomy, the leaders of the *millets* could call upon the civil officials of the Ottoman Empire to enforce a leader's decision upon an "errant flock."[22]

This scheme, according to the traditional view, meant that the Porte would not have to deal with individual Christians and Jews, but only with the titular head of their religious community.[23] Religion, therefore, provided a means of organizing society, and a way of establishing an individual's larger political community; those outside the *millet* had no way to engage the Ottoman state on their behalf.[24] But the conceptualization of the *millets* that asserts that their members lived apart in "sharply divided, mutually impenetrable religious communities" is "fundamentally wrong on almost every score."[25]

Recent studies of non-Muslim life in the Empire have critiqued these long-unquestioned assumptions about the workings of the *millet* system, pointing out that non-Muslim accounts about the *millets* were written centuries after the events that they claim to describe. In addition, scholars have challenged the notion that non-Muslims only used their communal courts except in those instances when they were engaging in legal matters with the state, or with others not of their faith.[26] Moreover, the leaders of the *millets*, the patriarchs and the chief rabbi, in fact exercised far less jurisdiction over their *raya* than that alleged by traditional accounts.[27] Furthermore, although the *millet* system theoretically applied throughout the Empire, the practicable application of the laws governing the *dhimmi* varied greatly throughout the Empire's long history.[28]

Judicial records provide one way of discerning how the *millet* system functioned, as a study of the workings of a local court in Aintab (Gaziantep) for the year September 1540 to October 1541 demonstrates. By that time, the Empire's European and western Asiatic territorial base had more than doubled through the acquisition of further territories to the east and southeast, including Syria, Palestine, Egypt, and the Hijaz. As a result of this expansion, the Ottoman Empire had become the dominant power in the eastern Mediterranean and the greatest Muslim power in that era.[29] The provincial capital of Aintab and the surrounding region profited greatly by its location at the intersection of significant trade routes southward to Syria, Palestine, and Egypt, and eastward to what is now Iraq, Iran and the Persian Gulf. Despite the presence of various peoples, including *dhimmi*, in other parts of the Empire, the population of Aintab contained only a very small non-Muslim population, almost all Christian Armenians.[30]

The judicial decisions in civil disputes and criminal prosecutions in Aintab during 1540-1541 reveal that the activities of the court at the local level were far more complex than either Ottoman or Islamic law would suggest.[31] In addition, the court's disposition of those cases shows not only how local political economies and social practices functioned, but also the kinds of strategies that the people appearing before the court devised to respond to the court's intervention in their lives.[32]

Necessarily, the judge's decisions rested on the input that he received from members of the community.[33] The Aintab community's assistance to the court not only consisted of the testimony of witnesses, but also the mediation of disputes and ratification of decisions, thus ensuring public support for the judge's determinations.[34] Court records show that disputes in Aintab were also resolved by community leaders of many kinds, such as religious authorities, neighborhood and village headmen, tribal elders, urban magnates, and local officials such as the governor or chief of police.

The records resulting from the Aintab court's adjudications reveal that the business transacted in this local court was far more complex than either Ottoman or Islamic law would suggest.[35] Although the court endeavored to provide justice to the poor and lowly, individual rights sometimes had to be compromised in order to protect the social order of the community.[36] Moreover, despite the commitment to justice, the records show that the court devoted less effort to cases involving the impoverished, women, non-Muslims, slaves, and members of tribal societies.[37]

The Aintab decisions also demonstrate that the women of that community used the court frequently. Both Islamic and imperial law, however, reinforced the societal and religious view of women as subordinate to men. Consequently, obstacles faced by women when using the Aintab court required them to develop methods that enabled them to obtain their rights.[38]

Despite their small number, the Armenians of Aintab used the court frequently to authenticate routine business transactions, most of which involved their Muslim colleagues. Perhaps these Armenians believed that court endorsement of a business transaction might give them better recourse should the Muslim in some way not perform as agreed.

The Aintab Armenians also employed the court to mediate such delicate matters as a wife's alleged sexual indiscretions or a quarrel between brothers.[39] Other examples of Armenian use of the Muslim court include divorcing a wife for failing to observe the Muslim requirement of segregation of women from men (called "*muhaddere;*");[40] obtaining a court order for the partition of property jointly owned by an Armenian man and his brother;[41] divorcing according to Muslim practice, with the wife renouncing her claim to property in exchange for custody of the children; and seeking the court's ratification of a "mutual guarantorship" of Armenians established to obtain and administer the local tavern's tax-farm.[42] An Armenian man also looked to the Muslim court to enforce a promise made by another Armenian to marry his daughter.[43]

The court's decisions suggest that the Armenians like the Muslims viewed the court as a means of help in managing the day to day business of their lives.[44] They also reveal that the Armenians were a socially diverse group, ranging from pillars of the small community to troublemakers, and even an alleged murderer.[45]

The system of judicial governance in the Arab areas of the Empire may have functioned for non-Muslims much like the court in Aintab.[46] The Jewish *millet* in Jerusalem, for example, had since the sixteenth century selected their own rabbis, whose names would then be registered with Jerusalem's chief qadi, as the community's political and religious leaders.[47] In the Ottoman province of Basra, Jews followed a similar procedure, electing the leader to represent the community and registering him with the Muslim authorities. Although the chief secular leader in Baghdad was selected without input from the community, his recognition by the court allowed him to wield considerable political power in the community.[48] Nor was this practice of registering local officials limited to Jews. In seventeenth century Aleppo, for example, large delegations of Christian laymen appeared before the local *qadi,* to identify their leaders, including a metropolitan who had been selected outside the church's traditional synods.[49] Once a religious group was registered with the *qadi*, its leadership could look to the Muslim authorities for aid in enforcing its own communal internal discipline.[50]

Non-Muslims living in Damascus in the eighteenth and nineteenth centuries found use of the Muslim courts of that city to be a strategic necessity, because the court served as the registry and depository of all official documentation and maintained a pragmatic approach to marital and familial issues. Consequently, non-Muslims necessarily became skilled in Islamic legal practice.[51] "[I]ndifference, perhaps tinged with contempt ..., rather than overt hostility seems to have been the emotional norm governing intercommunal relations in the period before the sectarian outbursts of the nineteenth century."[52]

A study of the judicial rulings (*fatwas*) issued by a centralized Ottoman court with jurisdiction over lower courts describes similar flexibility. A prominent jurist, Ebussuud Efendi, issued *fatwas* that illustrate the "complex web of social relationships connecting Muslims, Christians, and Jews in the Ottoman Empire."[53] Although Ebussuud denigrated non-Muslims by referring to them as "infidels" and asserted that Muslims must not speak the language of non-Muslims, he also found that gestures of friendship between Christians and Muslims such as receiving red eggs at Easter or reciprocal sharing of sacrificial meat at Bayram might be acceptable.[54] Another jurist favored the non-Muslim minorities and defended those Sufi masters who had been criticized for their leniency towards the non-Muslims of the Empire.[55] Yet the courts were not universally well disposed to minority litigants. While certain cases suggest that Christians could bring breach of contract cases and requests for divorce for adjudication, a Muslim murder of a Christian was left unaddressed and without penalty because only Christian witnesses were available to testify to it.[56] While these examples of non-Muslim use of the Muslim courts suggest a relaxed tolerance of Christians and Jews, the impact of European merchants on local economies, coupled with rising European military power, would slowly undermine the relationships between Muslims and Christians within the Empire.[57]

By the seventeenth century, the Ottoman Empire held vast lands in western Asia, North Africa, and southeastern Europe. Although Ottoman armies had been repelled when trying to conquer Vienna in 1529 and 1683, the Ottomans had occupied southeastern Europe for two hundred years or more.[58] They held most parts of the present-day countries of Turkey, Syria, Lebanon, Iraq, Israel, Palestine, Jordan, and Saudi Arabia until 1922.[59] The growth of the Empire's size created new opportunities for trade and other forms of commerce in which members of the *millets* could engage.

One century later, the Empire continued to be a polyglot of peoples. The population of the Asiatic provinces was largely Muslim, mostly Turks, Kurds, and Arabs, with significant Christian and Jewish minorities, while in the Balkans, the composition of the population was reversed; the majority was Christian with large Muslim minorities.[60] Moreover, although Islam was theoretically "one and indivisible," Muslims in the Empire included not only the predominant Sunnis, but also Shia.[61] But the Empire's toleration of all of its minorities would be tested in the years to come.

In a sixteenth century attempt to curb the influence of the Venetian traders, the sultan had entered into an agreement with France, called a "capitulation," granting that nation special dispensations for trade, usually in the form of lower than customary tariffs.[62] By the end of the eighteenth century, almost every western nation had a capitulatory treaty with the Empire. These agreements not only granted those realms exemption from Ottoman taxes and custom duties, but also granted the European merchants exemption from Islamic provisions pertaining to their personal status and permitted them to reside in areas of the Empire previously prohibited.[63] Moreover, they could call upon their home countries to support them whenever they had disputes with the Ottoman authorities.[64] The presence of these Europeans also led to penetration of the Empire by both Catholic and Protestant missionaries. Contact with the West also resulted in the rise of a class of "notables," Christians, Jews, and Muslims who possessed money and influence, some of whom were Ottoman governors, rich merchants or bankers, large landholders, or religious dignitaries, who could assert power and force the government to accept them as intermediaries.[65]

The nineteenth century brought about a radical restructuring of the Empire. Recognizing that the loss of Greece in the War of Independence and Mohammad Ali's seizure of power in Egypt signaled rapid decline, the Ottomans launched a series of reforms to modernize and westernize both the regime and the society of the Empire.[66] But at the same time that the Empire initiated programs of reform, fresh views of society, religion, and politics kept seeping into the realm as a result of the burgeoning European contact. Ottoman Christians began to freely embrace the innovations espoused by the westerners, further distancing themselves socially, economically, and even psychologically from their Muslim neighbors.[67] As the minorities began to emulate and adopt European concepts of national identity, they also began to abandon the religious identity of the *millet* system that had for so long organized the Empire, and to embrace the view that only through their sectarian identities could they achieve political rights.[68] The deterioration of the Muslims' position as a result of European capital, Great Power intervention in internal Ottoman affairs, and the reforms sought by the Ottoman state helped promote the rapid decline of inter-communal relations.[69]

At the same time, contention arose among the various denominations of Christians, especially between Catholic and Orthodox Christians. As Catholics within the Empire sought to achieve *millet* status, the Orthodox clergy lobbied the Porte and reminded it that the conquering Mehmet had established three millets only.[70] Greek gold coupled with the reluctance to go against the traditions of the past temporarily suppressed the call for a Catholic *millet*, thus allowing the Orthodox Patriarch to maintain the same level of power for the time being.[71] The sultans may also have supported the Orthodox position because of fears that the Catholics might be a "fifth column," providing additional opportunities to meddle in the Muslim Empire.[72] After many years of conflict, the Porte finally recognized three new *millets*: an Armenian Catholic *millet* in 1831,[73] a Melkite Catholic *millet* in 1848,[74] and a Protestant *millet* in 1847.[75]

At the same time, the evolution of the Ottoman commercial economy and the European influence on the economy that occurred in the eighteenth and early nineteenth centuries were just a few of the early signs of the social and political disarray that the Empire suffered throughout the nineteenth century. Selim III, a reforming sultan who began his reign in 1789, tried to introduce the kinds of changes that would help the Empire move forward. These innovations included a strengthened military, a rational taxation system, and increased power of the central government against internal as well as external enemies.[76] Conservative forces induced his deposition in May, 1897, on the basis that his reforms violated the tenets of Islam.[77]

His successor, Sultan Mahmut II, and his son, Abdulmecit, instituted reforms more successfully.[78] The reform decrees of 1839 and 1856, known collectively as the *Tanzimat*, proposed to end corruption, abolish tax farming, and establish full equality for all subjects in the eyes of the state and each other.[79] They introduced a modern bureaucracy, language training, military reforms, and a larger standing army. A procedure created by the reformers allowed the central government and an assembly of clerics and laity to periodically review the status of the *millets* and helped break the clerical stranglehold over them.[80]

Yet in extending conscription to all males, including non-Muslims, while permitting only non-Muslims to purchase exemptions, the reformers created resentment amongst Muslims who were required to risk their lives to serve the Empire, while Christians were not.[81] In addition, while the introduction of the telegraph, railroads, and photography permitted the state to upgrade its transportation and communication methods, it also enabled the government to establish networks of spies to control, weaken, and destroy domestic rivals.[82] Nevertheless, the reforms were ultimately incorporated in a constitution in 1876, in which Christians, Jews, and Muslims were all to enjoy the status and benefits of Ottoman citizens without discrimination.[83]

Despite the western stereotype of the "shrewd and crafty Armenian merchant," most Armenians in the Ottoman Empire were peasants.[84] The financial and other burdens imposed on the powerless Armenian rural population were horrendous. These included "onerous taxation, corvee, misuse of their lands by others, illegal appropriation of their products, expropriation, forced loans, and cheap labor."[85] The rural Armenians were required to pay a variety of exploitive taxes: the tithe, supposedly ten percent of the annual produce, but often collected at a higher rate, ranging from twelve and one-half percent to as high as fifty percent; property taxes imposed on houses, land – including pasturage, animals and fruit-bearing trees; and special taxes on births, marriages, deaths, transfers of goods, and the use of roads.[86] The amount of the taxes varied from year to year, their arbitrary nature causing extra hardship to the hard-pressed taxpayers.[87] In addition, the Ottomans often imposed exceptional war taxes to help pay for military ventures, but once a war tax was assessed, however, it continued indefinitely, thus creating a permanent levy.

Added with all of these payments to the Ottoman tax farmer were taxes paid to local Turkish or Kurdish aghas for village "protection". Armenians were subject to other burdens as well. In many regions, Kurdish nomads pastured sheep and cattle on Armenian lands, destroying cultivated fields and orchards. Every summer, for example, some twenty-four Kurdish tribes migrated from Mosul to Van to graze their sheep.[88]

Armenian peasants were also subjected to political oppression. Whether landless and poor, or landowning and well off, as *dhimmi*, Armenians had no claim to political rights. Moreover, by the nineteenth century, the term "raya," or "flock," had been redefined as "cattle," illustrating the contempt felt towards them by their Muslim overlords. At the same time, intercommunal relations declined far more quickly than in the past, further restricting the opportunity to rectify these injustices.[89]

In contrast to the rural population, some members of the urban Christian population continued to prosper economically through their commercial contacts in Europe and elsewhere.[90] The economic success of the Christians was exacerbated in the Muslims' eyes, not only by the visible presence of foreigners doing business, but also by the grant to Ottoman non-Muslims of "*berats*." These certificates gave the holders the same tax benefits and privileges as granted by the capitulatory treaties, including exemptions from the jurisdiction of the Ottoman courts.[91] Because these agreements had acquired treaty status, European opposition thwarted Ottoman attempts to withdraw some of the privileges granted by the capitulations and *berats*.[92]

The Muslim population observing these innovations experienced a profound sense of unease as it contemplated a new world no longer based on immutable principles, a society in which the earlier laws governing Christian-Muslim relations had been altered at their expense.[93] Especially galling were the building of new churches, the presence of public religious processions, and the Christians' alliance with the despised yet powerful Europeans.[94]

The Ottoman province of Mount Lebanon provided a miniature version of the complexities faced by a multi-confessional society and the pressures upon it. By 1860, the Druze notables, the Maronite sheikhs, and the Maronite Church all benefitted from communal understandings that did not pit one against the other. The episodes of violence that broke out in Lebanon and Syria, however, reflected a new political orientation in which groups saw their separation as more meaningful than their common experience.[95] Muslim anger there exploded, resulting in eruptions of violence in the nineteenth century against their Christian neighbors, most notably in Lebanon and Damascus (1860), but also in the cities of Aleppo (1850), Mosul (1854), Nablus (1854), Jedda (1858), and in Egypt (1882).[96] The riots reflected the end of a commitment to the multi-confessional society and the rise of sectarian identity as the only "viable marker of political reform and the only authentic basis for political claims."[97]

Christian elites in the nineteenth century further articulated and refined their religious identity, through which they sought political power.[98]

Europeans who believed their role was to reform and humanize the Ottoman Empire failed to understand the underlying philosophy of the Empire in which the multi-ethnic and multi-religious peoples lived together peacefully. Instead, they viewed the Empire as a large Muslim state with a significant number of persecuted Christians scattered throughout the Empire's various cities and provinces. Referring to the minorities as the "subjugated classes," the Europeans saw reforming the Muslim state as part of their "civilizing mission."[99] They attributed the nineteenth century's rise in violence to Islam, which they considered to be inherently bigoted, and failed to look for other causes.[100] The Ottomans, however, believed that the changes they sought to make through the Tanzimat programs of reform would resolve the problems of the Empire by creating a centralized, modern economy, able to compete with the European powers.[101]

The arrival of Protestant missionaries from Germany, Britain and the United States in the mid-nineteenth century exerted additional pressures on the established Ottoman order.[102] While the missionaries offered new educational opportunities to the people in the Empire, they also exacerbated separatist tendencies in the *millets*, especially within the Armenian *millets* where they had their greatest success.[103] But by preaching that the traditional Christianity practiced by the Armenian Church was a backward, paganistic form of Christianity, the missionaries helped to further diminish the power of the Armenian *millet*.[104] When the missionaries helped the Protestant Armenians obtain their own *millet* in 1847, the unity of the Armenians' religious identity was further shattered.

The breakdown of the *millet* system occurred while territorial changes continued to roil the Empire. In Balkan, Anatolian, and Arab provinces alike, new movements emerged that advocated breaking away from the Empire altogether. Territory was no longer lost by military defeat, but instead by revolts and rebellions against the sultan by his own subjects.[105] In Serbia, for example, a local prince with the support of Russia established a claim of hereditary rule in 1817; Serbia's independence was confirmed by the Treaty of Berlin in 1878.[106] Bessarabia was similarly separated from the Ottomans by the Treaty of Bucharest.[107] As these territorial losses mounted in the nineteenth century, the central government in Constantinople tried to stem the Empire's decline, exercising greater control over the outlying provinces. Yet influences beyond the Empire's control continued to promote its breakup.

Fiscal matters became crucial. Despite the excessive tax burdens placed on the Empire's agrarian population, the revenues lost through inefficiency and rampant greed left the Ottomans unable to maintain their armies and to sustain the Empire. Consequently, the Ottomans in the mid-nineteenth century began to borrow heavily from European bankers and Ottoman Christian bankers. When, however, the Empire was unable to repay the loans, the Porte permitted the lenders to establish the Turkish "Debt Administration," a consortium of foreign creditors who supervised part of the Ottoman economy, and directed the revenues received to repay the loans. By 1870, the debt service cost one-third of the Empire's revenues. A large part of the new borrowing was devoted to paying the interest and the principal on earlier loans.[108] To help reduce its debt, the Ottomans offered investment in public utilities and ports as security, thus further accelerating their dependence on their creditors.[109] Yet the Europeans wanted to keep the Empire intact. While a revolt by an Ottoman province might meet with success here or there, the international community, fearful of Ottoman disintegration or Russian expansion into Ottoman lands, would convene a conference, and "undo the worst results but allow some losses to ensue."[110]

By the end of the nineteenth century, the Empire was very much diminished. It had initially lost vast territories to Russia in the war of 1877-8, but the European Powers intervened, radically reducing Russian gains in the Treaty of Berlin of 1878. Nevertheless, the treaty declared that Serbia, Montenegro, and Rumania would be independent, acknowledging political realities; Bosnia and Herzegovina would remain nominally Ottoman, although already independent; one-third of Bulgaria would become independent; and Cyprus would be ceded to Britain. Most important for the Armenians would be the transfer to Russia of the three easternmost vilayets in Anatolia, the provinces of Kars, Ardahan, and Beyazit, where large numbers of Armenians lived.[111]

While parts of the Ottoman Empire were being peeled off, Armenians still saw themselves as Ottomans and continued to petition the Porte for relief from corrupt officials and predatory tribes that plagued them. Except for a few rebellions such as that in Zeitun in 1862, Armenians remained the "loyal millet."[112] But the accession of Sultan Abdul Hamid II posed grave problems for Armenians. Although he had sworn to uphold the 1876 constitution created by the reformers, the new sultan prorogued the constitution and parliament and ruled as an absolute monarch for the next thirty years.[113]

The years of Abdul Hamid's reign were tumultuous. Ever fearful of deposition, he expanded the telegraph network, allowing him to monitor his subjects throughout the Empire. He also granted a concession to the Baghdad Railway Company, whose parent corporation was the Deutsche Bank, to expand rail service to Baghdad, perhaps so that troops could be quickly moved to rebellious provinces.[114] Whatever his intent, these innovations helped modernize the Empire, because they increased transportation and communication throughout his realm. But the sultan also fostered large scale corruption, rewarding his favorites, and impeding every attempt to implement the reforms of the *Tanzimat*.[115]

Because the heralded reforms had failed to materialize for Armenians, popular discontent and eventually rebellion spread gradually through parts of that community. The overwhelming majority of Armenians, however, continued to view themselves as Ottomans.[116] Armenian youth came home from study abroad imbued with western principles of liberty and self-government, but their attempts to introduce these ideas to the tradition-bound Armenian populace met with little success. The youth continued, however, to agitate for reform and began to initiate demonstrations demanding the rights guaranteed by the constitution, as well as unsuccessfully imploring the western powers to intervene. Looking at the nations in the Balkans that had successfully separated themselves from the Empire, some Armenians began to form political parties that would work not only for change, but also for independence.[117]

Abdul Hamid responded with an iron fist. He instituted centrally directed massacres that took place between September, 1895 and January, 1896 in Constantinople, Trebizond (Trabzon), Erzerum, Harpoot, Aintab, Marash, Urfa (Sanliurfa), and other locations. Some 100,000 Armenians were killed in an orgy of clubbings, knifings, and mutilations, while countless others were left destitute, having lost their homes, occupations, and lands.[118] Armenians waited in vain for some kind of European intervention to rein in the sultan.[119]

Disillusioned by the lack of European support, some Armenians began to form small guerrilla bands, usually led by a charismatic revolutionary, to try to punish local Muslims for their attacks on Armenians.[120] Despite the satisfaction felt by the local Armenians at these attacks, the limited size of the groups involved when contrasted with the power of the Empire produced nothing more than the mosquito's sting of an elephant. Moreover, the attacks invited harsh Ottoman response.

At the same time that the sultan ignored Europe's complaints about his treatment of his subjects, he looked to Germany for support. Germany had long cultivated its relationship with the Ottoman Empire. The Kaiser himself, sometimes described as "vain, unbalanced, and dictatorial,"[121] had come to Constantinople in both 1889 and in 1898, the latter visit occurring after the Armenian massacres of 1895. German military advisors also came to Constantinople to provide the kinds of military training that would revitalize the Ottoman Army and win Turkish support for Germany's policies.[122]

Although two armed attempts had tried to remove the sultan after he suspended the constitution, neither was successful. Nevertheless, a secret society based in Paris had been formed, spurred on by the internal suppression of the constitution and its liberties and the international repugnance expressed toward the sultan for the 1895-1896 massacres. Eventually called the Committee of Union and Progress (hereafter the CUP),[123] the group of reformers planned a coup for September, 1896, to capitalize on the unpopularity of the sultan; they were, however, betrayed, arrested, and for the most part sent into internal exile.[124] The CUP movement seemed to be over.[125]

In September 1906, another organization, the "Ottoman Freedom Society" was founded in Salonica, home base of the Ottoman Third Army. Many Army officers and bureaucrats, including Mehmet Talaat, a high level postal official, enrolled in secret cells of the society. Aligning loosely with the CUP, they sought the restoration of the constitution and the deposition of Abdul Hamid, while retaining the dynasty.[126] Armenian politicians agreed to support the reformers' efforts.[127] By 1908, the CUP asserted that its cell membership had reached at least 15,000 in Macedonia.[128]

The same year, mutiny broke out in Macedonia and spread to the capital, resulting in the CUP's seizure of control of the government.[129] To save his throne, the sultan was forced to reinstate the suspended 1876 Constitution. The reformers, including Armenians, were jubilant. After the failure of an attempted counter-revolution, led by forces loyal to the sultan, Abdul Hamid was deposed, and his younger brother, Mehmet V, was installed in his place.[130] Armenians again supported the new regime, optimistically expecting that their long suffering in the Ottoman Empire had ended.[131]

After 1909, the sultan "reigned but did not rule." Five of the CUP's members were ministers in the cabinet, including the Minister of the Interior, Talaat, and the Minister of Finance, Javid Bey. Subsequent elections of the deputies for parliament were "rigged" so that only a handful of non-CUP deputies were returned.[132] Several small wars, followed by the Balkan wars of 1912-1913, continued to plague the Young Turks, causing feelings of unstoppable dismemberment.[133] Faced with the continuing erosion of the Empire's territories, Enver, an army officer and one of the heroes of 1908, staged a coup in 1913, promising to save the state from further losses.[134] A triumvirate of Enver, Talaat, and Jemal now ruled the Empire.[135]

Under the CUP's regime, Ottomanism, the equality of all Ottoman subjects, without regard to ethnicity or religion, was replaced by a newer idea, Turkism, in which every man in the Empire was to be made conscious of belonging to the Turkish "nation." Since a modernized Islam was an essential part of the concept of Turkism, the Armenians and other Christians living in the Empire were necessarily excluded.[136]

Because the situation of Armenians had not improved, they continued to request European intervention in Turkey to protect them from the ongoing depredations they were experiencing. Finally, through a 1914 compromise agreement by all six European powers, including Germany and Austria-Hungary, the Europeans forced the Young Turks to permit two European inspectors-general to live in the eastern provinces of the Ottoman Empire to observe the Young Turks' actions against Armenians, Greeks, Assyrians, and other Christians.

The inspectors-general, one from Norway and the other from the Netherlands, arrived in Turkey in 1914 to take up their posts.[137] Armenians were again full of hope that their sufferings in the Ottoman Empire were over. But before the inspectors-general could begin to work, the First World War broke out. The inspectors-general returned to their own countries immediately.

Perhaps dreaming of a greater Ottoman Empire, and the reconquest of territories lost, the CUP entered into an alliance with the Central Powers of Germany and Austria-Hungary during the First World War. But the CUP had backed the losing side in the conflict. At the war's conclusion, the five hundred-year Ottoman Empire was no more.

During the first quarter of the nineteenth century, a radical movement emerged in the United States that would affect not only the Ottoman

Empire, but many other parts of the world as well. While sheltered in a haystack to seek refuge from a sudden, summer shower, Samuel J. Mills, Jr. and a few fellow students from Williams College, Massachusetts, prayed together. During what later came to be called the "Haystack Prayer Meeting of 1806," the young men dedicated themselves to serve as Protestant missionaries in foreign lands.[138] The concept of missionaries in overseas fields was a new idea in the United States. Previously, the missionary efforts of American Protestants had focused on converting the "heathen" of North America, the Native Americans.[139]

To prepare himself for foreign service, Mills attended Andover Seminary, founded as a counterweight to the Unitarian influence at Harvard College. But when he and similarly interested students approached the leaders of the Congregational Church for help in establishing foreign missions, they were told that their proposals smacked of "infatuation."[140] Persevering, Mills and his colleagues had, by 1810, organized themselves formally and obtained support for foreign missions from a group of local ministers. Together, they incorporated the organization known as the American Board of Commissioners for Foreign Missions (the Board),[141] whose aim was "to evangelize the heathen in foreign lands."[142] Wildly successful, at its height the Board employed missionaries all over the globe.[143] In its first fifty years alone the Board sent out over 1,250 missionaries, men and women who had been trained in the classical tradition, and knew Latin, Greek, and Hebrew. This training in the structure of language gave the missionaries the skills necessary to learn the new languages required of them.[144]

To initiate their Near Eastern mission, two Board missionaries, Levi Parsons and Pliny Fisk, set sail in November, 1819, from Boston for Turkey to conduct explorations about the feasibility of evangelism in the Levant. Landing at Smyrna (Izmir), Turkey, they traveled in the Near East, including Palestine, where they explored starting a mission to convert the Jews. Failing to make any converts, they decided that such missionary efforts would most likely be ineffective. Turning to the Muslims instead, they quickly learned that a Muslim's conversion to Christianity created an insurmountable problem: it was against the law to convert from Islam and doing so was punishable by death.[145] With no prospects of success with Jews or Muslims, the missionaries instead began to look at the established Christian churches, including those of the Armenians (Gregorians), Nestorians,[146] Greeks, and Syrians.

The missionaries' evaluation of the Gregorian Church was harsh. These churches, stated Edwin Munsell Bliss, a veteran Board missionary, employed charms, relics, and miraculous pictures; they conducted idolatrous rites in unknown languages; and the clergy was "ignorant and bigoted."[147] Nevertheless, in the cities, a number of Armenian men expressed an interest in the evangelical faith promoted by the Protestant missionaries. By expanding the number of revitalized Armenians worshiping as God intended, the missionaries reasoned, pressure would be exerted on the Gregorian Church to reform.[148] These revitalized Armenian Christians would serve as such splendid examples of Christian living that the Muslims too would be stirred to seek such a faith for themselves, the missionaries hoped.[149]

The Gregorian Church, however, did not take kindly to the meetings of prayer and worship conducted by the Protestant missionaries and attended by small numbers of Armenians. The success of the missionaries aroused the ire of the Armenian Patriarch. In 1846, the Patriarch issued an anathema and bull of excommunication against those Gregorians who sought spiritual guidance from the missionaries. The Patriarch's order meant that all Gregorians were forced to end any contact at all with the new believers. Although the missionaries were reluctant to establish a new church, the Patriarch's orders forced them to rethink this issue. In November 1847, just one year later, a Protestant church with its own millet was formed,[150] a result in part of support from the Ambassador of Great Britain to Turkey, Lord Cowley.[151]

Under the missionaries' tutelage, the Protestant movement spread rapidly throughout Ottoman Turkey, Syria, Persia, Armenia, and Kurdistan.[152] The Board chose cities for mission work that were surrounded by large populations, and where the climate was considered adequately healthy for Americans.[153] By 1860, the missionaries had organized forty Protestant churches and twenty two fully operational mission stations throughout Ottoman Turkey.[154] Since Bible study was at the heart of the missionaries' evangelical faith, the missionaries realized they had not only to establish a printing press to furnish Bibles in the local languages, but also to provide schools to teach children to read.[155] One of the unique features of the Board's program in Turkey was the education of girls. As early as 1860, girls' boarding schools had been established at Constantinople, Harpoot, Marash, Marsovan, Mardin, Bitlis, Aintab, and Erzerum,[156] an enviable record in a country where many maintained that girls could never learn to read!

The missionaries also realized that they needed colleges and seminaries – institutions of higher learning at which young Armenian men and women would get the kind of Christian education needed to prepare them for service as teachers, college instructors, pastors, and evangelists.[157] Since serving the sick represented part of their Christian message, the missionaries also established hospitals with well-trained physicians to provide needed medical care.[158] By 1914, the Board operated nine mission hospitals in Turkey.[159]

Gradually, the hostility between the missionaries and the Gregorian clergy subsided. The children of both Gregorian and Protestant parents who sent their children to the same schools would meet at school functions and become acquainted, easing some of the tension. Some of the Gregorians went so far as to study for the Gregorian priesthood in the Protestant missionary colleges. In addition, the missionaries were often asked to speak at Gregorian services, thus demonstrating to the congregants that few differences existed in religious authority between the Protestants and Gregorians.[160]

In addition to the missionaries, other Americans resided in the Ottoman Empire. The United States maintained an embassy in Constantinople staffed by an ambassador, as well as a number of consular offices in several Ottoman cities. Some of the consular officials operated in the more remote parts of the Empire. Despite the long distances separating the ambassador from these consuls, he maintained regular, confidential contact with them by cipher. The reports the consuls filed with the ambassador kept him informed about the events in their localities and especially about the well-being of Americans working in their consular districts.

By the beginning of the twentieth century, the Board operated twelve stations and 270 outstations in "Asiatic Turkey;" by 1913 its staff numbered 209.[161] The presence of this number of foreigners did not, however, moderate Turkish hostility towards Armenians. When the Ottoman Empire joined the Central Powers in declaring war against Russia, France, and Great Britain, the diplomats, businessmen, and missionaries from those countries went home. So did the inspectors-general who were to oversee the treatment of Armenians. Turkey was now free to launch its genocidal destruction of the Armenian people without intervention by any other power. Yet because the United States was not yet a belligerent in the First World War, its diplomats and missionaries remained in the Ottoman Empire.

In 1915, the Young Turks attacked the Ottoman Armenian populations with unparalleled ferocity, setting into motion a mass murder that will remain the most indelible and dark recollection in the modern history of the Armenian people.[162] Turkish actions against the conscripted Armenian soldiers serving in the Ottoman Army signaled the first salvos in the process of extermination. In the last ten days of February 1915, the Turks disarmed these soldiers and transferred them to labor battalions where they were subsequently worked to death.[163] Consequently, the healthy young Armenian men were eliminated early on so that they could provide no resistance to any action taken by the authorities. Soon after, the Young Turk leadership unleashed their plan to eliminate most of the Armenians of Turkey. The genocidal scheme involved deporting Armenians to locations far from their homes where they would be without food, water, and shelter of any kind.[164] The Young Turks initiated the operation by serving the first order of deportation on April 8, 1915, in the town of Zeitun, Cilicia.[165]

Turkish troops then began "a massive and systematic operation against Armenians throughout almost all of the Empire," which, in the words of Christopher Walker, was "noteworthy for (within designated areas) its simultaneity and for its thoroughness, its pattern, and the scale of its organization."[166] Overwhelming numbers of observers recorded these and subsequent events: members of the Central Powers, such as German and Austrian military and diplomatic agents, American diplomatic agents, German and American missionaries, and persons employed in various capacities all witnessed these tragic events.[167] The location of the American missionaries and consuls proved particularly significant. Posted to areas far from the more developed parts of the country, such as the cities of Constantinople and Smyrna,[168] they saw what was unfolding in the hinterlands. Their reports about the deaths and deportations are therefore particularly important.[169]

The Turkish dragnet followed a regular pattern. In towns and villages the gendarmes first rounded up any Armenian men who had not been conscripted into the Ottoman Army. Typically they were led to an out-of-sight spot where they were murdered. Then Turkish authorities informed the remaining Armenians – women, children, and old men – that they were to be deported to locations where they would be safe during the war. Although Armenians sometimes had a couple of days to prepare for deportation, in some towns, they were given as little as two hours.

The conditions of the camps to which the deported Armenians were sent were beyond human comprehension. A boy of fifteen, deported on July 29th from the town of Tchorum (Chorum) in northern Asia Minor where his father had been a well-to-do business man, arrived with his family at the refugee center known as Katma, and described the camp:

> There is a terrible stink that tears every one's nose. Everywhere is (?) covered with unburied, rotten human waste, corpses, etc. Besides that, ten thousand people have left their filth, and have contaminated the whole area, and it is not possible not to choke. ... However, the night was terrible, for toilet we had to go further [sic] away, outside of the tent, but wherever we went, it was difficult to find a place to step. When we were advancing in the field, suddenly we felt an open hole in front of our feet. Although it was dark, we could see a dead man in the bottom of the hole. Fearfully screaming, we went running back. And now in front of us there was another hole, and another dead corpse in it. And like this, in every side holes and the unburied dead– men, women, elderly and children. All of them were bare and without clothing, some laying on their faces, and some on their backs, or on their sides.[170]

Another deportee, Elise Hagobian Taft, had arrived at the same camp in late December 1915, having traveled four months since her family was exiled from Bandirma. She wrote:

> After the rains finally stopped, father and I left our tent in search of drinking water. The sight before me was horrible beyond description. Hundreds and hundreds of swollen bodies lay in the mud and puddles of rain water, some half-buried, others floating eerily in rancid pools, together with rotted bodies and heaps of human refuse accumulated during the week-long rain. Some victims – only the upper torsos emerging from the mud and puddles – were breathing their last. The stench rose to the heavens. It was nauseating beyond belief. The scene was like a huge cesspool laid bare and made to stink, even more under a hot sun.... It was the ideal breeding ground for the incubation of typhus, typhoid, cholera, smallpox, dysentery and other scourges resulting from such unsanitary conditions.[171]

Other Armenians have offered similar descriptions of the camps where they stopped on the way to the desert.

Although the then American ambassador Henry Morgenthau tried to maintain his confidential contacts with his consuls in the field, the Turkish leaders refused to allow him to use cipher any longer. Consequently, he was unable to keep in touch with the American officials. In addition, Turkish authorities throughout the Empire subjected all letters, including mail to the ambassador, to rigorous censorship, and imposed restrictions on the right to travel.[172] Despite this, some Americans, mainly missionaries, managed to reach the capital and inform the ambassador about what was transpiring. Their reports about the treatment of the Armenians shocked Morgenthau deeply.

> For hours, they [missionaries] would sit in my office [he wrote] and, with tears streaming down their faces, they would tell me of the horrors through which they had passed. Many of these, both men and women, were almost broken in health from the scenes which they had witnessed. In many cases they brought me letters from American consuls, confirming the most dreadful of their narrations and adding many unprintable details.[173]

Morgenthau continually sought to determine the fate of the Armenians and the Americans who lived with them. On occasion, persons who were free to travel, such as German missionaries and medical personnel, would bring him letters from his own consuls and American missionaries telling him about the massacres and deportation of Armenians.[174]

In a letter dated June 15, 1915, one of Morgenthau's consuls, Jesse Jackson, stationed in Aleppo, described the stream of Armenians flowing through that city. Guarded by Turkish gendarmes, groups comprising 300 to 500 old men, women, and children arrived in Aleppo, staying a short time before being driven out of the city and into the desert where neither shelter, food, nor any means of living existed, Jackson wrote. Observers reported that thousands of Armenians were strewn across the burning desert to starve or die of disease.[175]

By early September 1915, Morgenthau felt he had gathered enough information to provide a clear picture of what was happening and to ask for monetary help for the refugees. He telegraphed the State Department, urging the formation of a committee to raise the funds needed to try to save at least some of the Armenians. He thought $100,000 would be sufficient.[176]

Morgenthau identified several prominent philanthropists whom he thought would be willing to help. To add urgency to his request, Morgenthau wrote that "the destruction of the Armenians of Turkey was underway and proceeding rapidly."[177] Not content to rely solely on the State Department, Morgenthau also wrote to one of the philanthropists, Cleveland Dodge, a close friend of President Woodrow Wilson from their college days at

Princeton University, urging Dodge to go to the State Department himself and read the dispatches Morgenthau had been sending. Among other things, Dodge then contacted Dr. James L. Barton, the Foreign Secretary of the Board; Barton and Dodge set up a meeting in Dodge's offices in New York City for September 16. At this meeting, the men assembled and discussed what could be done to save the Armenians. Shortly after, the men issued a report that described the situation and began the process of raising the needed funds.[178]

This book examines how two contemporaneous publications depicted the tragic events that occurred in the Ottoman Empire during the five years of the First World War, and how these two very different sources informed and aroused the compassion of the American people to contribute generously to the relief organizations. It also discusses in depth the kinds of stories provided to the American public to help them decide to donate their limited resources to assist Armenians.

Rather than participate in the debate over whether the Armenian Genocide occurred, I have accepted the findings of Armenian and independent scholars that the Young Turks engaged in a planned genocide when they eliminated Armenians in the Ottoman Empire who lived outside of the cities of Constantinople and Smyrna. The arguments advanced by Turkish partisans do not nullify the wealth of evidence from primary and secondary sources that demonstrates conclusively that the Young Turks decided to eliminate Armenians in a carefully planned scheme. Consequently, I have freely used the term "Armenian Genocide" throughout this book to mean an intentional act on the part of the Ottoman government. Furthermore, although it was not the purpose of this essay to evaluate the claims of genocide, the material provided in both publications reviewed overwhelming supports that conclusion.

The two publications reviewed are the *New York Times* (the *Times*) and the *Missionary Herald* (the *Herald*). This study looks at their reporting to see how the publications portrayed different groups: Armenian, Turkish, American missionaries, American consular officials, and others, and how they described the situations confronting them. I chose the *Times* and the *Herald* because of their diversity and their representation of two distinct types of news reporting. The *Times* was (and still is) the pre-eminent newspaper in the United States, publishing timely information daily for sophisticated and literate members of American public. Because of its secular, mainstream orientation, it would presumably bring hard-nosed integrity and realism to its reporting about the treatment of the Armenians in the Ottoman Empire.

As this work demonstrates, the newspaper took an exceptionally active role in reporting the Armenian Genocide throughout the war years, and kept its readers informed not only about the events in Turkey but also about the relief efforts of Americans to save the Armenian people. The relief committee decided to avoid paying for publicity, but according to James L. Barton, Chairman of the committee, it decided instead to :

> trust to the loyal and spontaneous support of the press. From the day the first official dispatches setting forth the need of help were released, the press of the entire country has been sympathetic, helpful and liberal to the last degree. Without its unanimous support the work of relief never could have been carried through. The [relief] Committee and the people who have received help are indebted beyond words to its generous and unfailing support.[179]

Barton also pointed out that the relief committee furnished verified information as quickly as possible to other newspapers and magazines, enabling those publications to keep their readers well informed about the rapidly unfolding events in the Near East.[180] Indeed, the *Times* fulfilled its role of publicist exceedingly well.

The *Times* followed the standard publication practice for American newspapers in the early years of the twentieth century. In its first section, it presented a front page with newsworthy stories, an editorial page, and a letters page. Larger editions were published at weekends. These included separate sections of the paper, such as an entertainment section and a classified advertising section.

To identify articles pertaining to Armenians during the war years, I used two sources. One was the *Index of the New York Times,* which provided detailed references to the *Times'* news reports, which I then read on microfilm. I also found photocopies of important *Times'* articles in a compilation titled, *Armenian Genocide: News Accounts from the American Press: 1915-1922.*[181]

In contrast to the daily news provided by the *Times*, the *Herald,* house organ of the Board since 1821, published monthly accounts about the mission fields where the Board's missionaries served. Global Ministries, the modern-day successor to the Board, recently characterized the *Herald* as a window to the world. Descriptions of native customs, history, economic activities, and geographical features were included along with accounts of the influence of the Gospel on these far off lands. In a day before TV, radio, or rapid communication, such missionary reports became prime information for many Americans about foreign lands.[182]

The monthly issues of the *Herald* included significant content about the work, experiences, and observations of the missionaries in Turkey. The *Herald* also followed a certain pattern in each of its monthly issues. Its title page set forth its name, the *Missionary Herald*, followed by the added designation *"containing the proceedings of American Board of Commissioners for Foreign Missions with a view of other Benevolent Operations for the year...."* After its title page, the publication contained editorials, reports about meetings and conferences, and sections designated as the "Home Department" and the "Foreign Department." The Foreign Department included news articles written by the journal's staff as well as articles written by the missionaries themselves. At the end of the journal, several features provided information for readers about relevant books, brief news about mission fields, and a chronicle of departures and arrivals of missionaries and their families. Each volume had an index.

Because the index lacked sufficient detail for use in this paper, I reviewed the *Herald* page by page for the war years and photocopied articles that pertained to Ottoman Turkey. This was not particularly difficult because of the limited number of pages published each month. This kind of review also gave me a better understanding of the Board's work as a whole, since I looked at the entire text and not just the pages pertaining to Turkey.

While both the *Times* and the *Herald* told the story of the Armenian Genocide well, the publications had both similarities and differences. Both news sources provided "hard-hitting" stories that described in similar ways the tragedy unfolding inside the Ottoman Empire. A regular reader of either the *Times* or the *Herald* could not fail to gain a full appreciation of the grave situation facing those Armenians subject to Turkish control. Yet while the stories provided by both news sources described the events in Turkey in similar ways, they had different emphases. The *Times* described not only the horrors facing Armenians, but also the means by which Americans could participate in relief efforts. Consequently, every account in the *Times* about the events occurring in Turkey included the name and address of Charles A.

Crane, the secretary of the relief organization set up to aid the refugees. Not only would Americans be informed about the desperate conditions facing Armenians, they would also know how they could help in their rescue.

Because of its different constituency, the *Herald* emphasized the valor of American missionaries living and working in Turkey at that time. These individuals were described in heroic terms, as well they might, for their deeds reflected compassion and sacrifice, including death, in the service of the Armenian people among whom they worked. Rather than returning home to safety, the missionaries strove mightily to save as many Armenians as possible.

As indicated in the following chapters, the *Times* and the *Herald* played an exceedingly important role in telling the story about events so evil that they were deemed unbelievable. They provided the information necessary to galvanize the public opinion of the citizens of the United States to support relief efforts for the victims and thereby managed to save countless Armenians from starvation and death.

End Notes to Introduction

1. Mordechai Nisan, *Minorities in the Middle East: A History of Struggle and Self-expression*, 2d ed. (Jefferson, NC: McFarland, 2002), 157; Merrill D. Peterson, *"Starving Armenians:" America and the Armenian Genocide, 1915-1930 and After* (Charlottesville, VA: University of Virginia Press, 2004), 5. Peterson, Professor of History Emeritus at the University of Virginia, wrote his book after living for a brief period in the modern Republic of Armenia as a Peace Corps volunteer.

2. John Patrick Douglas Balfour, Baron Kinross, *The Ottoman Centuries: The Rise and Fall of the Turkish Empire* (New York: Morrow Quill Paperbacks, 1977), 554.

3. Peterson, *"Starving Armenians,"* 15.

4. Nina Garsoian, "The Arsakuri Dynasty (A.D. 12-[180]-423) in *The Armenian People: From Ancient to Modern Times*, vol. I, *The Dynastic Period: From Antiquity to the Fourteenth Century*, ed., Richard G. Hovannisian (New York: St. Martin's Press, 1997), 81-84

5. The official name of the branch of the church founded by St. Gregory the Illuminator is the Armenian Apostolic Church.

6. Richard G. Hovannisian, "Introduction," in *The Armenian People from Ancient to Modern Times*, vol. I, *The Dynastic Period from Antiquity to the Fourteenth Century*, (New York: St. Martin's Press, 1997), vii.

7. Roderic H. Davison, *Turkey: A Short History*, updated Clement H. Dodd, 3d ed. (Huntingdon, England: Eothen Press, 1998), 18; Balfour, *The Ottoman Centuries*, 16.

8. Ibid., 18.

9. Robert Bedrosian, "Armenia During the Seljuk and Mongol Periods," in *The Armenian People: From Ancient to Modern Times*, vol. I, 244-247.

10. The Ottomans were called "Osmanli" by the Turks. See Balfour, *The Ottoman Centuries*, 95-100.

11. Davison, *Turkey: A Short History*, 22-28; Stanford J. and Ezel K. Shaw, *The History of the Ottoman Empire and Modern Turkey*, vol. 1 (Cambridge: Cambridge University Press, 1976), 12-22.

12. Davison makes the point that the looting was probably not as devastating as the looting attributed to the Crusaders who captured the city in 1204 on their way to the Holy Land. See Davison, *Turkey: A Short History*, 29.

13. Davison, *Turkey: A Short History*, 29; Balfour, *The Ottoman Centuries*, 95-100.

14. Balfour, *The Ottoman Centuries*, 112.

15. Shaw, *The History of the Ottoman Empire and Modern Turkey*, 62.

16. William L. Cleveland, *A History of the Modern Middle East*, 2d ed. (Boulder, CO: Westview Press, 2000), 52.

17. Bruce Masters, *Christians and Jews in the Ottoman Arab World: The Roots of Sectarianism* (Cambridge: Cambridge University Press, 2001), 19; Donald Quataert, *The Ottoman Empire, 1700-1922* (Cambridge: Cambridge University Press, 2000), 64-65; Erik J. Zurcher, *Turkey: A Modern History* (London: I. B. Taurus, 2004), 10.

18. *The Encyclopedia of the Modern Middle East,* s.v. "Millet System," 1224; Masters, *Christians and Jews in the Ottoman Arab World,* 61. Contrary to the traditional accounts, *"millet"* originally meant Muslims within the Empire, and Christians outside it. Quataert also asserts that the term *"millet"* dates from the reign of Sultan Mahmut II, in the early nineteenth century. See Quataert, *The Ottoman Empire, 1700-1922,* 173. Barsoumian asserts that the use of the *millet* designation for non-Muslims dates from the reign of Sultan Mahmut II in the early nineteenth century. See Hagop Barsoumian, "The Eastern Question and the Tanzimat Era," in *The Armenian People From Ancient to Modern Times,* vol. II, 182-183.

19. The name given to the Ottoman government as the portal (door) through which supplicants for largesse had to pass.

20. Shaw maintains that Mehmet created only a Greek *millet,* and that the Armenian and Jewish *millets* were created much later. See Shaw, *The History of the Ottoman Empire and Modern Turkey,* 59.

21. Youssef Courbage and Philippe Fargues, *Christians and Jews Under Islam,* trans. Judy Mabro (London: I. B. Tauris, 1998), 91.

22. Masters, *Christians and Jews in the Ottoman Arab World,* 61; *The Encyclopedia of the Modern Middle East,* 1224.

23. Ibid., 1224.

24. Masters, *Christians and Jews in the Ottoman Arab World,* 61; *The Encyclopedia of the Modern Middle East,* 1224.

25. Quataert, *The Ottoman Empire, 1700-1922,* 173; Erik J. Zurcher, *Turkey: A Modern History* (I. B. Taurus, 2004), 10.

26. Leslie Peirce, *Morality Tales: Law and Gender in the Ottoman Court of Aintab* (Berkeley: University of California Press, 2003), 59-60; *The Encyclopedia of the Modern Middle East,* 1224.

27. *The Encyclopedia of the Modern Middle East,* 1224.

28. Masters, *Christians and Jews in the Ottoman Arab World,* 6.

29. Peirce, *Morality Tales,* 22, 58.

30. Ibid.

31. Ibid., 4.

32. Ibid., 1-2.

33. Ibid.

34. Ibid.

35. Ibid., 4.

36. Ibid., 5.

37. Ibid., 5-7.

38. Ibid., 2.

39. Ibid., 60. Peirce does not indicate if a court for the Armenian *millet* was available to the Armenian litigants in Aintab. It is possible that the Armenians had to use the Muslim courts in the absence of any other.

40. Apparently Armenians also adopted one of the Muslim requirements for women.

41. Leslie Peirce, *Morality Tales*, 216.
42. Ibid., 231-232.
43. Ibid., 86.
44. Ibid., 60.
45. Ibid., 60.
46. Masters, *Christians and Jews in the Ottoman Arab World*, 17.
47. A qadi is a judge in a court. See Shaw, *The History of the Ottoman Empire and Modern Turkey*, vol. 1, 135.
48. Masters, *Christians and Jews in the Ottoman Arab World*, 62-63.
49. A metropolitan is the equivalent of a bishop. See Masters, *Christians and Jews in the Ottoman Arab World*, 62.
50. Ibid., 63.
51. Peirce, *Morality Tales*, 60.
52. Masters, *Christians and Jews in the Ottoman Arab World*, 38.
53. Ibid., 29.
54. Ibid., 29.
55. Ibid., 30.
56. Ibid., 32.
57. Ibid., 7.
58. Donald Quataert, *The Ottoman Empire, 1700-1922* (Cambridge University Press, 2000), 1.
59. Ibid., 2.
60. Erik J. Zurcher, *Turkey: A Modern History* (I. B. Taurus, 2004), 10.
61. Ibid., 10-11.
62. Masters, *Christians and Jews in the Ottoman Arab World*, 68.
63. Ibid., 68-69.
64. Ibid., 68-69; Donald Quataert, *The Ottoman Empire, 1700-1922* (Cambridge University Press, 2000), 77-78.
65. Erik J. Zurcher, *Turkey: A Modern History* (I. B. Taurus 2004), 10.
66. Donald Quataert, *The Ottoman Empire, 1700-1922* (Cambridge University Press, 2000), 50-51.
67. Masters, *Christians and Jews in the Ottoman Arab World*, 7.
68. Ibid., 11; Quataert, *The Ottoman Empire, 1700-1922*, 173.
69. Ibid.
70. Ibid., 99.
71. Ibid.
72. Ibid.
73. Ibid., 108.
74. Ibid., 111. It had taken the Catholics from 1627, the date of the first arrival of Latin missionaries in Aleppo, to 1848 to gain their own *millet*. The Melkite *millet* had a

patriarch who had authority over the community's churches in Antioch, Jerusalem, and Alexandria.

75. Barsoumian, "The Eastern Question and the Tanzimat Era," *The Armenian People From Ancient to Modern Times*, vol. II, 185-187.

76. Zurcher, *Turkey: A Modern History*, 21-23; Davison, *Turkey: A Short History*, 80-84.

77. Zurcher, *Turkey: A Modern History*, 22-23; Davison, *Turkey: A Short History*, 83.

78. Zurcher, *Turkey: A Modern History*, 39-45.

79. Quataert, *The Ottoman Empire, 1700-1922*, 65; Barsoumian, "The Eastern Question and the Tanzimat Era," *The Armenian People From Ancient to Modern Times*, vol. II, 181.

80. Masters, *Christians and Jews in the Ottoman Arab World*, 138-139.

81. Quataert, *The Ottoman Empire, 1700-1922*, 65; Masters, *Christians and Jews in the Ottoman Arab World*, 134-138; Barsoumian, "The Eastern Question and the Tanzimat Era," *The Armenian People From Ancient to Modern Times*, vol. II, 182.

82. Quataert, *The Ottoman Empire, 1700-1922*, 63.

83. Masters, *Christians and Jews in the Ottoman Arab World*, 140.

84. Richard G. Hovannisian, "The Armenian Question in the Ottoman Empire, 1876-1914," in *The Armenian People From Ancient to Modern Times*, vol. II, 204.

85. Barsoumian, "The Eastern Question and the Tanzimat Era," in *The Armenian People: From Ancient to Modern Times*, vol. II, 193.

86. Ibid.

87. Ibid.

88. Ibid.

89. Quataert, *The Ottoman Empire, 1700-1922*, 68-69.

90. Ibid., 64, 67.

91. Ibid., 78; Zurcher, *Turkey: A Modern History*, 11.

92. Quataert, *The Ottoman Empire, 1700-1922*, 67, 78; Zurcher, *Turkey: A Modern History*, 11.

93. Masters, *Christians and Jews in the Ottoman Arab World*, 132.

94. Ibid., 132.

95. Ussama Makdisi, *The Culture of Sectarianism: Community, History, and Violence in Nineteenth-Century Ottoman Lebanon* (Berkeley: University of California Press, 2000), 6, 95.

96. Masters, *Christians and Jews in the Ottoman Arab World*, 130.

97. Makdisi, *The Culture of Sectarianism*, 2.

98. Ibid., 132.

99. Ibid., 9-10.

100. Masters, *Christians and Jews in the Ottoman Arab World*, 129; Ussama Makdisi, *The Culture of Sectarianism*, 9.

101. Makdisi, *The Culture of Sectarianism*, 10.

102. The presence and effect of Protestant missionaries in the Ottoman Empire is more fully discussed below.

103. Masters, *Christians and Jews in the Ottoman Arab World*, 149-150.

104. Ibid., 145-150.

105. Ibid., 55.

106. Ibid.

107. Ibid.

108. Zurcher, *Turkey: A Modern History*, 64-65; Davison, *Turkey: A Short History*, 114.

109. Quataert, *The Ottoman Empire, 1700-1922*, 55.

110. Ibid., 57.

111. Ibid., 58-59.

112. Barsoumian, "The Eastern Question and the Tanzimat Era," in *The Armenian People From Ancient to Modern Times*, vol. II, 200-201.

113. Hovannisian, "The Armenian Question in the Ottoman Empire," *The Armenian People:* vol. II, 207; Zurcher, *Turkey: A Modern History*, 76.

114. Davison, *Turkey: A Short History*, 112-113.

115. Quataert, *The Ottoman Empire, 1700-1922*, 64.

116. Barsoumian, "The Eastern Question and the Tanzimat Era," *The Armenian People From Ancient to Modern Times*, vol. II, 201; Quataert, *The Ottoman Empire, 1700-1922*, 189.

117. Hovannisian, "The Armenian Question in the Ottoman Empire," in *The Armenian People: From Ancient to Modern Times*, vol. II, 212-218; Davison, *Turkey: A Short History*, 115-116.

118. Hovannisian, "The Armenian Question in the Ottoman Empire," in *The Armenian People: From Ancient to Modern Times*, vol. II, 207; Zurcher, *Turkey: A Modern History*, 83.

119. Joseph L. Grabill, *Protestant Diplomacy and the Near East: Missionary Influence on American Policy, 1810-1927* (Minneapolis: University of Minnesota Press, 1971), 41.

120. Hovannisian, "The Armenian Question in the Ottoman Empire," in *The Armenian People: From Ancient to Modern Times*, vol. II, 226-227.

121. Christopher Walker, "World War I and the Armenian Genocide," in *The Armenian People from Ancient Times to Modern Times*, vol. II, 245.

122. Ulrich Trumpener, *Germany and the Ottoman Empire 1914-1918* (Princeton, NJ: Princeton Univ. Press, 1968; reprint, New York: Caravan Books, 1989), 3-20.

123. Hovannisian, "The Armenian Question in the Ottoman Empire," in *The Armenian People: From Ancient to Modern Times*, vol. II, 228; Zurcher, *Turkey: A Modern History*, 86-87; Davison, *Turkey: A Short History*, 114-116.

124. Zurcher, *Turkey: A Modern History*, 87; Davison, *Turkey: A Short History*, 116-117.

125. Zurcher, *Turkey: A Modern History*, 87-88.

126. Ibid., 88; Davison, *Turkey: A Short History*, 120.

127. Hovannisian, "The Armenian Question in the Ottoman Empire," in *The Armenian People: From Ancient to Modern Times*, vol. II, 229.

128. Davison, *Turkey: A Short History*, 115-116.

129. Ibid., 120.

130. Ibid., 121.

131. Quataert, *The Ottoman Empire, 1700-1922*, 64.

132. Davison, *Turkey: A Short History*, 127.

133. Quataert, *The Ottoman Empire, 1700-1922*, 59-61.

134. Ibid., 64.

135. Cleveland, *A History of the Modern Middle East*, 133.

136. Davison, *Turkey: A Short History*, 128-130.

137. Hovannisian, "The Armenian Question in the Ottoman Empire, 1876-1914," in *The Armenian People From Ancient to Modern Times*, vol. II, 237-238.

138. Sidney E. Ahlstrom, *A Religious History of the American People* (New Haven, CT: Yale University Press, 1972), 423-424.

139. Ibid., 423-424.

140. David H. Finnie, *Pioneers East: The Early American Experience in the Middle East* (Cambridge, MA: Harvard University Press, 1967), 114.

141. Edwin Munsell Bliss, *A Concise History of Missions* (New York: Fleming H. Revell Company, 1897), 130-131.

142. Rev. Dr. Vahan H. Tootikian, *Highlights of Armenian Christendom* (Southfield, MI: Armenian Evangelical World Council, 2002), 280.

143. *Global Ministries of the Christian Church (Disciples of Christ) and United Church of Christ*, website at www.globalministries.org/index.php?option=com visited 18 February 2007. Global Ministries is the current name of the successor organization of the American Board of Commissioners for Foreign Missions.

144. Ibid.

145. Joseph L. Grabill, *Protestant Diplomacy and the Near East: Missionary Influence on American Policy, 1810-1927* (Minneapolis, MN: University of Minnesota Press, 1971), 7.

146. Nestorianism is the doctrine that Jesus exists as the man Jesus and the divine Son of God, or Logos, rather than a unified person. It derives its name from Nestorius ©. 386-451), Patriarch of Constantinople. This view of Christ was condemned at the Council of Ephesus in 431. Today's Church rejects the "Nestorian" label, preferring Church of the East, or Assyrian Church. Christine Chaillot, "The Ancient Oriental Churches," in *The Oxford History of Christian Worship*, ed. Geoffrey Wainwright, Karen B. Westerfield Tucker (Oxford, England: Oxford University Press, 2006), 131.

147. Grabill, *Protestant Diplomacy and the Near East*, 129.

148. Tootikian, *Highlights of Armenian Christendom*, 275-300.

149. Had this happened, the missionaries would have still had to address Muslim law, which inflicted capital punishment for apostasy.

150. James L. Barton, *Daybreak in Turkey* (Boston: Pilgrim Press, 1908), 166-168.

151. Tootikian, *Highlights of Armenian Christendom*, 288.

152. Barton, *Daybreak in Turkey*, 138.

153. Ibid., 188.

154. Ibid., 166-168.

155. The Red House Press is still a viable organization in Istanbul and is especially well known for its dictionaries of the Turkish language. I purchased a Turkish dictionary published by the Red House Press in Turkey in 2003.

156. Robert L. Daniel, *American Philanthropy in the Near East 1820-1960* (Athens, OH: Ohio University Press, 1970), 97.

157. Barton, *Daybreak in Turkey*, 174-175.

158. One of the hospitals that the missionaries established in what is now the city of Gaziantep is still called the "American Hospital" by the local residents.

159. Daniel, *American Philanthropy in the Near East 1820-1960*, 106.

160. Barton, *Daybreak in Turkey*, 175.

161. Suzanne E. Moranian, "The Armenian Genocide and American Missionary Relief Efforts," in *America and the Armenian Genocide of 1915*, Studies in the Social and Cultural History of Modern Warfare, ed. Jay Winter (New York: Cambridge University Press, 2003),186-187; Daniel, *American Philanthropy in the Near East 1820-1960*, 94.

162. Mordechai Nisan, *Minorities in the Middle East: A History of Struggle and Self-Expression*, 2d ed. (Jefferson, North Carolina: McFarland, 2002), 167; Quataert, *The Ottoman Empire, 1700-1922*, 184.

163. Christopher J. Walker, "World War I and the Armenian Genocide," in *The Armenian People from Ancient Times to Modern Times*, vol. II, 245.

164. Quataert, *The Ottoman Empire, 1700-1922*, 184-186; Vahakn N. Dadrian, *The History of the Armenian Genocide: Ethnic Conflict from the Balkans to Anatolia to the Caucasus*, 3d ed. (Providence, Rhode Island: Gerghahn Books), 225-226.

165. Christopher J. Walker, "World War I and the Armenian Genocide," in *The Armenian People from Ancient Times to Modern Times*, vol. II, 249-251. Walker argues that the date of the deportations from Zeitun is of significance in resolving one of the questions about the Armenian Genocide. Turkish apologists have typically asserted that the deportations of Armenians began as a *result* of the Armenians' revolt at Van. Yet the self-defense exercised by Armenians at Van did not begin until April 20, 1915, *after* the Turks had killed all of the 2,500 men in the town of Akantz, northeast of Van. This massacre, coupled with the deportation begun in Zeitun *before* the revolt at Van, signaled to Armenians that the Young Turks had already decided to exterminate them.

166. Ibid., 246.

167. Ibid., 246, 247.

168. The Armenians of Constantinople and Smyrna were not deported, probably because a large number of foreigners resided in those cities during the war years and could observe what the Turks were doing. For the most part, the deportations took place in areas far from those cities.

169. Jay Winter, "Under Cover of War: The Armenian Genocide in the Context of Total War," in *America and the Armenian Genocide of 1915*, Studies in the Social and Cultural History of Modern Warfare, ed. Jay Winter (New York: Cambridge University Press, 2003), 37. Winter, Professor of History at Yale University, is the author of many

books on the First World War. He also served as chief historian and co-producer for the Emmy-award winning television series, "The Great War and the Shaping of the Twentieth Century." He is a director of the Historial de la Grande Guerre, and the International Museum of the First World War at Peronne, Somme, France. Winter maintains that without understanding the Armenian Genocide, later genocides such as the Holocaust cannot be understood.

170. Quoted in Hilmar Kaiser, *At the Crossroad of Der Zor; Death, Survival, and Humanitarian Resistance in Aleppo, 1915-1917*, in collaboration with Luther and Nancy Eskijian (Princeton, NJ: Gomidas Institute Books, 2001), 19-21. For the original citation, see Vahram Dadrian, *To the Desert: Pages from My Diary* (Agop Hacikyan, trans; by Ara Sarafian, ed and intro), (London: Gomidas Institute, 2006).

171. Ibid., 21-22.

172. Henry Morgenthau, *Ambassador Morgenthau's Story* (Doubleday: New York, 1918; reprint, London and Princeton: Gomidas Institute, 2000), 218 (Page citations are to the reprint edition).

173. Ibid., 218.

174. Ibid., 225.

175. Ibid., 219-223.

176. James L. Barton, *The Story of Near East Relief (1915-1930), An Interpretation* (New York: Macmillan Co., 1930), 4. James L. Barton served as the Foreign Secretary of the American Board of Commissioners for Foreign Missions. He was knowledgeable about the Near East, having served as a missionary there.

177. Ibid., 4; Peterson, *"Starving Armenians"*, 15.

178. James L. Barton, *The Story of Near East Relief (1915-1930)*, 4-6.

179. Ibid., 14.

180. Ibid., 15.

181. *The Armenian Genocide: News Accounts From the American Press: 1915-1922*, comp and ed. Richard D. Kloian, 4th ed. (Richmond, CA: Heritage Publishing, 2005).

182. www.globalministries.org/index.php?option=com. 2/13/2007.

Chapter 2

THE YEAR 1914

The beginning of the First World War unleashed forces in Ottoman Turkey that resulted in the genocide of Armenians and the end of efforts made by the American Board of Commissioners for Foreign Missions to spread the Christian Gospel in Turkey.

THE NEW YORK TIMES

With the outbreak of the First World War, the interest of *The New York Times* (the *Times*) in the Near East intensified. The *Times* had long been concerned about the welfare of Armenians in the Ottoman Empire, a small group of Christians whose status in the Muslim Ottoman Empire had always been precarious. Its reporting about the massacres suffered by Armenians in 1895-1896 had provided its readers with descriptive news stories that portrayed the kinds of harm inflicted.

The details about the Armenians' misfortunes provided by the newspaper left an indelible impression on the reader. One news story published on March 16, 1895, bearing the headline "Turks Torture the Survivors of the Massacres in Sassoun," reported the demand made by Turkish officials that two Armenians sign a document blaming Kurds (rather than Turks) for some recent killings. When the Armenians refused to do so, the Turkish gendarmes placed heated triangles around their necks.[1] Another story, appearing in the *Times* of September 10, 1895, with the headline "Another Armenian Holocaust," described an attack on a company of gendarmes by brigands that Turkish authorities attributed to Armenian revolutionaries. Although no factual basis existed for this assertion, a force of one thousand Turkish troops destroyed Armenian villages and tortured men, women, and children.[2]

The *Times*' reports also described the economic oppression that plagued the Armenians. Tax farmers regularly extracted the maximum taxes from the villagers, far above the government's requirements. When one Armenian villager complained, the tax farmer sent sheep to devour the Armenian's crops. Forced labor without pay on Turkish or Kurdish farms, reported the *Times*, limited the time Armenians could spend on their own farms.[3] These journalistic examples illustrated the kinds of day-to-day harassment perpetrated by Turks and Kurds on the Empire's Armenian subjects. Ultimately this kind of sympathetic reporting probably aroused the news reading public in favor of the beleaguered Armenians.

Similar articles appeared around the time of the massacres of 1909. The *Times* again used such inflammatory headlines as "Moslem Massacres Take 5,000 Lives," and "Moslems in Antioch Wipe Out Armenians."[4] Even women and children, wrote the *Times*, were subject to massacre because the credo of the Turks held that no twig of the accursed race shall be suffered to live. These stories, describing massacre and pillage, albeit on a smaller scale than in 1895, used language that again would assuredly elicit the readers' sympathy. Such reporting guaranteed that when the Turkish government launched what would become the Armenian genocide of 1915, the *Times*' readers were already familiar with the Armenian people and their persecution in the Ottoman Empire.

The outbreak of the First World War led to a rapid deterioration of the Armenians' situation in Turkey. Only three months after the war's start, the *Times* ran a story with the headline, "Report Christians in Peril in Turkey," where it reported that "[r]efugees from Constantinople who had arrived in Petrograd, Russia, indicated that the state of affairs in Turkey was appalling. Brigandage, murder, and atrocities were commonplace, Armenians being the chief victims, but all Christians and foreigners were in great danger."[5] By using the term "Christians" in its headline, the *Times* not only invited support for Armenians but broadened the class of persons who were in danger, thereby enhancing the story's relevance to all Christians and not just Armenians.

Two weeks later, the *Times* reported on events in the eastern Turkish city of Erzerum, where a large military fort located only forty-five miles from the Russian border protected Turkey's eastern flank. "Erzerum Fanatics Slay Christians" read the headline over the story about a mob that had answered the call to holy war. Throngs of "fanatical Muslims" had demolished all Armenian clubs, churches, and schools of Erzerum, reported the *Times*. Four Armenians, including one woman, were killed during the riot.[6] By using such terms as "Christians," "fanatics," "holy war," and "peril" throughout these stories, the *Times* provided information that would have caught the attention of its readers, most of whom were probably Christians. Although younger readers might have known little or nothing about the Armenians, it would have been easy for older readers to recall previous stories about the persecution of Armenians and link those stories with the latest reports. For the Board's directors who may have been readers of the *Times*, the stories must have given rise to concern for the welfare of the Board's employees. The Board had no way of contacting those persons, because the Turkish government had imposed total censorship, and mail service had been interrupted by the war.

The *Times* continued to bring more news to its readers about the situation in Turkey. A Petrograd dispatch to the *Times* of London was published by the *Times* with the headline "Hang Christians in Street," with a sub-heading of "Armenians' Position at Erzerum is Very Precarious." Because of their alleged Russian sympathies, hundreds of Armenians had been summarily imprisoned and many hanged in the streets, wrote the *Times*. The story also reported mobilization of 300,000 Turkish soldiers at Erzerum.[7] On the same day, another story appeared with the dateline Petrograd that reported Turkish women rioting against the war in the streets in Erzerum by throwing stones. When ordered to disperse, the women "rent their garments and paraded the streets almost in a state of nudity," compelling the guards to retire in obedience to Islamic law. They forced the vali[8] to dispatch a telegram to Constantinople protesting the war. The rest of the article repeated much of the same information about the Armenians of Erzerum, adding that:

"... the prisons are full of Armenians and Greeks suspected of espionage. They are hanged in the streets and squares without trial and the corpses are suspended for weeks from the street lamps. In passing Turks spit on the bodies and compel Christians to do the same."[9]

The story mentioned the presence of 200,000 Turkish soldiers in Erzerum and that "German officers control everything in the town and fortress."[10]

The news story about the Turkish women appears fanciful. It is difficult to imagine Turkish women of that or any other era parading in the street without adequate clothing. In addition, the facts surrounding the event have not been reported in any of the other sources used in this book; it seems highly unlikely that such an unusual incident would not have been mentioned elsewhere. Also of significance is the discrepancy between the number of troops reported in this story and the number reported in the previous one, a difference of 100,000 soldiers. This divergence points out the difficulty in obtaining accurate news about events in eastern Turkey, which was far from the cities where journalists covering the war would have been located.

In less than a year, and despite the challenges confronting the *Times'* reporters and information sources, the newspaper's reports proved instrumental in giving rise to relief efforts on behalf of Armenians by an American public willing to contribute escalating amounts to keep Armenians alive. Children would be invited to share their pennies, and adults their nickels and dimes, while whole families were entreated to fast for a meal and to give the funds saved for Armenian relief. President Wilson himself announced an Armenian relief day in which all of America would be asked to contribute to the Armenian cause. The *Times'* role in making the Armenians and their travails known was crucial to the campaign.

THE MISSIONARY HERALD

At the beginning of 1914, a feeling of optimism had swept through both the Board's missionary community in Turkey and its supporters back home. With a deeply felt confidence in the future of missionary work in Turkey, the Protestant evangelists looked forward to more promising opportunities to convert Muslims, using education, medical service, and other works of philanthropy. They also saw the possibilities of expanding their existing efforts with the Armenian community, so that the tradition-bound "Gregorians"[11] could experience the kind of revitalized Protestant brand of Christianity preached and practised by the American missionaries.

But the advent of war in the summer of 1914 ended the possibility of future growth of missions in Turkey and eventually led to the end of the Board's efforts to spread the Christian Gospel in Turkey. By August 1914 Great Britain, France, and Russia were engaged in war against the Central Powers, a conflict which Turkey soon joined.

The Board lamented that despite the threats of war in previous years, it was nevertheless shocking to witness its actual outbreak. "It is a spectacle to make angels weep," editorialized the *Missionary Herald* (*Herald*), the journal of the Board, as Christian nations disregard solemn treaties "as if they were waste paper, turning their backs on ... all the fine phrases of peace in a mad rush to gain the advantage of the first blow." Despite the widespread promotion of peace, the espousal of arbitration of disputes, and the forward progress of civilization, all was discarded in a rapid slide "into a whirlpool of blood-lust and revenge," lamented the *Herald*.[12] "How hypocritical Christian nations must appear to all those native lands to whom missionaries have preached Christian love," the *Herald* added. The journal's typical optimism, however, led it to urge its readers to look forward to the *end* of the war, when "a more stable and Christian structure shall arise to express the civilization of the twentieth century."[13]

In the months immediately preceding the outbreak of war, missionary activities had continued much the same as always. In Marsovan, Anatolia Girls' School, Anatolia College, and Marsovan Theological Seminary held successful graduation ceremonies. In the area surrounding Marsovan, new schools were forming and existing schools were improving standards. The Gregorians had established a gymnasium, almost wholly on college lines, thanks to the leadership of Anatolia College graduates. The Greeks were trying to do the same. Even the Turks, according to Anatolia College's president, were diverting funds from the *Evkaf*, the Muslim Ministry of Pious Funds, into educational institutions. This, wrote President George E. White of the college at Marsovan, is one of "the most significant plans formed in many a day."[14]

In Sivas, the largest city in the interior of Asia Minor, two of the Board schools, the Teachers' College (for boys) and the Girls' High School, held commencement activities outside the city, at a new building located on a tract of land where the rest of the school would be built as soon as it was funded. The commencement speaker, Principal Roupen Racoubian, had returned to Sivas two years earlier after completing study at Columbia Teachers' College in New York City. The Girls' School was celebrating the fiftieth anniversary of its founding.[15]

Missionary complacency was soon jolted by the Turkish decision on October 1, 1914, to abrogate the capitulations. In three separate articles, the *Herald* addressed at length the subject of the capitulations. The capitulations, explained the missionary journal, were treaties by which foreigners had been exempt from local jurisdiction in both civil and criminal cases. Abrogation of the capitulations meant that the Board's missionaries were suddenly stripped of the special legal protection, which their governments had secured for them. Although at first this decision appeared to have wide ramifications that would disturb the Board's staff and elicit apprehension from them, the Board with its usual upbeat attitude indicated that it did not think there was any need for concern: "but we incline to think that Turkey does not mean to put oppressive or unlawful hands on any American, be he missionary or merchant, or to crowd out of her territory those ... [who] have shown themselves the true friends of her people." Besides, said the Board, "our government in Washington is fully aware of the role Americans play in Turkey, and will quickly join with the other Great Powers to see that the rights and privileges of foreigners in Turkey are protected."[16] This illustrates well the Board's optimistic view that it was playing a special role in Turkey, one widely supported by the Turks who could be counted on to protect the missionaries from the restrictions placed on other nationalities.

For a few months after the onset of war, Turkey's status as a belligerent was unclear, but rupture in the financial order of the world had forced the Board to use the services of the Standard Oil and Vacuum Oil companies as their bankers in paying missionary expenses.[17] Earlier problems with the mail service in Turkey had been resolved, easing the Board's anxiety about keeping in touch with its staff in Turkey. As of September 12, the missionaries remained safe, and "were not expecting any catastrophe."[18] Besides, wrote the *Herald*, the "Eastern lands" harbour good will towards the missionaries; and "even the lawless elements of the East have [respect] for the power and resources of the West whence the missionaries come."[19]

Despite the question of war, missionary activity continued apace in the latter part of 1914. The Board's staff filed many accounts about end of school year activities and the celebrations at its schools, colleges, and theological seminaries that accompanied them. In Marsovan, twenty-five men made up the teaching staff of Anatolia College, one of the seven colleges connected with the American Board. The college also planned to employ a native speaker to teach Turkish, joining the existing teaching staff of six Americans, one Swiss, one Russian, eight Armenians, and nine Greeks. Four student clubs conducted musical and athletic activities; of these, the Greek and Armenian clubs were the largest and published their own newspapers. A museum with 6,000 specimens and a library of 6,000 volumes had been established; Gregorians, Greeks, and Turks used the library and 200 persons per week visited the museum. Sir Edwin Pears, the pre-eminent foreign resident in Constantinople, gave the school's commencement address, asserting that the most important need for the people of Turkey was the kind of non-sectarian education provided by Anatolia College.[20]

The ominous build-up to war could not, however, be ignored. As early as August 1914, Turkey had informed its subjects that all men, including Christians, between the ages of nineteen to forty-five would be subject to the draft. For those schools educating or employing men in this age group, the conscription created great uncertainty.[21]

Unbeknown to the missionaries, Turkey and Germany had entered into a secret alliance on August 1, 1914. On October 28, the Turkish fleet bombarded Russian ports on the Black Sea. Eight days later, Britain, Russia, and France declared war on Turkey, which would now be fully engaged in the European conflict. The missionary supporters in the United States became alarmed and worried about the well-being of the many Board employees in Turkey. This anxiety increased when breakdowns in the mail service between Turkey and the United States made it hard for the Board to keep in regular touch with its workers in Turkey.[22]

The Board took pains to educate its supporters by describing in detail the history of the capitulations and why the Board believed their abrogation would not affect its operations in Turkey. Long-time Board missionary, Rev. Charles T. Riggs,[23] writing on September 12 from Constantinople, described how the news was announced in that city. On September 9, "in the most pompous style, heralds were sent around the town with drums to tell the people to assemble at specified places to hear the latest news."

In his neighborhood, wrote Charles Riggs, the herald announced that Germany had experienced a great victory; everyone was ordered to go and help celebrate it. When the crowd assembled, representatives of the governing cabinet told the crowd that the "awful disgrace" of the capitulations by which Turkey had been pushed down by other nations had ended forever. "Most of the ordinary people have no idea what the capitulations are," Charles Riggs went on to report, "and many have been misinformed so as to think they can now do whatever they like to foreigners."[24]

Charles Riggs stated modestly that he did not consider himself "well qualified" to guess what the abrogation would mean to the Board's missionary enterprise in Turkey, but he noted that foreign powers, including Germany and Austria, had also objected to this unilateral decision by the Turks. Charles Riggs maintained that the Board's many properties in Turkey nevertheless remained free from Turkish control, not because of the capitulations, but because they were owned by philanthropic institutions, and would therefore be treated no differently than property held by Turkish philanthropies.

Charles Riggs did, however, express a cautionary note. Each separate non-Muslim community, the Armenians, the Orthodox, the Jews, and so on, he explained, was subject to its national head, who was held responsible by the Porte for the collection of taxes, records of marriages, births, and for the settlement of controversies among its own people. He said that the Turks may decide to eliminate the millet system as well as the capitulations. "Time alone will tell," he mused.[25]

While Charles Riggs refused to speculate about the future of the millet system, he felt confident that he understood why the Turks had abolished the capitulations. Abolishing the capitulations, he wrote, is the only way for Turkey to save face after mobilizing as many as a million men for war.

Germany had hoped that Turkey would be drawn into the war, he argued, in order to fight the Russians in the Caucasus. Since that had not happened, speculated Charles Riggs, Turkey was left with this huge army. But the Turks could only demobilize without shame if they gave the Turkish people something to be proud of. Abolishing the special privileges of the Europeans will have that effect. Now that the Turks have acted, he said, the country will quietly demobilize.[26]

Despite long service as a Board missionary and resident in Constantinople, Charles Riggs completely misread the situation facing the Board and the Armenians. He failed to understand that the government of Turkey would join the Central Powers and use the cover of war to destroy its Armenian population and to create a Turkey for only the Turks.

Dr. James L. Barton, the Board's Foreign Secretary, weighed in on the matter. Abrogation of the capitulations, he wrote, would end the special privileged relationship of foreigners living inside the Ottoman Empire, an immunity called extra-territoriality conferred by the capitulations. Those rights had prevented Muslims from entering the homes, arresting, or interfering with the work or life of a foreigner, except through the foreigner's own government. The practical effect of these exceptions to Turkish sovereignty, wrote Dr. Barton, meant that foreigners escaped the "misrule" to which the rest of the inhabitants of the Empire were often subject.

The danger to the work of the missionaries lay, Barton felt, not so much in the character of Turkish laws as in their administration. Although foreigners had been permitted to hold real property in Turkey, those property holders still had to submit to Ottoman jurisdiction. There should be no problem, however, for the Board's missionary work in Turkey, stated Barton optimistically, because relations have been "so satisfactory and even in places cordial" between the missionaries and the Porte.[27]

Whatever the case about the capitulations, Turkey continued to mobilize for war. Rev. Chambers described the effects of mobilization in Adana during the week of August 2-9, 1914. First, all men, including Christians, between the ages of eighteen and forty were called up. Later that order was changed and Christians between the ages of twenty and thirty-two only were conscripted. Finally, wrote Chambers, orders were changed again. He did not describe the contents of the third order, but he did report that orders kept changing, and their contents were confused and indefinite.

On the day Chambers wrote, the Allies had demanded that Turkey demobilize, and Chambers hoped that Turkey would comply. Already, he said, the existence of the war had affected Turkey. Business had stagnated and the lack of money in circulation made commerce increasingly difficult. Gathering the ripened crops was impossible; in the upland areas the men had already been conscripted and the farm animals needed for harvesting had been requisitioned. On the plains, the cotton crop was ready for picking, but no men remained to do the work. The earlier wheat and barley harvest had been poor because of heavy spring rains. "It makes my heart sick to think of the destitution and suffering," Chambers said. "One of my prayers has been that I might be spared the experiences of any more relief work. It seems to me I have had more than my share. It is the most trying and stressful kind of work." Yet, the local situation remained tranquil, the missionary wrote, and he thought there was little probability of local difficulties. Chambers wondered what he could say to Turks about the war. The Turks, he said, are already saying: " '[t]he dogs are biting each other–let them bite.' "[28]

Matters were not so tranquil in other parts of Turkey. On August 2, wrote President White, of Marsovan's Anatolia College, mobilization orders were read in the Marsovan mosque after evening prayers. Martial law had been imposed almost immediately, he reported. Although there had not been a declaration of war, a regiment of Turkish soldiers had seized the new Board hospital in Marsovan and converted it into their barracks. Requisitioning supplies from the city's people had proceeded "in a most ruthless manner."[29]

As an educator, White's concerns ran most directly to the question whether Anatolia College could go forward with the fall semester. The staff would make every effort to do so, he said, but the college was plagued by lack of currency; none was in circulation and no checks could be cashed. Students might not be able to travel, or to bring currency or checks to pay their fees. The number of teachers available for the fall was unclear. Although many teachers had been required to register for military service, it was not clear how many would actually be called up. Every day, White wrote, "we wait for this wicked war wave to pass by, and expect more favorable times later.... If we can keep the college going, it will be one of the best ways of helping to maintain public confidence."[30]

The Board continued to lament the war. The editorial pages of the *Herald* described the anguish the missionary board felt: "the horror of it increases; the sense of multitudinous suffering, wholesale slaughter, and of irreparable ruin oppresses the heart like a nightmare. How can we stand the daily agony of this awful combat?"[31] But, the *Herald* added, "there are a few streaks of light in a sky that is undeniably black."[32] Even though the Sheik-ul-Islam at Constantinople had called for jihad, a holy war, by the faithful in support of Turkey, Muslim subjects of Great Britain had not responded.[33] Furthermore, stated the *Herald*, even though Turkey has declared war against Great Britain, France, and Russia, the American missionaries in Turkey are:

> probably the safest of all people in that land, and most likely to be protected. Turkey has never been given to harming them. She has blocked their plans, tried their patience, and tested their faith by her more or less veiled opposition; but she has not taken their lives or driven them out.... In all the ninety-five years that the American Board has operated in Turkey, only four of her missionaries have been murdered, and but one of these by an act of religious persecution.[34]

The *Herald* further told the Board's supporters that it had received positive assurances that the missionaries in Turkey were all fine. The *Herald* was particularly pleased that not only could the Board protect the lives of its missionaries, but also that the Board's work could go forward unhampered. Putting a positive spin on these troubling circumstances, the *Herald* reported that the Board expected new opportunities resulting from the war would provide for further growth. It was, stated the Board, "the chance of a lifetime.[35]

Notwithstanding the optimistic rhetoric of the editorial pages, the rest of the December issue of the *Herald* described the situation in Turkey in quite a different way. W. W. Peet, the Board's savvy treasurer, who wrote before Turkey had joined the war, shared insights from his post in Constantinople. Ongoing mobilization (despite the assurances from the Turks that it would end), requisition of all kinds of supplies needed by the troops, placement of troops all around Constantinople, the paralysis of business, and the seizure of hospitals for military purpose all strongly suggested that Turkey would enter the war, stated Peet. The Board had already received this information, no doubt, at the very time it indicated it did not think Turkey would join with the Central Powers.[36] The Board apparently did not feel it appropriate to share this information at that time with its supporters via the *Herald*.

The Board provided information about the situation in Erzerum, a flourishing missionary station established in 1839, that now had five missionaries, high schools for both boys and girls, and an active Sunday school. The missionaries had established nine outstations, each with its own church, with a total of 342 communicants and adherents numbering 1,065 individuals. Because the well fortified city was only forty-five miles west of the Russian border and was considered the key to Turkey's eastern defense, the missionaries (and others) assumed that Erzerum would be the first point of Russian attack. The *Herald's* article described the Armenian massacres of 1895, in which Erzerum and Trebizond were "filled with blood, fire, and pillage," but failed to address the possibility of current harm to Armenians.[37]

The *Herald* provided similar stories from sources in other parts of the interior of Turkey. In many places the effects of mobilization were already visible: a superb harvest ungathered, shepherds leaving their flocks untended, supplies needed by the army requisitioned without payment, and men ineligible for military service made idle by the end of industrial work.[38] According to Dr. W. S. Dodd, the American hospital in Konia had been seized for military purposes; Dodd, its medical director, would remain in charge of the hospital, with the help of one Turkish physician with him who would be officially in charge. The hospital presently held thirty beds; the military wanted the hospital to furnish 500 beds.[39] From Dr. Ussher in Van came an account of his and his colleagues' trip to the annual meeting of the Eastern Turkey Mission held in Harpoot that year. The trip took eleven days each way; they were on the road from 7:00 AM to 9:00 PM. He reported the conditions of various towns they went through. All were suffering from the effects of mobilization. Ussher observed that "the military had seized nearly all foodstuffs, kerosene and sugar, and were impressing into the army every male from twenty to forty-five years of age, leaving many families without food and only the women and children to care for the fields."[40] In Harpoot, Euphrates College, a Board school, had about 500 students in a city of 20,000. Rev. H. H. Riggs[41] was in charge of the school and described the problems resulting from mobilization and requisitioning of supplies. Turkish officials now placed soldiers in one of the halls, and H. H. Riggs was able to deliver his Christian message to the soldiers in the hospital.[42] And so the year ended. The missionaries were adjusting to operating evangelical programs in a country that had now joined in what was known as the "Great War." They knew that they were dealing with radically new conditions that hampered their abilities to pursue their aims. Yet 1914 was just the first year of the war. The optimism and faith in the future expressed by the Board through its journal, the *Herald*, would be sorely tried during the coming year.

Endnotes to The Year 1914

1. "Persecution of Armenians," *New York Times*, 16 March 1895, 5.
2. "Another Armenian Holocaust," *New York Times*, 10 September 1895, Part One, 1.
3. "Kurds and Christians," *New York Times*, 16 January 1895, 9.
4. "Moslem Massacres Take 5,000 Lives," *New York Times*, 21 April 1909, 2; "Moslems in Antioch Wipe Out Armenians," *New York Times*, 24 April 1909, 2.
5. "Report Christians in Peril," *New York Times*, 12 November 1914, 3.
6. "Erzerum Fanatics Slay Christians," *New York Times*, 29 November 1914, II, 2.
7. "Hang Christians in Street," *New York Times*, 14 December 1914, 2.
8. "Vali" is the term for an appointed governor of a province.
9. "Turkish Women Revolt," *New York Times*, 14 December 1914, 2.
10. Ibid.
11. This is the name given to the members of the Armenian Apostolic Church, founded by St. Gregory the Illuminator of Caesarea (Kayseri).
12. "The War in Europe," *Missionary Herald* CX (September 1914), 377.
13. Ibid. The Board was probably under the same delusion as the general public about the length of the war. Most expected it to end quickly in a matter of months. Instead the war lasted four years.
14. "Word From Marsovan," *Missionary Herald* CX (September 1914), 403.
15. "Commencement in Sivas," *Missionary Herald* CX (September 1914), 404-107.
16. "Turkey's Sudden Move," *Missionary Herald* CX (October 1914), 434-435.
17. "Financing Missions in War Time," *Missionary Herald* CX (October 1914), 431. Mail service became problematical again as the war went on.
18. "Pressing Questions and Answers," *Missionary Herald* CX (October 1914), 431.
19. Ibid.
20. "America's Contribution to Turkey's Education," *Missionary Herald* CX (October 1914), 455.
21. "War Rumors at Bardezag," *Missionary Herald* CX (October 1914), 455. Conscription of Christians would make it impossible for the Board to maintain all of their programs because many of the Board's teachers were Armenian or Greek men, and the pastors of the Armenian Protestant churches were all men.
22. "The Missionary Situation in Belligerent Turkey," *Missionary Herald* CX (December 1914), 554.
23. For Charles T. Riggs and H. H. Riggs, both active missionaries in Turkey during the years included in this book, I have included first names to avoid confusion.
24. Charles T. Riggs, "Those Abrogated Capitulations," *Missionary Herald* CX (November 1914), 493-494.
25. Ibid.

26. Ibid. This article demonstrates the difficulty of staying abreast of the events occurring in Turkey. It also shows the problem with publishing a monthly journal, outdated before it even leaves the printers.

27. James L. Barton, "Turkey and the Abolition of the Capitulations and Extraterritoriality," *Missionary Herald* CX (November 1914), 495-497.

28. "Mobilization Around Adana," *Missionary Herald* CX (November 1914), 508.

29. "From Marsovan," *Missionary Herald* CX (November 1914), 508-509.

30. G. E. White, "From Marsovan," *Missionary Herald* CX (November 1914), 508-509.

31. "The World of Battle," *Missionary Herald* CX (December 1914), 553.

32. "Some Streaks of Light," *Missionary Herald* CX (December 1914), 553.

33. "The Dividing of Islam," *Missionary Herald* CX (December 1914), 553.

34. "The Missionary Situation in Belligerent Turkey," *Missionary Herald* CX (December 1914), 554.

35. "A Cheering Message," *Missionary Herald* CX (December 1914), 555.

36. W. W. Peet, "Darkening Prospects in Turkey," *Missionary Herald* CX (December 1914), 558-559.

37. "Erzroom in the War Zone," *Missionary Herald* CX (December 1914), 566-567.

38. "From the Varied Fields," *Missionary Herald* CX (December 1914), 571-572.

39. "The Konia American Hospital Taken," *Missionary Herald* CX (December 1914), 572.

40. "Traveling in Eastern Turkey," *Missionary Herald* CX (December 1914), 572.

41. The Riggs family was active in Turkey. Rev. C. W. Riggs was resident in Constantinople; Rev. H. H. Riggs worked in Harpoot at Euphrates College.

42. "Conditions in Harpoot," *Missionary Herald* CX (December, 1914), 574-575.

Chapter 3

THE YEAR 1915

The deportation and murder of Armenians in Turkey was launched in April, but relief efforts did not get underway until September.

JANUARY - MARCH 1915

THE NEW YORK TIMES

Although the Board clung to its upbeat outlook about its future in the Ottoman Empire, the *Times* viewed the wartime situation without "rose colored glasses." The contrast in the style of reporting between that provided by the *Herald* and that provided by the *Times* was evident and indeed striking. While the Board's missionaries might not have been directly threatened by Turkey's actions, the *Times*' reporting strongly suggested that the Empire's Christians were in great danger. In keeping with its motto, "All the News That's Fit to Print," the *Times* was sensitive to the desire of its readers for information on the fast-moving events of the Near East and the dire straits of an Armenian population obviously in grave danger. A *Times*' story published in early January, 1915, reported that the Turkish government had no fear of Allied intervention in its internal affairs. "If the Straits are forced," warned the German Ambassador to Turkey, "the Turks will vent their wrath by a massacre of the Christian population."[1] Germany was using the threat of massacre to try to influence Allied wartime tactics.

Turkey's position was described in an interview given to the Associated Press (AP) by Talaat Pasha, Ottoman Turkey's Minister of the Interior and the man whom the *Times* called the most important in Turkey. Addressing the issue of the welfare of the minorities in Turkey, Talaat claimed that Britain and Russia had forced Turkey to go to war, but the Allies' own Muslim subjects would rise up in holy war against them once they witnessed the victories of the Turkish Army. "Christians in the Ottoman Empire who are participating in the destiny of their country are not suffering from conditions brought about by the present state of affairs, and any statements to the contrary are a result of British, French and Russian intrigues...," he informed the reporter.[2] Although he said nothing further to clarify what he meant by "Christians ... participating in the destiniy of their country," his words seem to imply that Christians who remained loyal to the Empire and who did not support the Allies would not be harmed. This statement may have reassured those Armenians who remained loyal to the Empire but were worried about how the war might affect them. However, while Talaat's words were soothing, they were in fact utterly false, as the events of the next month would show.

As early as March 20, little more than a month after Talaat had spoken to the AP reporter, the *Times* published an inauspicious story with a London dateline, bearing the headline "Whole Plain Strewn By Armenian Bodies," whose factual message contradicted Talaat's words. "The whole plain of Alashgerd,"[3] wrote the *Times*, "is virtually covered with the bodies of men, women, and children." When the Russians withdrew from this district, the *Times* explained, the Kurds fell upon the helpless people and shut them up in mosques. The men were then killed, and the women carried away to the mountains. The Red Cross Fund reported that this massacre had left 120,000 Armenians destitute in the Caucasus.[4]

This report from the Armenian Red Cross of London was based on information provided by an Armenian physician. The physician may not have been a neutral observer, but the wording and prominence of the headlines suggested that the *Times* believed the story to be accurate and wanted to publicize it. By identifying the source of information and the ethnicity of the doctor, the *Times* let the reader decide what weight to give the story.

The news report about the massacre at Alashgerd described an emerging pattern of warfare on the Turkish-Russian-Persian border that continued until 1918, when the Russians finally withdrew from the war. The Russian army would invade Turkish or Persian territory and engage the Turkish army. The Christian minorities would relax, believing that the presence of Russian troops guaranteed their safety. When military necessity required Russian withdrawal from an area, Christians who were physically able to flee with the Russians did so. Those who could not were slaughtered by Turkish troops or Kurds.

The *Times*' reporting on Turkey during the first three months of 1915 demonstrates a pro-Armenian bias. While the newspaper was willing to publicize the views of a Turkish leader like Talaat, the newspaper generally did not try to offer the Turkish viewpoint on the reported events. The headlines the *Times* employed in its news reports also imply strong support for the Armenian version of events.⁵ This is not to suggest that the stories were inaccurate; in fact, the conditions faced by Armenians at that point were far worse than the *Times* reported. But the veracity of its stories does not alter the fact that the *Times* did not publish the Turkish viewpoints on events. While it may have been extremely difficult to obtain such views, reporters or wire services could have been used to obtain other explanations of the events described.

THE MISSIONARY HERALD

While the *Times* focused on publishing hard-hitting stories about the massacres of Christians in Turkey, the Board remained concerned about its missionary staff, especially those unable to communicate with the Boston or Constantinople office. The pace of the war was accelerating. While the Board's staff may not have been in any danger, the missionaries were confronting enormous practical problems, including Turkish requisition of the Board's supplies and occupation of its buildings. In the city of Urfa the Turkish military had seized wheat, oil, rugs, hemp, and other goods from both rich and poor.⁶ In Aintab (Gaziantep), nearly all of the accumulated property of the community, draft animals, sheep and goats, and all food supplies, had been requisitioned, impoverishing the residents.⁷ Conscription of teachers and withdrawal of students through lack of money or difficulty of travel made it challenging to operate the Board's schools and colleges.⁸ Communication with missionary staff proved problematical. To get their messages through without censorship, the missionaries of Talas resorted to code. In a letter to Peet, the Board's long-serving treasurer in Constantinople, they cited Bible verses from the Old Testament. To understand their situation, wrote the missionaries, read these verses.⁹ Nevertheless, the Board heard from the State Department that all of the Canadian and American missionaries in Turkey were well.¹⁰

Although it was reassured about its staff, the Board was not pleased about the abrogation of the capitulations and the new regulations that Turkey had enacted to redefine relationships between the Turkish state and the foreigners living in it. The *Herald* stated:

> Following a sudden abrogation of the ancient agreements by which she has mainly dealt with foreign residents and interests in her empire, Turkey has ... promptly issued some new rules governing foreign schools, hospitals, and benevolent institutions within her borders.

These new rules are harsh, unreasonable, and drastic. They reveal an unmistakably hostile attitude.[11]

Apparently the Board no longer felt that Turkey appreciated its Christ-like service.

While the language of the new regulations may have been strident, local Turks adopted a lackadaisical approach to implementing them. White, President of Anatolia College, Marsovan, wrote that the new rules had gone into effect there on December 1, 1914. Although the local Turkish government had threatened to close the school if it did not comply, the officials seemed comfortable with its level of adherence.[12]

Despite the Board's annoyance about the capitulations, it sought to be helpful to the Turks in the midst of war. The Constantinople Chapter of the American Red Cross, of which Peet was the treasurer, sent the Turkish War Department a list of available hospitals in Asia Minor, with the number of beds each one could provide to meet the War Department's needs. Of the list of fifteen hospitals, ten were Board institutions.[13]

The *Herald* also gave its readers an inkling of the difficulties to come, by describing the experiences of the Erzerum mission, the first station to come within a battle zone. The government had seized the mission's buildings, including the boys' and girls' schools, for use as infirmaries to address the typhus epidemic. The mission staff in Erzerum had to request help from the Sivas station to deal with the medical crisis. Mrs. Sewney, wife of Dr. Sewny; Miss Graffam, the principal of the girls' high school in Sivas; Miss Zenger and Dr. Clark all went from Sivas to Erzerum during the dead of winter to provide assistance to the Erzerum staff.[14] This would not be the last time that missionary help would respond to the havoc created throughout Turkey by epidemics of cholera and typhus.

The *Herald's* overall theme for the first three months of 1915 was one of optimism: the missionaries were safe; they expected to remain in Turkey throughout the war; and they thought it likely that they would be in Turkey when the war was over, possibly in even greater numbers. Yet the Board was well aware of the murder of 200,000 Armenians during 1895-1896 and in 1909. The possibility, if not the likelihood, of a recurrence of such massacres under cover of war remained very high.

Nevertheless, the *Herald* mentioned nothing about the potential for attacks on Armenians and other Christian minorities, who could no longer look to the Allied powers for protection, and whose status in Turkey could become even more precarious. This omission is particularly bewildering because continuing service to Armenians was essential to the realization of the Board's long time goal of converting the Muslims of Turkey. Without the Armenians to serve as "shining examples" of the kind of Christianity the Board was promoting, the Board would have to approach the Turks directly.[15]

While its primary focus during 1915 had to be the safety of its staff, the Board's failure to express any significant concern about the welfare of Armenians in the Ottoman Empire is puzzling.

APRIL - JUNE 1915

THE NEW YORK TIMES

While the *Herald* had begun to tell its readers about the enormity of problems faced by the Board's mission staff in Turkey, it had yet to tell its readers about the potential harm to the Christian minorities. In contrast, by the month of April, the *Times* had begun to run in rapid succession a series of informative news stories about conditions in Turkey.

The *Times* published two brief accounts of the persecution of Armenians on April 19, 1915.[16] On the following day, it added a lengthy story that described its interview with Enver Pasha, Turkish Minister of War – the first given by him to the American press. In this highly flattering story, the reporter extolled Enver as "the world's youngest Commander-in-Chief" and the "handsomest man in the Turkish Army." The interview, conducted in German, although Enver spoke "excellent French," discussed his reasons for going to war.

Enver, much like Talaat, stated that the Russians had forced the Turks into war by encroaching on Turkish territory in the Caucasus and causing trouble on the Black Sea. Turkey remained friendly to the Americans in Turkey, he said, even though American arms and ammunition had been exported from the United States to the Allied powers. "We are not savages, who hold the innocent responsible for something that isn't their fault," he said.[17]

For the most part, the *Times* story simply quoted Enver, giving him an opportunity to describe Turkey's position without any significant questioning by the reporter. Enver spoke in platitudes only, describing the war effort, the reforms by which he had revitalized the army, and the expectation that Turkey and Germany could not help but be successful against the Allies.[18] Since the reporter failed to ask any meaningful questions, he became Enver's unwitting publicist.

On April 24, 1915, only four days after the report of the interview with Enver was published, the Ottoman government unleashed its plan to exterminate the Armenians in Turkey. On that date, the Ottoman Ministry of the Interior rounded up several hundred Armenian intellectuals, community and business leaders in Constantinople and many more in other areas, allegedly because they engaged in anti-government or nationalist activities. Most of those arrested were killed.[19]

Armenians who had been conscripted into the Ottoman Army were killed outright or transferred to labor battalions where they were worked to death.[20] Most of the remainder of the Armenian population, largely old men, women, and children, was deported in the summer to the "waterless tracts of inland Syria and Mesopotamia," desert areas reached after many months of travel, mainly on foot under inhumane conditions and without any of the provisions necessary to sustain life, such as food, water, shelter, and medical care.

The deportations took place far from the eyes and empathetic care of the civilized world. The distances traveled by the deportees were often long: for example, Armenians deported to the desert from towns as far away as Bayburt, had to travel a distance of 1000 kilometers.[21]

The conditions of deportation were abysmal.

> Along the deportation routes, they were subject to massive and repeated depredations– rape, kidnap, mutilation, outright killing, and death from exposure, starvation and thirst – at the hands of Ottoman gendarmes, Turkish and Kurdish irregulars, and local tribes. The Ottoman army was also involved in massacres. The kidnapped and other surviving women, and many orphans, were then subject to enforced conversion to Islam as a means of assimilation into the "New Turkey."[22]

The few survivors who were able to make it to the desert were often marched from one desert camp to the other, and then ordered back to their earlier camp. The aim was to kill them through exhaustion and despair and to claim that they had died "of natural causes."[23]

On April 26, just six days after it had published its reporter's interview with Enver, the *Times* published two more accounts about the Armenians in Turkey. The first, headlined "Kurds Massacre More Armenians," described the slaughter of Armenians at Erzerum, Berjan,[24] Zeitun, and ten villages near the city of Van. The story included the news that the Catholicos, the ruling head of the Armenian Church, had cabled President Wilson an appeal to the people of the United States. In response, the Secretary of State, William Jennings Bryan, requested that Ambassador Morgenthau convey to the Turks a request that "steps be taken for the protection of imperiled Armenians and to prevent the recurrence of religious outbreaks."[25] A subsequent request of the Catholicos led Secretary of State Bryan to take official notice of "the reported Armenian massacres."[26] Ambassador Morgenthau, along with other members of the diplomatic corps in Constantinople, had already taken up the matter "vigorously" with the Ottoman authorities.[27]

The second story published by the *Times* after the interview with Enver carried the headline "Great Exodus of Christians." It reported that during the first two days of January, 1915, the Russian troops pulled out of Urmiah and twenty to thirty thousand Armenians and Nestorians[28] had fled in panic for Russia and its relative safety. The terrified mob, stated the *Times*, fled on foot through knee-deep mud across mountain passes in freezing weather, with little food and even rarer shelter, some of them taking three weeks to make the trip. Crazed women who could no longer stand the cries of their children suffering from hunger and cold threw them into the Araxes River or into pools of water to put them out of their misery quickly. Those who lived – wrote the *Times* – envied those who had died.[29] The *Times* article described poignantly and sympathetically the kind of terrible events that would soon become commonplace as the genocide and war continued.

On May 6, the *Times* published a story with the dateline Tiflis, Transcaucasia,[30] and the headline "Routed Turkish Army Pursued by Russians" describing a Turkish–Russian military clash on the border of Turkey and Persia. Included in this story was a description of the fighting at Van[31] where Armenians of that city had decided to defend themselves rather than be murdered or deported. The outcome was as yet unknown as four Turkish regiments with artillery advanced from the city of Erzinjan, reported the *Times*. Van's Armenians, stated the paper, were requesting diplomatic intervention by the United States or Italy.

The *Times*' account also identified two related problems that would later be of major significance. It related that "[t]he existing state of terror has prevented the planting of crops and a famine is impending. The city of Erzerum in Turkish Armenia, has 300 cases of typhus fever today."[32] A subsequent *Times*' account addressed the welfare of the Van missionaries who lived in the "eastern suburbs of the vilayet." Since a vilayet is a province, a large area of land, and not a city with suburbs, the veracity of the story's other content was discounted by the Board and others familiar with Van. Yet the report did note that during defense of Van, the Turks had fired altogether 17,000 shells on Van's defenders.[33]

Five days later, the *Times* ran a story about a "flood of communications" inundating the State Department from all parts of the United States urging that action be taken on behalf of the threatened "native Christians" in Armenia and other regions under Turkish control. The *Times* reported that the State Department was preparing a reply to these letters, which would include Ambassador Morgenthau's request that *Turkish* troops be sent to Urumiah to restore order. The article included the following prescient observation:

> It was pointed out today that the feud between the native Christians in Persia and Turkish Armenia and the Kurds had endured for centuries, and [that] the present disturbed situation created by the European war was almost certain to be reflected in new outbreaks.[34]

The story the *Times* published about Ambassador Morgenthau's request for Turkish troops was obviously untrue, since it was the prospect of the arrival of Turkish troops in Urmiah that had led to the crazed flight of the civilians to Russian territory. In addition, the news story reported the hostility reflected in the State Department's observation that the depredations against the Armenians were much like a permanent tribal feud like the "Hatfields versus the McCoys" and would soon dissolve. Within five months, the State Department would awaken from its ignorance of the truth and state of denial and play an active role in the fund-raising program that would raise enormous amounts of money for the relief of the Armenians, Syrians, and other persecuted groups. Prominent in these efforts was Cleveland H. Dodge, a close personal friend of President Wilson.[35]

Standing in contrast to the State Department's reported assessment, the *Times* provided a spate of stories about the Armenians' plight in rapid succession. From May 17 through May 25, a space of eight days, seven articles appeared in the *Times*. On May 17, the *Times* printed a brief story about an uprising of Armenians in Zeitun, a mountain village located in Cilicia, a revolt of such importance that two Turkish reserve divisions were dispatched to quell it. The article also reported a massacre of 2,000 Armenians in

"Transcaucasia."[36] The following day, bold headlines announced that 6,000 Armenians had been slain by the Turks at Van, information attributed to a dispatch received in London from the Russian consul in Persia.[37]

A few days later, the *Times* published two more stories about Armenians, this time on the first page of the paper. One carried the headline, "Massacres by Wholesale." It reported that "[o]ne of the first sparks fanned into flame in the East by the European War was that of the old hatred between the Armenian Christians in Asiatic Turkey and Persia and the Mohammedan Turks and Kurds."[38] Although, at first glance, the *Times* appeared to be reiterating the State Department's expressed view that this ancient conflict was so deep and enduring that it could not be resolved, subtle changes in the story made it more pro-Armenian. It does not describe the conflict as a family "feud," thereby eliminating the suggestion that this was an ancient and ongoing quarrel of little or no importance. The article also characterizes "Armenian Christians" as being in "constant danger," thus triggering the sympathies of the *Times*' Christian readers. The Armenians too are painted as "victims" rather than perpetrators.

The second first-page story describes the issuance of a statement by the Allies specifically condemning Kurds and Turks involved in massacring Armenians with "the connivance and help of the Ottoman authorities."[39] The Allies threatened to hold the Turkish authorities responsible for these massacres, the article reported.[40]

On the following day, the *Times* published a story with the exhilarating headline, "Russians Save Armenians," which told of the liberation of Van by Russian troops and the concomitant retreat of the Turkish army.[41] The story was short and received little emphasis, as well as being inexplicably placed on page four when earlier stories about the revolt at Van had been page one news.

A subsequent story, on June 6, reported that the Kurds had fled from the approaching Russian troops, committing atrocities as they fled west "in the districts of Bitlis, Moush, and Diyarbekir."[42] No information was given by the *Times* about the fate of the Turkish troops also fleeing west to escape the Russians. This story repeated the Allies' threat to hold Turkish officials responsible for the "outrages" inflicted on Armenians.

After a month of intensive reporting on the situation in eastern Turkey, two articles appear in the following month of June 1915. The June 1 edition included a story with the dateline Constantinople via Bucharest, headed "40,000 Turkish Wounded," in which it was said that Constantinople hospitals were overwhelmed by the influx of military casualties. Despite these headlines, the bulk of the story pertained to a witness's report of the situation in the eastern provinces.[43] It is "perfect hell," reported the unidentified but seemingly reliable observer. The inhabitants are "maddened by war, typhus, and famine," quoted the *Times*' reporter.[44] The witness reported further

> bands of Kurdish horsemen [had] made a concerted rush into the Armenian quarters at Moush, a town west of Van, first attacking the shopkeepers in the bazaar, burning, looting and murdering as they went.... Fully 250 men were killed. The women, if old and ugly, were murdered or beaten; if young and pretty, they were taken away. The children generally were spared, but a few were put to death for sheer amusement.[45]

A subsequent report in the *Times*' Sunday edition dated June 6 added that Armenian volunteers were attempting to protect the Christian population from the Kurds.[46] The articles published in June 1915 employ images of atrocities made more believable because of the specificity in the descriptions of the sufferings of the Armenian victims – men, women, and children.

The stories published in April, May, and June 1915 provided the kind of information that would inspire the paper's sophisticated American readers to identify with the Christians of the Ottoman Empire. Their identification with Ottoman Christians and their knowledge of the atrocities would also lay a foundation for similar efforts by future fund-raising committees.

THE MISSIONARY HERALD

By early 1915, the Allies had initiated their attempt to force the Dardanelles[47] with the aim of seizing Constantinople. The Board had to be concerned about possible Turkish retribution against its staff, both in Constantinople and in the interior of Turkey. Ambassador Morgenthau addressed that concern in a message to the Board that said, "I never felt any doubt about the safety of the American missionaries and I am now assured by the proper authorities that they will treat all the Canadians and Englishmen connected with American missions with the same consideration."[48] The Ambassador's report was good news to the Board, and it helped to make the Board's typically optimistic reports to its supporters and staff more reality based than wishful thinking. It also reaffirmed the Board's point of view that the Turks honored the missionaries for their selfless, Christ-like ministry.[49]

Nevertheless, by April 1915, the Board also had a clearer understanding of the difficult situations that some of its missionaries in Turkey were facing. Much of the mail received by the Board at its headquarters in Boston and also in Constantinople showed signs of censorship, and missionary officials suspected that other mail from the Board's staff simply never arrived. The Turkish censors had even confiscated some editions of the *Herald* itself because of its "objectionable" content.[50]

The war caused some of the Board's missionaries to redirect their energies from evangelism to desperately needed medical work, a shift the Board would now recognize as imperative.[51] To maintain its supporters' interest in the missionaries' activities, the *Herald* began publishing exciting stories about the kind of unique experiences being faced by the staff during this time of war.

In one of these reports, from the city of Trebizond, the Rev. L. S. Crawford wrote in code that the "bombardment from people of the north was underway" [meaning the Russians] "but so far the mission had escaped any damage." Rev. Crawford also reported that two hundred destitute mothers had to be provided with food, mostly bread and condensed milk, for the babies whose mothers' milk had been dried up by the bombardment, as well as a little money.[52]

In a report from Harpoot, the *Herald* told its readers that the American hospital had been converted to a Red Cross hospital for military causalities, creating a vastly increased workload for Dr. Atkinson, its long time medical chief. The missionaries expressed their belief that the sacrificial work Dr. Atkinson carried out did a great deal to make the Board's Christian ministry and the spirit that underlay it clear to the Turks.[53]

Although the missionaries did not expect any untoward behavior by the Turks, overall wartime conditions posed a very serious threat to their work. Typhus raged at the mission station in Erzerum, exhausting the missionaries' ability to provide care for either their charges or each other. To minister to the sick, mission buildings previously used as barracks for Turkish troops were sterilized and converted to hospital use. Dr. Case, the station's medical director, had been forced to request that staff from the Sivas station come to Erzurum to help care for the victims of the epidemic, Christians and Muslims alike. Responding to Dr. Case's call for help, as described earlier, Miss Graffam, Mrs. Sewny, Miss Zenger, and Dr. Clark journeyed from Sivas to the Erzerum station. The trip, which normally took ten days, lasted twenty-one days because of snow and bad roads.[54]

Things at Erzerum became progressively more difficult as one after the other of the missionaries succumbed to typhus. Rev. Stapleton, his physician wife, Dr. Stapleton, and their two children all caught typhus but recovered. In a village nine hours from Erzerum, Dr. Sewny also contracted typhus but was too ill to be moved. His wife, accompanied by Miss Graffam, got there in time to speak to him before he died, but found it difficult to get a wooden box to bring his body back to Erzerum. Despite her own grief, Mrs. Sewny had to nurse Dr. Case and his wife, both of whom had contracted typhus, as a result of which Mrs. Case died. Two German nurses working in Erzerum, the city's pharmacist, and the chief Turkish doctor, also came down with typhus and were nursed to health by Miss Zenger, who herself later caught the fever and died. The Board's missionaries, reported the *Herald*, were absolutely overwhelmed and exhausted from nursing all of these seriously ill colleagues. At the same time, those who survived were gradually recovering.[55]

These stories could only begin to tell the *Herald*'s readers about the sufferings of some of the Board's staff in Turkey. The heroic record of the missionaries' sacrifices may have helped stir American readers to contribute an accelerating flow of funds needed to help relieve the Armenians' misfortunes.[56] Not everyone could go to serve in foreign lands, but almost everyone, including school children, could contribute something, no matter how small, to help the Armenians and the missionaries who worked with them. It was a point in the history of America where its people "stood tall" with a unified, national, selfless response that paralleled the missionaries' own courageous efforts.

Typhus was also rampant at the mission station at Harpoot, as well as in nearby Mezereh, where the Board's hospital was located. Sick soldiers, predominantly Turkish but also some Christians, lay in the street in the mud, because the military hospital was unable to care for all of them. Conditions were, wrote Dr. Atkinson who was in charge of the Board's hospital, "indescribable." The government took over the college buildings at Harpoot for use as space for additional hospital beds, although the college staff (unsuccessfully) objected, because this would mean that typhus would be introduced into the school buildings. The facility, subsequently turned into a Red Cross hospital, created a great deal of additional work for Dr. Atkinson, but, wrote the *Herald* in typical missionary language, the effort served to show the Turks the real purpose and practical outcome of "Christlike service."[57]

In Mardin, near the Syrian border, the Red Cross and the Red Crescent hospitals had combined to provide the best possible care for the Ottoman soldiers in their charge. Dr. Thom treated typhus patients both there and in nearby villages, where typhus had been introduced by a single soldier. In Sivas, the typhus epidemic claimed three hundred victims a day and residents begged in the streets. Sivas' mission staff was depleted because of the large number who had gone to Erzerum to assist. The station head at Sivas, Mr. Partridge, could not risk visits on horseback outside the mission compound; if he traveled by horseback, the military would seize his and any other horses they might get their hands on.[58] But not all reports were bleak. At the Board station in Talas, Rev. Wingate wrote that the winter had been mild and that flour was plentiful.[59]

These reports, published in the April and May issues of the *Herald*, had begun informing the Board's supporters about the horrific situations facing the mission staff in Turkey. It had yet to inform its readers, however, about the deadly animosity of the Turkish government toward its Armenian subjects.[60] By June of 1915, the *Herald* felt it had to address the issue of whether Washington should break diplomatic relations with Germany, which was conducting warfare on the high seas and leading to the slaughter of "innocent women and children."[61] But the Board called for a rupture neither with Germany nor with Germany's ally, Turkey. The Board recognized that such a move might jeopardize the well-being of its missionary staff, which could be interned for the rest of the war. A break with Turkey might also lead to the confiscation of the Board's considerable mission property in the Ottoman Empire, as well as the expulsion of Henry Morgenthau, the Ambassador who understood the tragedy that was unfolding before his eyes, and in whom the missionaries were placing great trust.

Although the *Herald* took pains to reassure its readers that the Board was still receiving letters from its missionaries in Turkey, it remained difficult to know exactly what was happening in the mission field. Outside sources were reporting many events that were not yet being mentioned in the missionary letters, suggesting that censorship continued to interfere with missionary communications to the Board. In addition, the normal time lag in receiving and reporting missionary news had increased because of the war, contributing to the Board's ignorance about the status of its programs and the welfare of its staff. The Board's dilemma appeared particularly evident in the *Herald's* June 1915 issue.[62]

Although Associated Press (AP) dispatches from Tiflis had reported that the denizens of the Armenian city of Van had resisted the certainty of massacre and deportation by barricading themselves in the city, the *Herald* found that questionable. Thirty Americans and the boys and girls of the Armenian schools were holed up in a "suburb of the vilayet," was the report published in the *Times*. Yet, stated the *Herald*, the Board had received no word of such events and considered the report highly dubious. The *Herald's* article pointed out that "a suburb of a vilayet" does not really exist, because a vilayet covers a large area of land; in addition, fewer than thirty Americans resided in Van.[63] Moreover, it said, reports sent to the State Department included information that contradicted the AP story. Based on information from Dr. Ussher and Rev. Yarrow, both missionaries stationed in Van, the American consul at Harpoot had assured the State Department that all was well in that city. Schwester Martha, a German missionary in Van, was supervising the newly opened military hospital there, aided by Miss MacLaren, a Board missionary. It was also known that the college at Van had opened as planned in September 1914, despite its proximity to the battlefield, and that the lower schools were functioning well with 548 in the boys' school and 518 in the girls' school – "All of which," stated the *Herald*, "makes still more improbable the situation depicted in the recent dispatches from Tiflis."[64]

The *Herald's* outright dismissal of the AP story from Tiflis was a mistake. While it debunked the AP account of May 10 because of its erroneous terminology about a vilayet, an incorrect number of Americans in Van, and the positive reports received by it from the American consul, the story was essentially true. The *Herald* may have felt its position was somehow compromised by reports of Armenians vigorously resisting the depredations of Turks and Kurds, preferring that their readers view Armenians as docile recipients of American charity. Possibly, the Board also mistakenly thought its own missionaries had engaged in partisan warfare during the siege of Van, thereby impairing their impartiality and hindering their effectiveness in Van and elsewhere in Turkey.

The exhaustive list of missionary illness, recovery, and, in some cases, deaths reported in the *Herald* during the months of April through June 1915 demonstrates the extraordinary nature of the times and the selfless and courageous efforts by the Board's men and women missionaries. Inspiring tales of missionary heroes could not help but engender admiration and respect from the readers of the *Herald*. Through these stories, the *Herald's* readers were able to participate vicariously in a genuinely needed and to them abundantly meaningful human relief effort. When in coming months the *Herald* and *Times* would describe the needs of Armenian refugees, readers would be able to transform their emphatic identification with the events in Turkey to generous monetary support to save Armenian lives.

JULY - SEPTEMBER 1915

THE NEW YORK TIMES

If the readers of the *Herald* had found some of the events in Van during the spring puzzling if not incomprehensible, the readers of the *Times* continued to get more accurate and complete data and more thoughtful and inspiring analyses. The *Times* went to great efforts to provide regular and thoroughgoing reports about the situation in Turkey and the welfare of its Christian minorities. On July 12, 1915, the newspaper published a story with the dateline Athens, headlined "Turks Are Evicting Native Christians" with the descriptive sub-heading, "Greeks and Armenians Driven From Homes and Converted by the Sword, Assert Americans."[65] By attributing this information to unidentified American travelers coming from Turkey and adding eyewitness accounts of the treatment of the Christian population,[66] the *Times* conveyed a ring of authenticity to the story. These reports supported, stated the *Times*, what the "native sources" were advocating, namely, if action was not taken against Turkey immediately, "there would be no more Christians in the Ottoman Empire."[67] One day later, the *Times* ran a brief report bearing the headline, "Turks Hard Pressed in Turkish Armenia," describing the Russian pursuit of the Turkish forces fleeing west from Van. The Turks, it stated, had distributed 40,000 rifles to arm the Kurds for use against the Armenians. The story ended with a description of the organized massacre of Armenians in Bitlis, but noted that the defenders were strengthened by 160 Armenian volunteers from America.[68]

On July 15, just two days after the just-mentioned new articles appeared, the first solicitation of funds to aid the Armenians appeared in the *Times*. Bearing the headline, "Ask Aid For Armenians," the short, twenty-two line story announced an appeal for "destitute non-combatants of Armenia" by an organization called the American Armenian Relief Fund. The Fund's directors included Bishop Greer; Oscar S. Straus, former Ambassador to Turkey; the former President of Harvard University, Charles W. Eliot; Bishop Philip M. Rhinelander of Philadelphia; and prominent financier Isaac N. Seligman. The article reported that more than 100,000 Armenians had fled to Russia and were in a "pitiful condition," but that the condition of Armenians remaining in Turkey was even worse. All of the able-bodied men had been conscripted and thousands of families, denied their only breadwinners, had been " 'plunged into privation, while pestilence works its ravages and Kurdish savagery spreads terror and destruction.' "[69]

The article described what was actually the first American committee formed to aid destitute Armenians of the First World War years, and it set the pattern for the *Times*' reporting of the resulting relief efforts for years to come. It named each of the prominent Americans who had banded together and lent their names to the enterprise, and it articulated the reasons that relief was needed. The article included, at the end, the name of the committee's treasurer and the treasurer's address. By providing this information, the *Times* was also lending its name and prestige to the efforts made to save the destitute members of all ethnic and religious groups in Turkey, Syria, and the Caucasus. In the future, the *Times* would serve – in the same way – as publicist for successive relief committees, giving them free publicity, educating the reading public about conditions in the Near East, and concluding all articles with the name and address of the treasurer to whom funds for relief could and should be sent.

Two more articles about Armenians appeared in July 1915. One of these, a news story headlined "Wholesale Massacres of Armenians by Turks," reported the statement of the Earl of Crewe, Lord President of the Council of England, that the British Foreign Office was in receipt of information about "both wholesale massacre and wholesale deportations." Lord Crewe asserted that the presence of the Germans in Turkey was "an unmitigated curse both to the Christian and Moslem populations." Because of the anti-German sentiments of Lord Crewe, this appears to be little more than a piece of wartime propaganda without much content, but the *Times* headline does continue to present the massacres as fact rather than as allegations.

The *Times* carried a story from Paris dated August 4, 1915, which reported that an Armenian socialist political party had asserted that the Turks had massacred all of the men of Bitlis, and had then assembled 9,000

Armenian women and children, drove them to the banks of the Tigris, shot them, and threw their bodies into the river. To this story the *Times* added a disclaimer stating that "[t]hese advices have not been substantiated from any other source." The article also stated that the Armenian population of Cilicia had been subjected to persecutions, with more than 40,000 Armenians feared dead, that Armenians at Moks (Bahçesaray) and Diarbekr (Diyarbekir) had also been killed, and that twenty members of the Armenian Social Democratic Party had been publicly hanged because they supported a plan to establish an independent Armenia.[70] Since this was the first disclaimer in the numerous articles on the plight of Armenians published by the *Times*, it appears that the *Times* had some reasons for questioning the veracity of the story. Possibly the "socialist" information source led the *Times* to be wary. Despite any misgiving it might have had, the *Times* published the story on the front page, suggesting that it may have wanted to demonstrate to its readers that it evaluated all of its sources carefully.

Throughout the rest of the month of August 1915, the *Times* peppered its readers repeatedly with stories about the conditions of Armenians in Turkey. The headlines of the articles give the gist of these stories. An earlier article titled "Armenian Horrors Grow" reported information provided by Lord Bryce of the British House of Lords.[71] Next the newspaper included an article titled "Armenians Are Sent To Perish in Desert," by Aneurin Williams, Member of Parliament. This article reported that the roadways and the Euphrates River "are strewn with corpses of exiles and those who survive are doomed to certain death, since they will find neither house, work, nor food in the desert. It is a plan to exterminate the whole Armenian people."[72] This story includes some of the same information reported in the article of August 4, 1915, which purported to be based on "socialist sources" and for that reason had been accompanied by a disclaimer. Apparently the *Times* felt that if the information came from a member of the British Parliament rather than "socialist" sources, it must be accurate and a disclaimer was not needed. "Burn 1,000 Armenians: Turks Lock Them in a Wooden Building and then Apply the Torch," with a dateline Petrograd, appeared on August 20, 1915, and describes a particularly gruesome version of savagery but provides no specific source for the information provided.[73] "Turks' Sop To Armenians," published on August 25, described the Porte's promise to allow ten per cent of the Armenian people to remain in Turkey.[74] An article on the same subject, deportation, titled "Turks Depopulate Towns of Armenia," describes the 600,000 starving Armenian deportees who were still on the road. The *Times* presented the story, gleaned from information reported by a traveler who had just arrived in New York from Turkey, as authoritative.[75]

These reports, published in rapid succession, conveyed a heightened sense of conviction by the *Times* that the stories they were obtaining from their eyewitness sources were accurate and true to the facts. Considering the nature of the profound allegations contained in these reports, the *Times*' failure to seek corroborating evidence is surprising. It suggests that the *Times* was now fully committed to publishing whatever information it received about the massacre and destruction of the Armenian people without independent corroboration, if received from a reliable (non-Socialist) source.[76]

Although these accounts do use such terms as "horrors" and "massacres," the rhetoric thus far had not included the kinds of pejorative terms often used to describe Turks, such as "fiendish," "diabolical," and "cruel." The facts described, such as "burned to death," and "600,000 starving," were so grisly that additional inflammatory language was not needed. The *Times* vividly communicated that Armenians were facing deadly situations that would soon lead to their extermination. By providing such assertive reporting, and describing the desperation of the Armenians' situation, the *Times* prepared the American public for the next period of American-Armenian engagement – the attempts to save as many Armenians as possible from an otherwise predictable death.

During September 1915, the *Times* continued to signal its commitment to the cause of reporting all of the facts pertaining to the Armenians of Turkey by publishing a total of twenty-three articles about their deportations and murder. The *Times* followed the same pattern of using lurid headlines to gain the readers' attention and entice them to read the graphically headlined reports. These articles included such provocative headlines as "Answer Morgenthau by Hanging Armenians"[77] (in response to Morgenthau's objections to the massacres of Armenians), "Mission Board Told of Turkish Horrors,"[78] "Armenian Women Put Up At Auction,"[79] and "500,000 Armenians Said to Have Perished."[80] Of the articles published in September, the story titled "1,500,000 Armenians Starve"[81] best conveyed the overall picture of the deportations, complete with heartrending descriptions of convoys in which old men, women and children walked on endlessly without food, water, or shelter.

The article comments that the evacuation of Armenians living on the southeast Mediterranean coast of Turkey might have had some military justification, since the Allies could have easily attacked Turkey at that location, and that the presence of a large number of non-combatants might interfere with Turkey's defensive measures. Yet no such rationale could explain the deportations from deep within Turkey – from cities and towns such as Erzerum, Trebizond, Diyarbekir, Samsun, Caesarea, and Urfa. (See map.) Moreover, observers expected very few of the 1,500,000 deportees to reach their destination in the Syrian desert, for no steps had been taken to provide for their needs, and the authorities discouraged the provision of aid by townsfolk along the way through threats of death to those who would seek to provide it. For those who did reach the desert, conditions would not improve, for neither shelter, food, water, nor clothing were awaiting them. The *Times* recognized that the conditions facing Armenians in the Caucasus, in the Syrian desert, and in Turkey itself would destroy almost all of the Armenians of Turkey unless immediate external intervention was organized.

Recognizing what seemed to be an almost inevitable outcome unless remedial action was taken at once, the paper's rhetoric heated up, describing Turks in ever more antagonistic language. The articles in September included such terms as "diabolical cruelty,"[82] "fiendish massacres,"[83] "virtual slavery,"[84] and "atrocities of a nauseating and appalling character." It would be difficult for a reader who read these headlines to remain dispassionate about the fate of the Armenians.

Rather than change the tenor of its reporting about the travails of the Armenians, the *Times* made some attempts to provide balanced coverage by providing another viewpoint on the persecution of Armenians. It carried a story – dated September 29, 1915 – in which Count von Bernstorff, the German Ambassador to the United States, asserted that reports of "alleged atrocities in the Ottoman Empire were 'pure inventions,'" and that the penalties imposed on Armenians had resulted from their attempts to "stir up rebellion and revolt and treasonable activity," making Turkey's Armenian policy a war-time necessity.[85] By placing this story on the front page of the *Times*, the editors gave the Turkish government an extraordinary opportunity to influence American public opinion on the Armenian issue. However, the only follow-up to this story consisted of a page one article in October, which reported the United States' request to von Bernstorff to ask the German government to intervene on behalf of the Armenians of Turkey.[86]

Included among the many *Times* articles on Armenians was the report on the formation of the organization called the American Committee for Armenian and Syrian Relief (ACASR),[87] next named the American Committee for Relief in the Near East (ACRNE), and finally Near East Relief (NER).[88] Dr. James L. Barton, the Board's Foreign Secretary, and Charles R. Crane, an experienced traveler in the Near East and a wealthy businessman who served also as President of the Board of Trustees of the Constantinople College for Women,[89] visited the State Department and reviewed the accumulated reports of the Department's consuls inside the Ottoman Empire. The records of the State Department referred to the *Times*' "harrowing tales of the treatment of the Armenian Christians by the Turks and the Kurds." The State Department records also described a plan of extermination of the Armenians, especially those belonging to the Armenian Apostolic Church – called "Gregorian Christians" or simply "Gregorians" – the Church to which about ninety percent of the Armenian population belonged.

The *Times* reported that the two men, Barton and Crane, would attend a meeting within a few days to create a plan to appeal to the American people for funds to aid Armenians.[90] This story, while reiterating much of the same information about Armenians, differed from articles previously published by the *Times*, in that it included information obtained from the State Department's agents and from consular officials whose jobs required them to file written reports about conditions in Turkey and other parts of Asia Minor. As a result, the records cited by the *Times* could not be dismissed as pro-Armenian or pro-Allied propaganda.

On September 26, 1915, Professor Samuel Train Dutton, secretary of the newly formed American Committee for Armenian and Syrian Relief, made public a preliminary report on the investigation conducted by Committee members Crane and Barton into the allegations about Armenians. In a press release, the Committee stated that its representatives (Barton and Crane) had read and evaluated written testimonies of eyewitnesses, including not only Armenians but also Greeks, Bulgarians, Italians, Germans, Turks, Englishmen, Americans, businessmen, travelers, and various officials of different ranks. They all agreed, based on their own observations, that a program of extermination of non-Moslems was then underway in the Ottoman Empire, and the committee intended to do something about it. Importantly, the new group's preliminary report recited the pertinent facts:

The ostensible deportation of men, women, and children toward Mesopotamia is usually but a form of marching those starving, helpless, and frequently naked refugees out into the mountains to be outraged and butchered, sometimes by their guards, and sometimes by the Kurds who gladly co-operate in the work of destruction.

In addition, the Committee noted the pressure of the Armenians' "forcible conversion to Islam."[91]

Aside from Dutton, Barton, and Crane, the committee members included Cleveland H. Dodge, a close friend of President Wilson since their Princeton days, Arthur Curtiss James, Rabbi Stephen S. Wise, John R. Mott, Frank Mason North, William Sloane, D. Stuart Dodge, and others.[92] The committee mentioned that in certain localities American property had been seized and Americans harassed by the authorities, but admitted that this was of trivial importance compared to the ongoing destruction of the Armenian people. If the press of the United States would use all of its power to demand that the Turkish government cease "this crime against humanity," stated the committee, it would not fail to produce results.[93] The committee members doubtlessly remained unaware that many of Germany's military and civilian agents in Turkey viewed the deportations and atrocities with disgust, and were therefore already urging the Turkish government leaders to stop their inhumane treatment.[94]

One of the challenges facing the Committee was the need to make Armenians attractive to the American public, at that time largely white, Anglo-Saxon Protestants. Unlike the Board's constituency in the United States, who were regularly exposed to information about the Armenians through the *Herald*, Armenians were probably little known by the American news-reading public. The Armenian beneficiaries of the proposed relief efforts lived in areas not easily accessible for travel by Americans, spoke a language that was unintelligible to most Americans, wrote in an altogether unfamiliar alphabet, worshiped in a church that practiced a form of Christianity unknown to most Americans, and sometimes had a swarthy and somewhat Semitic appearance. In an effort to help Americans relate to the deported, sick, starving, and dying Armenians, the Committee pointed out that among the deportees there were pupils and graduates from American schools, teachers and professionals who had earned degrees in American and European universities. They included men and women who were forward thinking and had represented the brains and enterprise of Turkey for the last twenty years or more.[95]

Because of America's isolationist tradition, the press would have to "sell" the Armenians to the insular American public in order to generate a flow of funds adequate to the proposed mission of mercy. One of the ways chosen to attract support from Protestant America was to emphasize in reports the pressure on Armenians to abandon Christianity and become Muslim. As martyrs for Christ, Armenians could be linked to the Christian martyrs of the early Christian era and therefore be much more attractive to American Christians. These approaches, coupled with the avalanche of information published by the *Times*, would help make Armenians known to the American public.

THE MISSIONARY HERALD

By July 1915, the Board was pleased to have received written communications from some of its Turkish missionary staff, even though it was unable to reach many of them in return. These letters, according to the Board, reported the missionary staff safe and for the most part well. "Reference is frequently made to the strain of the times through which they are passing and to events that may not be described but are full of excitement," the Board wrote in the July 1915 issue of the *Herald*. The Board also acknowledged that it received information of importance "from outside." In fact, the Board owed its knowledge of conditions in Turkey to non-missionary sources. The information thus received included the steps taken to exterminate the Armenian people either by outright murder or deportation.

The Board had long been familiar with the persecutions and massacres of Armenians. What they had not witnessed were wholesale abductions from people's homes, carried out under conditions that were simply tantamount to murder. The deportations from Marash, stated the Board, meant the loss of the educated and able Christian population of this area and "a blow at American missionary interests, menacing the results of more than fifty years of work and many thousands of dollars of expenditure."[96] When talking about the destruction of Armenians, the Board tended to call attention to the staff time and dollars it had contributed to its ministry in Turkey that would now be lost. At a time when Armenians of Turkey were being massacred or sent to the desert to die of exposure or starvation, the Board's financial concerns seem embarrassingly trivial.

Despite the general lack of news from its staff, the Board had at last received a telegram from the mission station's doctor in Van, Dr. Clarence B. Ussher, which had been forwarded through the American Ambassador at Petrograd. Sent by Dr. Ussher when the Russians entered Van in May, Dr. Ussher informed the Board that the missionaries were safe, but that the one thousand Muslims who had flooded into the American mission headquarters in Van for protection from the Russians were starving. Assistance was urgently needed, Dr. Ussher said.[97] One month earlier, the missionaries had requested assistance for Armenians; this month the missionaries had solicited funds for Muslims.[98] "[H]ere is fresh evidence," crowed the Board, "that the missionaries are the friends and benefactors of all the people among whom they dwell," without regard to whether they are Armenians, Turks, or Kurds.[99]

Meeting the needs of both Turks and Kurds was an important missionary theme throughout this and the remaining war years, as the Board emphasized not only its work for Armenians, but also its long-term plan for converting Muslims. If the missionaries were seen as assisting the Christian population only, they would have little credibility in the Muslim community. The *Herald* addressed this issue quite openly:

> [The missionaries] are making a record for devotion, reliability, fair-mindedness, and good will which it would seem must entitle them to the favor of whoever may be the ruling power in that harassed land [Turkey] and to the gratitude of all races of its people.[100]

But despite numerous appeals for funds, few gifts had been earmarked by their donors for Turks. Perhaps Turkey was too remote, mused the *Herald*, or possibly the Turkish people's age-old reputation for "trickery, cruelty, and lawlessness" has "made the ears of the charitable less sensitive to Turkey's cry for help."[101] If the public showed lack of interest in helping Muslims, they did not have the same reservations about helping Armenians. The Armenians were Christians, albeit a kind of Christianity that was dissimilar to American Protestantism; they were the oppressed rather than the oppressor; and the American public had on occasion encountered Armenians. It was highly unlikely the public in that era was generally acquainted with any Turks or Kurds.

Although the Board sometimes got information directly from some of its missionaries, the information often proved incomplete. From Urfa, the Board received a disturbing letter from its missionaries in that town, Mr. and Mrs. Leslie. Despite the war, regular church work had continued and the members of the churches had shown a deeper spiritual interest than at any time in the past, the *Herald* reported. Lack of financial support in the latter part of 1914 and 1915 meant that some of the older boys could no longer stay in the Board's Urfa orphanage but would have to go out on their own. If funds were not provided quickly, said this report, the orphanage itself would have to close, even though most of their orphans were small boys.[102] The letter from the Leslies demonstrates the financial problems stemming from the war, and the emotional content of the missionaries' concerns for the welfare of those for whom they had assumed responsibility. Was there a reader of the *Herald* whose heart would not be touched by the thought of small orphaned boys put out of a closed orphanage? Additional stress may have been placed on the missionaries by Urfa's role as one of the stopping places on the way to the desert for many of the deported Armenians from locations farther north. Although the well-documented deportations and related atrocities would be natural subjects for the Leslies' letters to the Board, they did not mention either, suggesting that rigorous Turkish censorship limited what could openly be related to the Board.

A letter from Mrs. Lyndon S. Crawford of Trebizond published in the August 1915 *Herald* demonstrated the problems of censorship. Mrs. Crawford stated that she could not write about the conditions that were calling for relief, but that she had given out $400 in condensed milk, bread, and money in the month of April alone to three hundred families, whose numbers, she said, kept increasing. She furnished condensed milk to those too sick to eat bread, especially when it was made of corn meal, and to babies who could not get sufficient nutrition from their mothers' milk if the mothers only ate bread. The quantity of milk available for distribution was, she said, "a drop in the bucket" in relation to the need, and she had had to turn many away. Conditions about us are "tragic and appalling," she wrote.[103]

The *Herald* also struggled to reconcile the concept of warfare among Christian nations with the teachings of Christ. Board Secretary Edward Lincoln Smith[104] wrote an essay bearing the title, "The War's Contribution to Missions."[105] Although Christianity on the whole has been discredited by this war, Smith wrote, the religion espoused by Christ has to be separated from the responsibility for war activities in Europe.

Describing the war's effect on Muslims, Smith stated: "[i]t was a happy moment for the millions of Christian subjects of the Ottoman Empire when the very great majority of the Moslem suftahs[106] ignored the declaration of the holy war."[107] Mankind will expect a better world to emerge from this conflict, Smith stated; the next twenty years will be the greatest era ever for missions.[108]

By September 1915, the *Herald* abandoned its optimistic stance that things were well in Turkey. The style with which it wrote about Armenians also changed markedly. In a long article in its September 1915 issue titled "In Darkest Turkey," the *Herald* asserted that Turkey was engaged in a "systematic, authorized, and desperate effort on the part of the rulers of Turkey to wipe out the Armenians."[109] The account goes into great detail about the death and destruction that was being visited upon Armenians through the process of outright murder, or the slow, lingering, often painful death of the deportations.

The only bright spot, said the *Herald*, is that the American missionaries in Turkey continued to remain unmolested and are treated by the Turks with consideration and kindness. The missionaries were rendering important service, stated the *Herald*, for they must bear a "crushing load of distress and anxiety," inevitable in the situations they confront on a daily basis.[110] This information, the *Herald* reported, had not come from the Board's missionaries, who tended to be very circumspect (being subject to censorship), but from other (unnamed) sources.[111]

These statements mark a change in the *Herald's* reporting because for the first time they directly accused the Turkish government of planned and authorized actions against Armenians, rather than the actions of a renegade few. The *Herald* also clearly identified the kinds of daily challenges faced by the missionaries who always had too few resources to serve the needy around them.

By September 1915, the *Herald* also knew what exactly had happened at Van. After the Russian entrance into Van, the Board now had an unintended fully equipped mission station in Russian territory whose communications were not subject to censorship by the government.[112]

The *Herald* reported that a conflict had arisen between the Armenian residents of Van and the Turks. Each side took cover behind defenses that enabled them to attack the opposite side. The missionary compound, located in what was called the "Gardens" section of Van, was regularly bombarded by Turkish cannon set up atop the nearby fortress, although all of the mission's occupants were strictly unarmed.[113] Dr. Ussher, the only physician in the Armenian quarter, had the care not only of his patients, but also of the wounded Armenian soldiers and refugees. Four thousand Armenians from the neighborhood in which the mission compound was located took refuge in what they hoped would be a safe place, and they had to be supplied with food, shelter, and sanitation facilities during the siege.[114]

The Americans had the refugees organize into committees that could provide an administrative structure to address the needs of these uprooted persons. For the people outside the compound, the missionaries provided milk and eggs for infants and the sick, and bread for everyone. The siege lasted four weeks with increasing strain on the missionaries, their resources, and the combatants. Finally,

> [a]fter four weeks of such strenuous and exciting life, during which bullets peppered the walls and whizzed through rooms and shells from the cannon fell on the premises or exploded above them, while refugees kept increasing and provisions waning and all sorts of threats and rumors filled the air, at last on Saturday and Sunday, May 15 and 16, the Turks withdrew across Lake Van.[115]

On Tuesday, May the 18th, the advance guard of the Russo-Armenian volunteers arrived in Van, temporarily ending the Turkish threat to Armenians.[116] When the Russo-Armenian troops arrived, the Turkish residents of Van feared that they would be slaughtered by the Russian troops. One thousand Turkish women and children then took refuge in the mission compound, brought there by the Armenian soldiers as the only safe place for them. After sheltering four thousand Armenians for four weeks, the missionaries then had the task of helping one thousand Turkish women and children.[117]

The *Herald* could not extol their missionaries more. "Courage, adaptability, resourcefulness, self-sacrifice, sympathy, sanity: what quality of a rounded and capable Christian service was not displayed in the test hours of that month of siege," wrote the *Herald*.[118]

The significance of this story for the Board was the strict impartiality of the missionaries, who had provided everything possible to both sides of the conflict. Not only had they cared for the Armenians who had inundated their compound, terrified of both Turkish troops and Turkish and Kurdish civilians, the missionaries had offered the same sanctuary to the city's Turkish and Kurdish civilians when called upon to do so. In the best missionary tradition, the missionaries had offered assistance to all sides – Armenians, Turks, and Kurds – while maintaining rigid neutrality so that they could not be accused of partisan activity.

The *Herald* story was a heroic tale of deliverance, a romantic piece of missionary literature. The story also brought home to the readers of the *Herald* how difficult it was for the Board to know what was happening at its stations. The *Times'* report was published relatively soon after the events that were being reported, but until the Board received additional information from its staff, it was unable to evaluate the situation and act accordingly.

In a much calmer vein, the *Herald* reported that the Board had received a postcard from Mr. Merrill of Aintab that said nothing about the war, but only that the school's commencement had been cancelled because of a lack of graduates. But Merrill's postcard did not elaborate on the situation.[119] From Erzerum, the Board received a telegram from Mr. Stapleton, asking that his friends be informed that he was well, but also that he would be postponing his furlough.[120] The notes from the Board's staff, so lacking in detail, appear to have served as a way for the Board's staff to assure friends and relatives they were well. Sometimes the missionaries sent postcards to the Board, probably so that the censor could easily read the message and be assured that the message was innocuous and not subversive in any way.

Problems of delay in obtaining and reporting news about the missionaries in the Board's stations in Turkey continued to plague the Board. The September 1915 issue of the *Herald* is illustrative. While the Board extolled the "thrilling" events about Van in one section of the *Herald*, another section of the *Herald* describes a delay in publishing the September issue because of late breaking news about the missionaries at Van.

On August 16, 1915, the State Department notified Dr. Barton that the American consul at Tiflis had reported that all the Americans of the Van mission station were now in Tiflis, except Mrs. Ussher who had died of typhus in Van. The fifteen Americans had arrived safely but without funds or clothing. Dr. Ussher and Mrs. Raynolds were gravely ill,[121] and the remaining missionaries were exhausted from overwork and hardship.

The American consul in Tiflis requested instructions about the refugees' relief and repatriation. This information did not surprise the Board, since newspaper accounts (mainly the *Times*) had been providing news about the Turkish recapture of Van and the missionaries' escape for some time. The *Herald* listed the fifteen names and noted with pride that the Board had responded to the emergency by sending $4,000 immediately to Tiflis to be used for their care. It also informed its readers that some of the rescued missionaries were on their way home for furlough. This acknowledgment that the press could report accurate missionary news before the Board itself was aware of the unfolding events was a surprising admission by the Board, and one it had not made before.

OCTOBER - DECEMBER 1915

THE NEW YORK TIMES

The newly-formed American Committee for Armenian and Syrian Relief (ACASR) immediately set to work to raise funds needed for the Armenians. On October 3, 1915, the Committee issued a "detailed report," the result of weeks of investigation into the conditions facing the Armenians of the Ottoman Empire. The *Times* signaled its sympathy with the Committee's purposes and the integrity of its report by publishing its own lengthy investigatory report on the first page, first column, of its Monday, October 4, 1915 issue.[122] The story was indeed a "blockbuster" and must have been viewed as such by the *Times*' readers. After describing the Committee's findings in general terms, and in particular, its characterization of the government's treatment of Armenians "as an unsurpassed record of cruelty and horror that has not been equaled during the last thousand years," the *Times* chose to identify the signatories to the report. Both the names of the signatories and their affiliations were provided, thereby giving the report optimal authority.[123]

The *Times* article next provided a general statement about those individuals who had provided the information relied upon by the Committee. All of them were individuals of unquestionable veracity, integrity, and authority, wrote the *Times*, whose names, positions, and locations could not be revealed without causing "irreparable harm" to their persons or interests.[124] To make its lengthy news story about the massacres and deportations easier to read, the *Times* provided short subtitles throughout to help break up the dense narrative. The major sub-headings were "Deportation Was Begun in Zeitun" (decrying the lack of food, water, or shelter on the deportation routes); "Women Driven Under the Lash" (portraying the use of whips to force women in their last days of pregnancy or with little children to keep moving); "Prisoners' Feet Beaten to Pieces" (publicizing the consequences of the re-introduction of the bastinado); "Women of Sultan's Soldiers Deported" (providing a picture of how the deportations were carried out); "Beat Child's Brains Out on Rock" (illustrating outrages against women and children); "Woman Writes of Horrible Experiences" (detailing the tortures visited on the deportees as they walked on their way to the desert); and "Moslem Criminals Released for Pillage" (depicting the kind of criminals who had been released from prison so that they could participate in the destruction of the Armenians). The reports that followed the headings must be read at length to appreciate the character and horror of the conduct reported and the consequences to the victims.[125]

At the end of the article, the *Times* made a plea for funds to aid in saving lives by sending money to the Committee's treasurer, Charles R. Crane, 70 Fifth Avenue, New York.[126] Just as the *Times* had always included the name of the Brown Brothers as treasurer of the Armenian Relief Fund Committee, it now did the same for ACASR.

The language that the *Times* used so powerfully in this article could not have failed to arouse its readers to thought, sympathy, and action. Phrases like "torture, pillage, rape, murder, wholesale expulsion and deportation, and massacres," "torture by fire," "the burning out of the eyes of the poor victims," and "mutilated bodies of women, girls, and little children," presented a picture of such overwhelming cruelty that only the most indifferent reader could fail to be touched.[127] ACASR had decided from the outset that it would rely solely on news reporting rather than on paid publicity to raise funds for Armenians.[128] The *Times* proved a willing partner in that enterprise.

For the remainder of the month of October 1915, the *Times* kept the issue of Armenians in Turkey before its readers' eyes. The day after publication of its "blockbuster" article, the *Times* published a report that the State Department had responded to news about the massacre and deportation of

Armenians by addressing the Porte directly. The article reported in particular that "representations have been made to the Ottoman Government by the Government of the United States regarding the Armenian atrocities."[129] If the *Times* could demonstrate this level of interest, surely the officials of the State Department in Washington could no longer ignore the question. While the American Ambassador was knowledgeable and active, his communiques to the State Department had not produced results. The *Times'* report could help not only to raise funds to care for the victims, but also to pressure the State Department to take further action to influence the Turkish government. On October 6, 1915, the *Times* instructed its readers who wanted to help Armenians to send funds to the Ambassador or ACASR.[130]

In the same issue, the *Times* also informed its readers that the sixteen missionaries who had joined the Russians in their retreat from Van had finally arrived in the United States, bringing fresh tales of the Turkish siege. The article's headline read, "German Directed The Turks at Van," leaving no doubt in the minds of the *Times'* readers about who was behind the Turkish attack on the American mission compound and other parts of the city. Dr. Yarrow, one of the Van missionaries during the siege, provided a stirring account of the twenty-seven days spent fending off the Turks and Kurds, including a report that a German officer oversaw the artillery barrage on the mission compound.[131]

Throughout the rest of October 1915, the *Times* readers showered its readers with articles about some action or another pertaining to Armenians, including the refusal of the German government to intervene on behalf of the besieged minority. On October 7, the *Times* published a story with the headline "800,000 Armenians Counted Destroyed," which compared Germany to Pontus Pilate, a reference that would be understood by almost all American Christians, and a second story that announced that the Committee had already acquired $75,000 to help Armenians.[132] On October 9, three separate stories appeared: "A Hope For Armenians," "Why We Aid Armenians," and "Sends $100,000 To Aid Armenian Refugees."[133] Many things were happening and the *Times* sought to report them all, with sensitivity to human suffering and attention to detail that must have drawn tears to many of its readers' eyes.

At all times, the newspaper demonstrated the level of its sympathy for Armenians. In its Sunday edition of October 10, the *Times* published five articles altogether, each pertaining to the situation of Armenians in Turkey.

These highly factual news reports not only reported, but also commented on the various events and diplomatic efforts being made on behalf of Armenians and some of the responses to those efforts. "Armenian Appeal By Bryce In Full" described Lord Bryce's letter to a member of the British Parliament summarizing the events befalling the Armenians.[134] "Letters Tell Of Outrages" proved unique because it included not only a letter from a Board missionary, but one from a Turk living in Turkey written to his son in the United States, in which he decried the treatment of Armenians and the resulting loss of local business.[135] An article titled, "Defends Repression Of The Armenians" included a German military journalist's statement that "...it is Turkey's own affair how she deals with Armenian uprisings."[136] An AP story, "Pleas For Armenia By Germany Futile," portrayed Germany in a softer light, stating that the German government had sought to prevent deportation and massacre but had succeeded only in Constantinople, because it had no control over other areas.[137] An article dubbed "Turkish Statesman Denounces Atrocities" expressed the views of an exiled Turkish statesman, the former Grand Vizier, Mehmed Charif Pasha, as expressed to the editor of a newspaper in Geneva, denouncing the Turkish treatment of Armenians and indicating that it was based on a plan hatched several years earlier.[138] Although these stories contain powerful language in support of Armenians and show the breadth and depth of the paper's repugnance toward Turkish policy, the *Times* located the stories on page 19 of Section II of the Sunday *Times*. By placing them there, the *Times* to some extent "killed the story," because such a location would guarantee that many readers would miss the articles entirely. In view of the *Times*' vigorous editorial support of Armenians, this action is puzzling.

On the very next day, however, the *Times* again elevated the Armenian accounts to page four of the front section of the paper. "Spare Armenians, Pope Asks Sultan" described a letter from Pope Benedict to the Sultan;[139] "To Plead for Armenians" announced a mass meeting of the Armenian Atrocities Committee in a New York City theater[140] while "Prays for Morgenthau's Work" appeared on October 11, 1915.[142] Two days later, the paper again ran stories on page four in the first section. The article, "Armenian Protests Charged To Allies," presented the argument advanced by Germany that the Allies were manufacturing atrocity claims about the Turks and had themselves failed to stop *Armenian* massacres of *Turks*.[142] "Massacres Renewed, Morgenthau Reports" discussed the Ottoman government's failure to respond to the United States' warning about atrocities.[143] "Turks Fear Armenians" laid out the argument that the Turks had to massacre Armenians because they worried that the Christian minority might rise up against them.[144]

As a responsible newspaper, the *Times* also allocated space to the Turkish point of view. In "Turkish Official Denies Atrocities," the *Times* published a statement given to them by Djelal Munif Bey, Turkish Consul General in New York.[145] The Consul General asserted that the reports of Armenian atrocities were fabricated. ACASR had relied on statements of ill-informed missionaries and others who had not been identified, he claimed. All those who were killed had rebelled against the Turkish state and were therefore eliminated. He particularly criticized the Board's missionaries. This stance must have been a "hard sell" to the American public to whom the missionaries had long been portrayed as selfless, well-educated Americans who sacrificed a life of relative ease in the United States to serve in Turkey, a remote and barbarous country.

On the following day, the *Times* published two stories on the same page. Bearing the titles "We Can Do Nothing Further"[146] and "Says Only Germany Can Save Armenians,"[147] the articles reported the frustration of the State Department in its endeavor to alter Turkey's domestic and foreign policies.

Taking steps to meet the mounting challenges, ACASR intensified its fund raising activities, which were heralded by a mass meeting on Sunday, October 17. In a four-column story spread across page three, the *Times* reported that a "great audience that packed the Century Theater... assembled to respond to the atrocities in Armenia, passed resolutions condemning the acts of the Turkish government and offered to render assistance to the American Ambassador and others who were seeking to aid the Armenians." Dr. Barton, as would be expected, served as a prominent speaker, using the occasion to describe his research into the situation in Turkey. The meeting, according to the *Times*, focused more on denouncing the atrocities of the Turks than on assisting Armenians.[148]

The *Times* gave those espousing Turkish viewpoints on the deportations another opportunity to present their case. On October 18, 1915, it published a lengthy letter by Zia Mufty-Zade Bey headlined, "The Kind of Armenians a Turk Knows," and sub-headed, "They Betray Their Rulers, Take Refuge in Christian Missions, and Have to be Dealt With as Dangerous Rebels." The letter expressed in impassioned language the author's claim that disloyal Armenians had taken seditious actions against the government, which justified the actions taken against them.[149] The *Times* placed this letter in the first section of the paper to make it more accessible, demonstrating an attempt at impartiality, but in light of the flood of pro-Armenian articles published that month, the Turkish position probably found few adherents among the papers' readers. The *Times* had, however, not published Mufty-Zade's letter as written but had omitted three paragraphs. He objected and asked that the *Times* print the letter in its entirety; the newspaper complied the next day.

In the omitted lines of the letter, Mufty-Zade Bey affirmed that every nation has committed evil acts, and admonished the *Times*' readers that nations claiming to be Christian should honor Christ's saying that "let he who has no sin throw the first stone." The omitted lines also cited the United States' policy of relocating Native Americans to reservations, alluding to the close analogy between the respective situations. The Armenians, like native Americans, indeed, took unnecessary chances, he argued, and now must bear the consequences of "their rebellious and treacherous actions." Turkey, he wrote, is neither better nor worse than any other nation.[150]

But that day, the *Times* also published an article with the headline "Turkey Bars Red Cross,"[151] telling of Turkey's refusal to let the American Red Cross send doctors and nurses to aid Armenians. If Mufty-Zade Bey had garnered any sympathy for the Turkish position, this account of the Ottoman government's denial of humanitarian aid surely nullified it.

While continuing to publish stories sympathetic to Armenians, the *Times* did print a lengthy report of the Turkish government's accusations against Armenians. In an article headed "Accuse Armenians of Wronging Turks" and sub-headed "Ottoman Authorities Give Out Formal Charges of Widespread Outrages," the *Times* published allegations of "barbarous acts ... committed on Muslims along the Caucasian frontier by Russian troops, aided by members of the Greek and Armenian population of that region." The article detailed numerous heinous acts against Muslim women and children, beheadings of Muslims, and tortures of the same kinds that Armenians reported they had experienced.[152] These claims by the Ottoman government may have been true, but lacking independent corroboration of atrocities by Armenians, the *Times*' readers may have simply dismissed the article as Turkish propaganda.

At times, the New York daily seemed to abandon all editorial discretion and publish anything that pro-Armenian sources provided. An example is the article, "Turkish Spies in Hotel," alleging that four Turks had walked by a group of Armenians dining at a hotel restaurant and had cast ominous glances at the latter. One of the diners was the prominent Armenian spokesmen Arshag Mahdesian. By the time the hotel's detective was summoned, the four "spies" had left the hotel.[153] This story seems silly.

The *Times* continued to publish news stories sympathetic to Armenians. One titled "Armenians Thank Pope" was bound to appeal to American Catholics.[154] Another titled "Only 200,000 Armenians Now Left In Turkey," subheaded "More than 1,000,000 Killed, Enslaved or Exiled, Says a Tiflis Paper," sought to quantify the number of Armenians killed;[155] and a piece headed "Slay All Armenians in City of Kerasunt," subheaded "Turks Wipe Out Entire Population in Town on the Black Sea," kept the on-going massacres in the public eye.[156]

The *Times* continued to address the question of German complicity. An article with the headline, "Germany Says She Cannot Stop Turks," explained Berlin's position,[157] while "Can't Defend Armenians," referred to the statement of the Turkish leader, Halil Bey, that the Turkish public was so incensed over the Armenians' disloyalty to Turkey that he lacked the troops needed to hold back the Turks.[158] The *Times* also published a response to Mufty-Zade Bey written by Arshag Mahdesian.[159]

The many articles on Armenian issues published by the *Times* in October 1915 varied little from those published in September. As the most widely read and influential paper in the United States, and in keeping with its motto and mission, the *Times* proved relentless in its dissemination of information to the reading public on any aspect of the "Armenian Question" during this month. Any regular reader of the *Times* had to be fully informed about all of the issues pertaining to the genocide, including viewpoints expressed on behalf of Armenians, Turks, and many others. This emphasis must have reflected the importance of this topic to both the *Times*' editors and its readers.

By November 1915, ACASR adopted a standard format for disseminating information.[160] The Committee would put out a press release describing some facts about the current condition of Armenians, food relief programs, governmental assistance, or some other topic pertaining to its work, and the *Times* would then publish a story based on the information provided by the Committee. In each story, the *Times* would name the source, ACASR, and provide the names of a few members of the Committee "and other prominent men." The paper then disseminated the contents of the press release, shaped the language to fit its own style, and almost always concluded the account by noting that Charles Crane was ACASR's treasurer and that contributions to the committee could be sent to his office at 70 Fifth Avenue in New York City. This system had advantages not only for ACASR, but also for the *Times*. The Committee gained the free publicity it needed, and the *Times* put out news stories that would interest its readers with little effort on its part. This system worked so well that it was continued throughout the remainder of the war years.[161]

Negative publicity about Turkey continued to be published by the *Times*. The story "Aid For Armenians Blocked By Turkey" described Turkey's refusal to allow food and supplies to be given to the refugees, and provided its own estimate that 1,000,000 Turkish Armenians had been deported or had died.[162] The report also included a first person account by an official representative of one of the neutral powers:

> I watched them one time when their food was brought. Wild animals could not be worse. They rushed upon the guards who carried the food, and the guards beat them back with clubs, hitting hard enough to sometimes kill. To watch them one could hardly believe these people to be human beings.[163]

No information from Turkish sources could overcome a story like that.

On November 27, 1915, the *Times* published a three-column story titled "Armenians' Heroic Stand In Mountains," sub-headlined "Men, Women, and Children Fought with Knives, Scythes, and Stones." This article was based on a report authored by Viscount Bryce that "[s]urpass[ed] in horror, if that were possible, what has been published already." The *Times* article described in detail the destruction of the Armenians and the Chaldeans[164] of the regions of Van, Moush, and the hill country of Sasun."[165] The article is full of pejorative language about the "Turkish beast," his "atrocities," "unspeakable crimes," "Butcher battalions," and the "shocking, lingering agony," "death cries of the victims," "roasted to death," and "the odor of burning flesh" of the besieged Christians. The article's lurid pictures no doubt created images that would linger in readers' minds for a long time to come. Moreover, the same "loaded" words and images would be used to describe the Turkish conquest of Bitlis, Moush, and Sasun.

Some women knelt down and prayed amid the flames which were burning their bodies. Others shrieked for help, which came from nowhere, and the executioners, who seemed unmoved by this unparalleled savagery, grasped infants by one leg and hurled them into the fire...[166]

Viscount Bryce, a long time supporter of the Armenian cause, would provide even more gruesome stories in October 1916.

Of crucial interest to the public was the use of the funds they had contributed to ACASR. The *Times* explained in a news story published December 10, 1915, that $100,000 had been forwarded "to the sufferers" but that far greater amounts than originally estimated were needed.[167] (Morgenthau had naively estimated that $100,000 would be sufficient.) ACASR, recognizing the magnitude of the problem, accordingly sent a revised estimate to Morgenthau. The Committee soon realized, however, that even more funds had to be raised to prevent the death rate from decimating the refugees. The report also included news from ACASR that relief efforts were now underway to relieve the suffering of some 300,000 "non-Mohammedans" who had escaped from Turkey into Trans-Caucasia.[168] In the future, much of ACASR's relief efforts would be focused on the Caucasus.

In the middle of November, the *Times* ran a story headlined "Church Plea For Armenia" that announced that the Anglican and Eastern Orthodox Churches Union had petitioned President Wilson on behalf of Armenians. The American people, said the story, increasingly prejudiced against Turkey's ally, Germany, because of the latter's failure to halt the deliberate extermination of a Christian people, asked for the protection by the Wilson administration, and that American ships be sent to Turkey to transport as many of the Armenians as possible to Christian countries.[169]

The *Times* also continued to be a publicist for the Board. A story headed "A Missionary Poisoned" and sub-headined "The Rev. F. H. Leslie of Michigan killed at Urfa" told about the death of one of the Board's missionaries, the circumstances of which were being investigated by Ambassador Morgenthau, who had not yet reached any conclusions. Because of Leslie's location and his role in distributing monetary allowances to the 800 British, French, and Italian internees held by the Turks in Urfa, he had been asked to serve as United States Consular Agent. The Turkish government, however, had refused to recognize his appointment. Since 1912, Leslie had been the only missionary serving in Urfa, a "remote station in

North Mesopotamia," reported the *Times*. He was particularly noted for having set up a large industrial relief plant that employed several thousand refugees.[170] While Morgenthau had not yet reached a conclusion about Leslie's death, the headline, "A Missionary Poisoned," implied that the Board itself had.

Not all prominent Americans were supportive of American action. The Committee invited Theodore Roosevelt to take part in one of its public meetings, or to make some statement about his views on the Armenians' situation. In his response to the invitation, Roosevelt wrote to Samuel P. Dutton, Secretary of ACASR, that "a nation [the United States] too timid to protect its own men, women, and children from murder and outrage and too timid even to speak on behalf of Belgium, will not carry much weight by 'protest' or 'insistence' on behalf of the suffering Jews and Armenians."[171]

Roosevelt's letter, released by Dutton to the *Times*, stated that mass meetings to commiserate about the plight of Armenians were useless. The "peace-at-any-price men," and the "professional pacifists" do more harm than good. When America is willing to live up to its lofty morals with force, he wrote, it will be able to take an effective stand in international matters that will prevent "such cataclysms of wrong as have been witnessed in Belgium and on even graver scale in Armenia." Dutton released the letter, he said, not because Roosevelt's arguments about peace were necessarily without debate, but because ACASR hoped that the former president's support for the Armenian cause might inspire contributions to ACASR.[172]

Diplomatic efforts on behalf of Armenians continued. A story headlined "Pope May Make New Plea To Kaiser" described the activities of a British Armenian Committee led by T. P. O'Connor, quoted as being "full of despair about Armenia." O'Connor stated that the British Armenian Committee was "immensely encouraged by the information they received of the great wave of sympathy and of horror which had passed over America...." Lord Robert Cecil, Under Secretary of the Foreign Office, reported Mr. O'Connor, had informed the House of Commons that the Pope would be asked to make a direct appeal to the Kaiser as he had with the Sultan. The British Armenian Committee also asked the British government to use its armies and navy to try to rescue any Armenians where possible.[173]

On December 9, 1915, the *Times* published another lengthy, detailed and impassioned article about Armenians based on information from ACASR. Multiple headlines and sub-headings announced its interconnecting themes:

"Woman Describes Armenian Killings"; "German Missionary Says Turks Proclaimed Extermination as Their Aim;" "Fiends' Work in Harput;" and "'Let Your Christ Help You!' Was the Cry as Torture Went On – Dr. Knapp a Victim."

The *Times* article reported that the American Consul at Tiflis had informed ACASR that 180,000 destitute Armenians were in the Caucasus, spread among the provinces of Erivan, Elisavetpol, Kars, and Tiflis. (See Map.) In addition to the standard coverage of the devastation of the Armenian population and the pitiable state of individual Armenians and their families, this story contained details provided by a German missionary whose national affiliation must have given her statements more credibility. Her account included descriptions of grisly tortures in which Turks beat Armenians to death for the sheer pleasure of it, hammered nails into the feet of Armenians [called at the time "horse shoeing"], and taunted Armenians with slogans like "'Now let your Christ help you!'"[174]

During the rest of December 1915, the *Times* published only two other articles about Armenians. An AP story, datelined Berlin, quoted the Secretary of the Young Turks, Dr. Nazim Bey, saying that Turkey possessed all supplies needed. Interviewed by the AP, Dr. Nazim spoke calmly until asked about Armenians. On the latter issue, he angrily denounced the biased investigators who relied on the Greeks, Jews, and Armenians for this information. Although Turkish subjects have "grudges to air," said Nazim, "'[e]very time a Turk does something praiseworthy in this world, he is hailed as an Armenian; he continued, but every time he commits a crime or acts basely, he is a Turk – or something else.'"[175] This article is significant, because it indicates how the Armenian issue permeated any discussion of Turkey's role in the First World War. Even an article pertaining to Turkey's supply of commodities to its ally, Germany, raised the matter of the Armenian question.

The *Times'* final article of the year on the Armenians addressed the issue of German complicity in the Turkish crimes. Count Ernst von Reventlow, a "German naval expert," defended "Turkey's massacre of the Armenians" on the basis of military necessity. Nevertheless, on August 9, 1915 the German Ambassador in Constantinople himself had registered a protest with the Turkish government for all the horrific crimes that had occurred, reported Dr. Barton, ACASR's spokesman. "Impartial and reliable sources" indicated that Germany itself acknowledged that the massacres, plunders, and other acts of violence resulting from the deportations meant that most Armenians perished before reaching their destinations, Dr. Barton indicated. In Mardin, for example, all Christians without distinction of race or religion had experienced the same fate, the *Times* wrote. Thus, the *Times* reported, "Under such circumstances the [German] Embassy, by order of its Government, is obliged to remonstrate once more against these acts of horror."[176] If this account is accurate, it should have created some goodwill in the United States towards Germany, and it should also have lent support to the view that the Turkish government alone was responsible for the genocide of Armenians. So many articles in the *Times* had suggested that Germany was behind the Genocide that this statement seems to offer a strikingly "revisionist" assessment of the dynamics of the relationships existing at that time between Germany and Turkey.

THE MISSIONARY HERALD

During most of 1915, the *Times* informed its readership in vivid prose about Armenian affairs on a regular basis. As 1915 drew to a close, the *Herald* recognized that it needed to provide more informative reporting, so that the Board's supporters would be as familiar with the conditions facing the deportees in its Near Eastern mission field as the *Times*' readers were. The *Herald* began to devote more space to Armenian deportees, as well as to provide information about individual missionaries who still served in the most dangerous parts of the Ottoman Empire, under constant threat of harm and possibly death.

In its October, 1915 issue, the *Herald* described the deaths of Mrs. Ussher at Van, Mrs. Raynolds at Tiflis, and Miss Ely in Bitlis; this was old news to those *Herald* readers who also read the *Times*, which had already reported the deaths of Mrs. Ussher and Mrs. Raynolds some months earlier. In an article in the October, 1915 issue, the *Herald* attempted to shed some light on the issue of the deportations by publishing a lengthy article by Board missionary, Mary Louise Graffam.

Mary Louise Graffam had personally witnessed the deportations of Armenians of Sivas and had gone with the deportees as far as Malatya until she was forced to return to Sivas by Turkish officials.[177] Miss Graffam's eyewitness account described the conditions of deportation at the time that the Turks and Germans were still denying that such events were occurring. Even though Miss Graffam remained in Sivas throughout the war, the *Herald* identified Miss Graffam in its story. Both she and the *Herald* evidently believed she was immune from Turkish retaliation for reporting what was occurring.

An article in the same issue also told about the work of Misses Grisell MacLaren and Myrtle Shane. The *Herald* described their efforts at the Turkish military hospital in the Turkish section of Van, performed under the supervision of a German nun, Schwester Martha. Because of active warfare between Armenians and Turks in Van, Misses MacLaren and Shane resided in the Turkish hospital instead of the mission compound, where all the other missionaries lived. When the Russians appeared to liberate Van from the Turkish siege, the two missionaries decided to stay at the military hospital because the Armenian nurses who worked in the hospital feared that the departure of the two American women would result in their own deaths. Misses McLaren and Shane also remained with the Turks as the Turks retreated from Van on boats across Lake Van to Bitlis. Like so many missionaries in that region, Miss McLaren fell victim to typhus but was nursed back to health by Miss Shane. The two women hoped to remain with the Turks in Bitlis because they felt they were doing important work. "Even the Turks must admire such intrepid missionaries," stated the *Herald*.[178] The *Herald* also reported the arrival in the United States of sixteen missionaries whose experiences in the Near East represented "the most varied and thrilling" thus far in their lives.

In a lengthy report published in two parts in October and November 1915, the first of which was titled, "'Mid Toil and Tribulation," and the second, "Out of the Jaws of Death," the Board described the siege of Van, which had occurred in April and May 1915, and the illnesses from typhus of many of the mission staff during those days. While much of the information had already been reported by the *Times*, the *Herald's* account provided one for its own readers who may not have access to the *Times* article, but also included additional information for those who did.[189]

When the Russians retreated from Van, a chaotic flight of Van's Armenian population followed, some through narrow valleys where Kurds ambushed the fleeing party at will. Along the way, Mrs. Raynolds climbed down from her wagon, the horse bolted, and the wagon ran over her leg; Mrs. Raynolds then had to be carried in a cart over the difficult terrain.

On August 13, Mrs. Raynolds and her escaping caravan of refugees reached Tiflis, where they sought help from the American Consul, F.

Willoughby-Smith. But for the injured missionary, the help was of no avail. She died in Tiflis, two days before her husband reached that city from the United States.

From Tiflis, the missionaries continued on to Petrograd (St. Petersburg), from whence they found their way back to the United States. While in control of Van after the Russian pull-out, the Turks razed every part of the Board's mission plant. The *Herald* described this in far greater detail than it did the siege or the retreat, suggesting that the Board's main concern was the loss of its property.[180]

The opening editorial of the *Herald's* October 1915 issue described conditions in Turkey. The Armenians in the interior and the Greeks on the Asia Minor coast had been deported. The Board's interest in Turkey, the *Herald* wrote, was philanthropic and religious. It still had 200 American Board missionaries in the country, with twenty-one stations, seven colleges, nine hospitals, and 400 schools of all grades. The article stressed the Board's huge financial commitment to Turkey, which was now imperiled by the war. Once the war ended, the Board explained, a thorough review of the Board's "investment" would be made.[181] In the same issue, the Board reported that a missionary to Urfa served as an American consular agent and handled the funds for the Europeans interned in Urfa because of the war.[182] The Board did not mention or perhaps understand that Leslie's appointment as an American official might bring an end to his neutrality with the Turks.

The October issue of the *Herald* also furnished new information about the destruction of Turkey's Armenian population. One article described a plan in an unidentified city where Armenian men were arrested, tortured, set free on the road, only then to be slaughtered by Turks. The anonymous writer of this letter reported that the city's entire Christian population, Armenian and Syrian alike, was being deported, but with no water or food provided for the march. The author of the letter predicted that all of the deportees from this city would die.[183]

This description was helpful to the *Herald's* readers because it explained some of the mechanisms used to destroy the Armenian people. The article of the *Herald* was also significant because it addressed for the first time the question of Armenian disloyalty to the Ottoman state. The missionaries, stated the *Herald*, did not know if such treachery existed, but if it did, it occurred only among a few harebrained fools. The great majority of the Armenian population in the interior of Turkey remained loyal to the Empire.

Even so, old men, women and children could not be held responsible for the actions of a tiny minority, said the *Herald*.[184]

The next month, the *Herald* published a long article with graphic but anonymous reporting about the condition of Armenians of Turkey. The substance of the article is reflected in this sentence: "Torture, rapine, exile, and massacre have virtually exterminated the Armenians over wide areas of the country: family, property, life, all have been scattered and broken."[185] The article demonstrates that the *Herald's* reluctance to publish direct and informative descriptions of the events in Turkey had been replaced by a decision to report without reservation what was occurring. The Board had only limited knowledge of the situations facing its staff, but apparently it had received enough information from credible sources to be able to declare that "unbelievable outrages are being committed in the hidden interior of Turkey."[186] It is possible that the Board's awareness of the news reports in the *Times* may have led it to provide more thorough reporting to its readers. The *Herald* was doubtless mindful of the fact that while the United States government had protested the treatment of Armenians and had demanded that the atrocities end, Washington had no legal jurisdiction over Turkey, and, as the Germans said, continuing or abandoning the practice was an issue for Turkey alone to decide. The Board also complained that the Turks were destroying its missionary enterprise in Turkey. In its November 1915 issue, the *Herald* described in great detail the mission properties destroyed and the interference with the rights and liberties of its missionaries.[187]

The Board's message seemed to be confused at this point. The *Herald* again revived the question of the capitulations and their unilateral abolition. For the first time, the *Herald* used the highly pejorative term, "the mad Turk."[188] For almost a century, the Board had worked with Armenians, a people now faced with extermination. It was losing much of the mission plant it had built up during that period. Yet its original and primary goal was to convert the people it now called "the mad Turk." In addition, the suffering of the Armenians trivialized the Board's continuing concern about its property losses.

To reconcile some of these contradictions, the Board began to shift much of its work in Turkey away from evangelism and into relief activities, thereby regaining its footing and carving out a new role for itself in Turkey. Recognizing that it would be working with the Turks in the years ahead, the *Herald* tried to present images of "good Turks." A letter from a Turk to his son in the U.S. described all the terrible conditions the Cherkez Bashibazooks, Turkish irregular mercenaries, had heaped upon the "raya," the derisive term used by the Turks to describe non-Muslims. The writer objected to this treatment.[189] Publication of this letter reminded the *Herald's* readers that there were indeed good Turks and suggested that the missionaries were already thinking about a Turkey without Armenians, in which they could continue to work. Dr. Barton had already announced that when the conflict was over, reconstruction would need to begin. A "future of marvelous possibilities lies before our work in Turkey."[190]

At the same time that it was looking to its future after the close of the war, the Board continued to focus on the plight of the current victims of the conflict. The *Herald* reported the findings of the War Relief Commission, sent by the Rockefeller Foundation to investigate conditions in Turkey. The Foundation's conclusions, while confidential, were nevertheless made available to the Board.

The high praise heaped upon the Board's staff in Turkey pleased Board officials in Boston. The report resonated with Board ideals in yet another respect. It emphasized that refugees, to the extent possible, should work in industrial relief projects rather than simply be handed money and food. Of the twenty cities listed in the report, Board mission stations or staff operated in sixteen of them. The Board was pleased to see this validation of its values and effort.[191]

In November, the *Herald* informed its readers for the first time about the formation of the American Committee for Armenian and Syrian Relief (ACASR). This organization was an outgrowth of a meeting on September 16, 1915, consisting of representatives of American institutions and associations conducting philanthropic work in Turkey. At the September convocation, the participants discussed what could be done systematically to raise money for the relief of the destitute people living in Turkey.

Within three weeks, this "young and vigorous body" of men had organized, investigated conditions in Turkey, and published information that would persuade Americans to dip into their pockets to help victims of man's inhumanity to man in far-off lands – people whom they had never met and would never likely meet. As a result of its initial efforts, the Committee found itself able to send $100,000 to Morgenthau in Turkey for relief purposes.

The men who made up the committee planned to keep up their philanthropic activities because they anticipated an ongoing need for funds to ameliorate the suffering in the Near East. But they also hoped in some way to stop or limit the persecution of the Christian minorities in Turkey.[192] When that appeared impossible, they devoted their efforts to programs of relief.

Through the agency of the Federal Council of Churches, ACASR had requested successfully that President Wilson proclaim the second Sunday in November a national day of prayer. Surely these prayers had been heard, stated the *Herald*, because a "few rays of light appear over that darkened land."[193] By December 1915, relief funds had surpassed $800,000 according to the *Herald*, but much more would be needed.[194]

Thus ended the year 1915, a year in which the Turkish government launched its plan to eliminate Armenians in Turkey. Yet it was also the year in which relief activities to save the remnant of Ottoman Armenians started. In the following year, those efforts would accelerate. Whatever criticisms might be directed at the Board's policies, no doubt can exist about the missionaries' terrible sacrifices, including the loss of physical and mental health and even their lives. They were truly heroes.

End Notes to The Year 1915

1. "Says Turks Advise Christians to Flee," *New York Times*, 11 January 1915, 2.
2. "Talaat Says Turks Fight for Life," *New York Times*, 18 February 1915, 3.
3. Alashgerd is a sanjak, a political unit within the province of Van in southeastern Turkey.
4. "Whole Plain Strewn by Armenian Bodies," *New York Times*, 20 March 1915, 4.
5. It is possible that the *Times* did try to get the Turkish viewpoints on its news reports. If so, it could have informed its readers about those attempts. Since it did not, the reader is left to assume that it did not make any such attempts.
6. "War Conditions in the Heart of Turkey," *Missionary Herald* CXI (February 1915), 77-78.
7. "Pitiful Situation at Aintab," *Missionary Herald* CXI (March 1915), 127.
8. "War Conditions in the Heart of Turkey," *Missionary Herald* CXI (March 1915), 127.
9. *Missionary Herald* CXI (March 1915), 108. The verses cited in the letter refer to famine and destruction.
10. "Dissolving Views," *Missionary Herald* CXI (March 1915) : 129-130.
11. "Turkey's Hostile Regulations," *Missionary Herald* CXI (March 1915), 103.
12. "The Latest from Marsovan," *Missionary Herald* CXI (March 1915) : 128.
13. "Mission Hospitals Open to Turkish Soldiers," *Missionary Herald* CXI (March 1915), 104.
14. "Sivas Helps Wounded Soldiers, *Missionary Herald* CXI (March 1915), 127-128.
15. In the *Herald*, the Board never resolved the issue of the fatal consequences for Muslim Turks who converted to Christianity. Since it could not have envisioned a church with dead followers, they must have hoped for a change in Islamic law that permitted conversion.
16. "Pillage in Smyrna District," *New York Times*, 19 April 1915, 2; untitled, *New York Times*, 19 April 1915, 2.
17. "Enver Says Turks Had to Fight," *New York Times*, 20 April 1915, 2.
18. Ibid.
19. Henry Morgenthau, *Ambassador Morgenthau's Story* (Doubleday: New York, 1918; reprint, London and Princeton: Gomidas Institute, 2000), 217.
20. Henry Morgenthau, *Ambassador Morgenthau's Story* (Doubleday: New York, 1918; reprint, London and Princeton: Gomidas Institute, 2000), 200-202; Christopher J. Walker, "World War I and the Armenian Genocide," in *The Armenian People from Ancient to Modern Times*, vol. II, Foreign Dominion to Statehood: The Fifteenth Century to the Twentieth Century, ed. Richard G. Hovannisian (New York: St. Martin's Press, 1997), 246. Armenian physicians were often not killed because of their usefulness to the Ottoman troops.
21. Henry Morgenthau, *Ambassador Morgenthau's Story* (Doubleday: New York, 1918; reprint, London and Princeton: Gomidas Institute, 2000), 205-207. Morgenthau's account is particularly significant because as the United States Ambassador to Turkey

during the start of the genocide, he talked with many of the American missionaries who were working in the interior of Turkey at that time. See also Taner Akcam, *A Shameful Act: The Armenian Genocide and the Question of Turkish Responsibility* (New York: Henry Holt, 2006), 152-168.

22. Donald Bloxham, *The Great Game of Genocide; Imperialism, Nationalism, and the Destruction of the Ottoman Armenians* (Oxford: Oxford University Press, 2005), 1. Bloxham's account agrees with the concept of the Armenian genocide, but he argues that Armenian actions helped to trigger the Turks' actions. He denies, however, that the conflict was a civil war as Turkish apologists maintain.

23. Vahakn N. Dadrian, *The History of the Armenian Genocide* (Providence, RI: Berghahn Books, 1995), 221. It should be noted that although the genocide was initiated in Constantinople with the arrest described above, the Armenians of Constantinople and Smyrna (Izmir) for the most part escaped deportation. Armenians were largely deported from the Asiatic provinces, but also Thrace.

24. "Berjan" should probably have been "Terjan" near Erzerum.

25. "Kurds Massacre More Armenians," *New York Times*, 28 April 1915, 2.

26 "Appeal to Turkey to Stop Massacres," *New York Times*, 28 April 1915, 2. The Catholicos' request recognized that Wilson and America stood for morality in the world and therefore could protest or perhaps even intervene in Turkey's internal affairs. As the war progressed and the sufferings of the minorities of Turkey intensified, it became clear that the United States would not intervene in Turkey, but what the mission supporters did instead was to launch a mammoth campaign to try to bring succor to the helpless people of Turkey.

27. "Morgenthau Intercedes," *New York Times*, 29 April 1915, 2. It is not clear if the two requests were the same, but were channeled through different agencies.

28. The Nestorians were a Christian community spread through Turkey, Iran, and Russia. Their doctrine held that Jesus exists both as the man Jesus and the divine Son of God. (Christine Chaillot, "The Ancient Oriental Churches," in *The Oxford History of Christian Worship*, ed. Geoffrey Wainwright, Karen B. Westerfield Tucker (Oxford, England: Oxford Univ. Press, 2006), 131.

29. "Great Exodus of Christians," *New York Times*, 26 April 1915, 3.

30. The term "Transcaucasia" refers to the south Caucasus.

31. Van is a city located in eastern Turkey, not far from the Russian border. The Turks began killing villagers in the surrounding area. Rather than wait for certain death through murder or deportation, the Armenians of Van decided to defend their city and did so successfully for four weeks. They would have been forced to capitulate eventually, but the Turkish troops took flight as Russian troops arrived. See Clarence D. Ussher, *An American Physician in Turkey; A Narrative of Adventures in Peace and in War* (Boston: Houghton Mifflin, 1917; reprint, London: Sterndale Classics, 2002).

32. "Routed Turkish Army Pursued by Russians," *New York Times*, 6 May 1915, 3. The story of the defense of Van was also depicted by a Venezuelan mercenary in Turkish uniform, Rafael de Nogales, *Four Years beneath the Crescent*, (London: Charles Scribner's 1926; reprint, London: Taderon Press, 2004).

33. "Missionaries in Danger," *New York Times*, 10 May 1915, 9.

34. "Pleas for Armenians," *New York Times*, 15 May 1915, 6.

35. Dodge's relationship with President Wilson seems the most logical explanation for the State Department's change of heart. Wilson and Dodge had attended Princeton College together. In addition, Dodge served as Chairman of the Board of Trustees of Robert College, the oldest American College in the Near East. See James L. Barton, *The Story of Near East Relief* (New York: Macmillan Company, 1930), 6. Morgenthau's actions in support of the refugees may also have helped to change the State Department's outlook. The other members of the relief agency, the American Committee for Armenian and Syrian Relief (ACASR), founded in the fall, were also prominent Americans.

36. The term "Transcaucasia" refers to the south Caucasus. The source was attributed to unnamed Armenian newspapers.

37. "6,000 Armenians Killed," *New York Times*, 18 May 1915, 3.

38. "Massacres by Wholesale," *New York Times*, 24 May 1915, 1.

39. "Allies to Punish Turks Who Murder," *New York Times*, 24 May 1915, 1.

40. The question of Ottoman Turkish direction of the massacres and deportations has become part of the tangled historiographical issues surrounding the events of 1915. Historians following the Turkish state's position claim that the events were no more than local expressions of rage in retribution for alleged disloyalty. Most Western and some Turkish historians conclude, quite differently, that the atrocities were the focus of a centrally directed plan to eliminate the Armenian presence in Ottoman Turkey. The issue is the subject of a scholarly analysis by Turkish historian Taner Akcam titled, *A Shameful Act: the Armenian Genocide and the Question of Turkish Responsibility* (New York: Henry Holt & Co., 2006).

41. "Russians Save Armenians," *New York Times*, 25 May 1915, 4.

42. "More Armenian Massacres," *New York Times*, 6 June 1915, 2. In Bitlis and Moush, towns to the west of Van, the fleeing Turks are reported to have killed all the Armenians of those cities. Diarbekir is located in southeastern Turkey and would not normally be described as being within the area through which Turkish troops and Kurds had fled. This discrepancy suggests that the *Times* reporter was either ignorant of Turkish geography, or was referring to another situation entirely and had conflated that story with that of the Turkish and Kurdish flight.

43. The "eastern provinces" are generally considered to consist of the provinces of Turkey that were once historic western Armenia.

44. "40,000 Turkish Wounded," *New York Times*, 1 June 1915, 7.

45. Ibid.

46. "More Armenian Massacres," *New York Times*, 6 June 1915, II, 2. The Armenian volunteers mentioned in the story may be Armenians not subject to Russian conscription who offered to participate in the Russian army's invasion of eastern Turkey.

47. "To force the Dardanelles" means to use military means, largely armed ships, to overcome the Turkish defenses protecting the Dardanelles and thereby gain access to the Sea of Marmara and Constantinople. Turkish defenses included not only mines in the waterway, but also artillery on the adjacent land. I visited the Gallipoli peninsula in May, 2007 and was impressed by the difficulty of the British undertaking.

48. "Ambassador Morgenthau's Message," *Missionary Herald* CXI, (April 1915), 161.
49. "Burdened Missionaries in Turkey," *Missionary Herald* CXI, (May 1915), 211.
50. "Letters from Turkey," *Missionary Herald* CXI (April 1915), 161.
51. "From W. W. Peet, Constantinople, February 8," *Missionary Herald* CXI (April 1915), 161.
52. "From Rev. L. S. Crawford, Trebizond, January 23," *Missionary Herald* CXI (April 1915), 190-19; "Trebizond's Bombardment," *Missionary Herald* CXI (May 1915), 234.
53. "Fighting Typhus Fever," *Missionary Herald* CXI (May 1915), 235.
54. Ibid.: 234-235.
55. Ibid.: 234-236.
56. There is no denying the selflessness and devotion of these missionary Americans who could have spent the war years in comfort in their own homes in the United States.
57. "Fighting Typhus Fever," *Missionary Herald* CXI (May 1915), 236.
58. "A Sample Case of Missionary Devotion," *Missionary Herald* CXI (May 1915), 212.
59. "From Rev. Henry K. Wingate, Talas, January 23," *Missionary Herald* CXI (May 1915), 191.
60. Animosity existed towards the Nestorians and the Assyrians, but their numbers were so much lower that they did not draw forth the level of hostility of the Turks towards the Armenians.
61. "A Neutral Nation's Duty," *Missionary Herald* CXI (June 1915), 262.
62. "Rumors as to Van," *Missionary Herald* CXI (June 1915), 262.
63. "Later Word from Van," *Missionary Herald* CXI (June 1915), 262.
64. Ibid.
65. "Turks Are Evicting Native Christians," *New York Times*, 12 July 1915, 4.
66. Likely the eyewitnesses were missionaries.
67. "Turks Are Evicting Native Christians," *New York Times*, 12 July 1915, 4.
68. "Turks Hard Pressed in Turkish Armenia," *New York Times*, 13 July 1915, 4.
69. "Ask Aid for Armenians," *New York Times*, 15 July 1915, 3.
70. "Report Turks Shot Women and Children," *New York Times*, 4 August 1915, 1.
71. "Armenian Horrors Grow," *New York Times*, 6 August 1915, 6.
72. "Armenians are Sent to Perish in Desert," *New York Times*, 18 August 1915, 5.
73. "Burn 1,000 Armenians," *New York Times*, 20 August 1915, 7.
74. "Turks Sop to Armenians," *New York Times*, 25 August 1915, 25.
75. "Turks Depopulate Towns of Armenia," *New York Times*, 27 August 1915, 3.
76. This is not to say that the information is not true. Many independent sources have reported similar events, suggesting that these events had occurred. It is just unclear why the *Times* did not provide more information about why it believed its sources were accurate.
77. "Answer Morgenthau by Hanging Armenians," *New York Times*, 15 September 1915.
78. "Mission Board Told of Turkish Horrors," *New York Times*, 17 September 1915, 3.
79. "Armenian Women Put Up at Auction," *New York Times*, 29 September 1915, 2.

80. "500,000 Armenians Said to Have Perished," *New York Times*, 24 September 1915, 2.

81. "1,500,000 Armenians Starve," *New York Times*, 5 September 1915, II, 3.

82. "Tales of Armenian Horrors Confirmed," *New York Times*, 27 September 1915, 5.

83. "Armenian Women Put Up at Auction," *New York Times*, 29 September 1915, 3.

84. "Bryce Asks Us to Aid Armenia," *New York Times*, 21 September 1915, 3.

85. "Armenian Atrocities Scouted by Bernstorff," *New York Times*, 29 September 1915, 1.

86. "Asks Bernstorff's Aid to Prevent Massacres," *New York Times*, 1 October 1915, 1.

87. For a very brief period, the committee was called the American Committee on Armenian Atrocities. Robert L. Daniel, *American Philanthropy in the Near East 1820-1960* (Athens, OH: Ohio University Press, 1970), 150. See "Report of Committee on Armenian Atrocities, 4 October 1915" in Ara Sarafian and Eric Avebury, British Parliamentary Debates on the Armenian Genocide 1915-1918 (Princeton and London: Gomidas Institute, 2003).

88. James L. Barton, *The Story of Near East Relief* (New York: Macmillan Co., 1930), 3-7

89. James L. Barton, *The Story of Near East Relief* (New York: Macmillan Co., 1930), 5.

90. "500,000 Armenians Said to Have Perished," *New York Times*, 24 September 1915, p. 2.

91. "Tales of Armenian Horrors Confirmed," *New York Times*, 27 September 1915, 5.

92. The full make-up of the Committee was described in an article in the *Times* published on October 3, 1915.

93. 'Tales of Armenian Horrors Confirmed," *New York Times*, 27 September 1915, 5.

94. See Taner Akcam, *A Shameful Act: The Armenian Genocide and the Question of Turkish Responsibility* (New York: Henry Holt & Co., 2006), 161, 169-170, 185-186.

95. "Tales of Armenian Horrors Confirmed," *New York Times*, 27 September 1915, 5.

96. "In Disordered Turkey," *Missionary Herald* CXI (July 1915), 309.

97. "Russian Rule in Turkey," *Missionary Herald* CXI (July 1915), 331.

98. Ibid., 332.

99. Ibid.

100. "In Disordered Turkey," *Missionary Herald* CXI (July 1915), 309.

101. "Wanted! Good for Evil," *Missionary Herald* CXI (July 1915), 312.

102. "As Matters Stand in Oorfa," *Missionary Herald* CXI (July 1915), 332.

103. "Relief Work at Trebizond," *Missionary Herald* CXI (August 1915), 378-379.

104. The Board had two secretaries: Edward Lincoln Smith, general secretary and James L. Barton, foreign secretary. Also See "Report of Committee on Armenian Atrocities, 4 October 1915" in Ara Sarafian and Eric Avebury, British Parliamentary Debates on the Armenian Genocide 1915-1918 (Princeton and London: Gomidas Institute, 2003).

105. "The War's Contribution to Missions," *Missionary Herald* CXI (August 1915), 361-364.

106. "Suftah" is a Muslim dignitary – a person of honor and rank.

107. "The War's Contribution to Missions, *Missionary Herald* CXI (August 1915), 362.

108. Ibid.

109. "In Darkest Turkey," *Missionary Herald* CXI (September 1915), 401. These statements are crucially important, because after the war and the creation of the modern Turkish state, the Board's missionaries denied that the Turks wanted to exterminate the Armenians in 1915. They may have wanted to hang on to their large property holdings in Turkey, and felt suppressing the truth would enable them to do so.

110. Ibid., 401-403.

111. Ibid.

112. "At Our Russian Station," *Missionary Herald* CXI (September 1915), 417.

113. The missionaries were adamant about excluding arms from the mission compound. Dr. Ussher had a young son who was friends with an Armenian boy named Vasken Parseghian. Vasken's mother was Dr. Ussher's cook. In 1989, I met Dr. Parseghian, by then professor emeritus at Rensalaer Polytechnical Institute, Troy, New York, who told me that he and Dr. Ussher's son had played together in the Ussher home while it was being shelled by the Turks. The boys found the bombardment great fun.

114. "Four Thousand Refugees," *Missionary Herald* CXI (September 1915), 417-418.

115. "At Our Russian Station," *Missionary Herald* CXI (September 1915), 417.

116. Ibid.

117. "At Our Russian Station," *Missionary Herald* CXI (September 1915), 418.

118. "All Present or Accounted for," *Missionary Herald* CXI (September 1915), 396.

119. "Turks on the Run at Aintab," *Missionary Herald* CXI (September 1915), 418.

120. "Steady on Their Job," *Missionary Herald* CXI (September 1915), 395.

121. Dr. Ussher had typhus and had to be carried from Van in a litter when the Russians withdrew. His wife had already died from typhus. Mrs. Raynolds, who accompanied him on the flight to Russia, broke her leg on the same flight and was not able to recover. She died in Tiflis. See Clarence D. Ussher, *An American Physician in Turkey; A Narrative of Adventures in Peace and in War*, Grace H. Knapp, collaborating (Boston: Houghton Mifflin Co., 1917; reprint, London: Sterndale Classics, 2002), 301-332.

122. "Tell of Horrors Done in Armenia," *New York Times*, 4 October 1915, 1.

123. Following are the names and positions of the signatories of the document as they appeared in the *New York Times* on October 4, 1915: The Right Rev. DAVID H. GREER, Protestant Episcopal Bishop of New York; OSCAR B. STRAUS, former Secretary of Commerce and Labor, and ex-Ambassador to Turkey; CLEVELAND H. DODGE of Phelps, Dodge & Co (The comma between the name of the signer and his affiliation was omitted in Dodge's case); The Rev. Dr. STEPHEN S. WISE, Rabbi of the Free Synagogue, New York; CHARLES A. CRANE of Chicago, Vice Chairman of the Finance Committee of the Democratic National Committee during the last campaign; ARTHUR CURTISS JAMES, Director of many railroads and of the Hanover National Bank, the United States Trust Company, and of Phelps, Dodge & Co; The Rev. Dr. FRANK MASON NORTH (comma omitted) of the Board of Foreign Missions of the Methodist Episcopal Church; JOHN R. MOTT (comma omitted) of the International

Committees of the Young Men's Christian Association; WILLIAM W. ROCKHILL, former Ambassador to Turkey and former Ambassador to Russia; WILLIAM SLOANE, President of W. & J. Sloane, 575 Fifth Avenue; The Rev. Dr. EDWARD LINCOLN SMITH (comma omitted) of the American Board of Commissioners for Foreign Missions; The Rev. Dr. FREDERICK LYNCH (comma omitted) of the New York Peace Society; GEORGE A. PLIMPTON (comma omitted) of Ginn & Co., a trustee of Constantinople College; The Rev. Dr. JAMES L. BARTON, for many years a missionary in Turkey, and now the Secretary of the American Board of Commissioners for Foreign Missions; The Rev. Dr. WILLIAM J. HAVEN, one of the founders of the Epworth League; STANLEY WHITE, President of the White Advertising Corporation; Professor SAMUEL P. DUTTON, an authority on Balkan affairs.

124. "Tell of Horrors Done in Armenia," *New York Times*, 4 October 1915, 1.

125. Ibid.

126. Ibid.

127. Ibid.

128. James L. Barton, *The Story of Near East Relief* (New York: Macmillan, 1930) 14-15.

129. "Government Sends Plea for Armenia," *New York Times*, 5 October 1915, 3.

130. "Morgenthau Giving Relief," *New York Times*, 6 October 1915, 3.

131. "German Directed the Turks at Van," *New York Times*, 6 October 1915, 3.

132. "Already had $75,000 to Help Armenians," *New York Times*, 7 October 1915, 3.

133. "A hope for Armenians," "Why We Aid Armenians," and "A Hope for Armenians," *New York Times*, 9 October 1915, 3.

134. "Armenian Appeal by Bryce in Full," *New York Times*, 10 October 1915, II, 19.

135. "Letters Tell of Outrages," *New York Times*, 10 October 1915, II, 19.

136. "Defends Repression of the Armenians," *New York Times*, 10 October 1915, II, 19.

137. "Pleas for Armenia by Germany Futile," *New York Times*, 10 October 1915, II, 19.

138. "Turkish Statesman Denounces Atrocities," *New York Times*, 10 October 1915, II, 19.

139. "Spare Armenians, Pope Asks Sultan," *New York Times*, 11 October 1915, 4.

140. "To plead for Armenians," *New York Times*, 11 October 1915, 4.

141. "Prays for Morgenthau's Work," *New York Times*, 11 October 1915, 4.

142. "Armenian Protests Charged to Allies," *New York Times*, 13 October 1915, 4.

143. "Massacres Renewed Morgenthau Reports," *New York Times*, 13 October 1915, 4.

144. "Turks Fear Armenians," *New York Times*, 13 October 1915, 4.

145. "Turkish Official Denies Atrocities," *New York Times*, 15 October 1915, 4.

146. "We Can Do Nothing Further," *New York Times*, 16 October 1915, 8.

147. "Says Only Germany Can Save Armenians," *New York Times*, 16 October 1915, 8.

148. "Thousands Protest Armenian Murders," *New York Times*, 18 October 1915, 3.

149. "The Kind of Armenian a Turk Knows," *New York Times*, 18 October 1915, 3.

150. Zia Mufty-Zade Bey, *New York Times*, 19 October 1915, 10.

151. "Turkey Bars Red Cross," *New York Times*, 19 October 1915, 4.

152. "Accuse Armenians of Wronging Turks," *New York Times*, 22 October 1915, 3.

153. "Turkish Spies in Hotel," *New York Times*, 29 October 1915, 15.
154. "Armenians Thank Pope," *New York Times*, 21 October 1915, 4.
155. "Only 200,000 Armenians Now Left in Turkey," *New York Times*, 22 October 1915, 3.
156. "Slay All Armenians in City of Kerasunt," *New York Times*, 26 October 1915, 1.
157. "Germany Says She Cannot Stop Turks," *New York Times*, 23 October 1915, 3.
158. "Can't Defend Armenians," *New York Times*, 25 October 1915, 6.
159. "The Light That May Go Out in Turkey," *New York Times*, 28 October 1915, 10.
160. Robert L. Daniel, *American Philanthropy in the Near East: 1820-1960* (Athens, OH: Ohio University Press, 1970, 150.
161. The public's interest in news about intrepid missionaries was not as farfetched as it might sound. As recently as 1955, an American missionary was killed by preliterate tribesmen in Ecuador. A long article about this event appeared in *Life* magazine, and his wife wrote a book, *Through Gates of Splendor*, that remained on the best seller lists for a long time.
162. "Aid for Armenians Blocked by Turkey," *New York Times*, 1 November 1915, 4.
163. Ibid.
164. Chaldeans are Nestorians who accepted the jurisdiction of the Pope.
165. The reference to Samsun is puzzling. Samsun is located on the Black Sea Coast. The town adjacent to Moush is Sasun, but Viscount Bryce provided another story published in the *Times* on January 25, 1916 about the massacre of Armenians at Sasun. It is possible that the 1916 story is about Samsun, the Black Sea town.
166. "Armenians' Heroic Stand in Mountains," *New York Timesv*, 27 November 1915, 1.
167. "More Aid for Armenians", *New York Times*, 10 December 1915, 8.
168. Ibid.
169. "Church Plea for Armenian," *New York Times*, 14 November 1915, II, 19.
170. "A Missionary Poisoned," *New York Times*, 13 November 1915, 2.
171. "Roosevelt Heaps Blame on America," *New York Times*, 1 December 1915, 4.
172. Ibid.
173. "Pope May Make New Plea to Kaiser," *New York Times*, 9 December 1915, 5.
174. "Woman Describes Armenian Killings," *New York Times*, 12 December 1915, II, 6.
175. "Looks to Germany to Set Turkey Free," *New York Times*, 12 December 1915, 3.
176. "Germany Protested Armenian Massacres," *New York Times*, 23 December 1915, 3.
177. "Two Women in Turkey," *Missionary Herald* CXI (October 1915), 460.
178. Ibid.
179. "Mid Toil and Tribulation," *Missionary Herald* CXI (October 1915), 456; "Out of the Jaws of Death," *Missionary Herald* CXI (November 1915), 512.
180. "Out of the Jaws of Death, *Missionary Herald* CXI (November 1915), 512.
181. "American Interests in Turkey," *Missionary Herald* CXI (October 1915), 443-444.
182. "A By-Product of Missions," *Missionary Herald* CXI (October 1915), 444.
183. "A Typical Deportation," *Missionary Herald* CXI (October 1915), 465-466.

184. Ibid., 466-467.
185. "An Orgy of Unbridled Hate," *Missionary Herald* CXI (November 1915), 497.
186. "One Instance," *Missionary Herald* CXI (November 1915), 497.
187. "American Interests in Turkey Violated," *Missionary Herald* CXI (November 1915), 498.
188. Ibid.
189. "A Turk's Account," *Missionary Herald* CXI (November 1915), 454.
190. "Reconstruction," *Missionary Herald* CXI (November 1915), 537.
191. "A Relief Commissioners' View of the American Board," *Missionary Herald* CXI (November 1915), 500.
192. "A Timely Organization," *Missionary Herald* CXI (November 1915), 499.
193. "Sunday, November 14," *Missionary Herald* CXI (December 1915), 558.
194. "Joining in Relief Work," *Missionary Herald* CXI (December 1915), 558.

Chapter 4

THE YEAR 1916

The year 1916 saw the *Herald's* emphasis shift from the conditions of the Armenians to relief efforts. In contrast, the *Times* continued to keep the ongoing massacres, deportations, and persecutions of Turkey's Armenians before the public's eye.

JANUARY - MARCH 1916

THE NEW YORK TIMES

The *Times* published a letter on January 3 with the heading, "Turkey's Past and Future." Written by Mr. S. S. Kaish, it reminded readers that Turkey's Armenians had suffered massacres both in 1895-1896 and in 1909. Pointing out that history repeats itself, Kaish told the *Times*' readers that 950,000 Armenians had recently "met their deaths either by massacre or by starvation in the desert."[1]

In what would become a familiar refrain, Kaish asserted that the military might of the Turkish army stemmed from "German brains, German guns, and German submarines." Remove these German props and the Turkish army would collapse, claimed the writer.[2]

Arshag Mahdesian, a frequent letter writer on Armenian issues, also emphasized the German connection by linking the sinking of the USS *The Persia* to the Armenian situation. The ship, he said, was sunk by a submarine manned by fez-wearing sailors with arm bands inscribed with the words "Mohammed is the prophet of God" – a ruse that was perpetuated, he claimed, by Germany to shift the blame away from Germany and arouse American hostility toward Ottoman Turkey. Turkey, he scoffed, lacked both submarines and the crews to man them. Germany had devised this latest "Teutonic trick" to lead the United States to sever diplomatic relations with Turkey, which in turn would allow *Germany* to continue to exterminate the Armenians.[3]

That Germany had instigated the deportations, Mahdesian argued, was a fact acknowledged by both Turkish officials and imams. The Berlin to Baghdad Railway, still under construction, would pass through lands then occupied by Armenians. Deporting Turkey's Armenians to the Syrian deserts would free those lands for colonization by Germans. On the other hand, failure to deport Armenians would end Germany's opportunity to settle in these areas. Mahdesian argued that funds provided to Armenians came from American Embassy and Consular officials, as well as American missionaries, and that it was these monies that were keeping Armenians alive. If the United States ended diplomatic relations with Turkey, the flow of funds from these sources would end or be greatly reduced. The goal of the German scheme to sink *The Persia* was to cause the United States to end diplomatic relations with Turkey, thereby ending American official and missionary presence in Turkey. America should take care, he warned, lest it fall into the "Teutonic snare."[4]

If letter writers such as Kaish and Mahdesian promulgated assessments of relations among Americans, Turks, and Germans that might be considered highly speculative, the *Times'* news stories reported the brutal facts. Headlined "500 Armenians Slain Under Turkish Order," with the subheading, "Forced by Cold and Hunger to Surrender, Men, Women, and Children Were Put to Death," a story published in January 1916 described the plight of five hundred Armenians of Sasun[5] who resisted the order of deportation and took refuge in a mountain fast. Forced by cold and hunger to surrender at last, the Armenians of Sasun – described by the *Times* as the most "manly part of the Armenian nation" – did so under an agreement of amnesty. Despite that agreement, said the *Times*, they were all killed. The men of Sasun were massacred, and the women and children were drowned in the Euphrates River. This account had been telegraphed to Lord Bryce by an Armenian refugee worker, and a London Armenian association gave it to the London press.[6] Although the *Times* did not editorialize about the Turks, it did not need to. The Turks were portrayed as perfidious and, therefore, untrustworthy because they violated their pledge of amnesty. The story's depiction of the method of execution – massacre and drowning – added to the negative image of the Turks. By publishing this story at the beginning of 1916, the *Times* sent a strong signal that it would continue to publish news highly critical of the Turks.

Three days later, the *Times* published a story with the headline, "Saved By American Consul," and a subheading that read, "Armenian Refugees Hope Others Will Be Rescued From Slavery." The report described the "energetic action of the American Consul at Aleppo [Jesse Jackson], who adopted a strong attitude with Turkish military authorities, thereby saving thousands of

Armenian lives at Aleppo, while the German Consul took no action to rescue any of the Armenians."[7] By using the terms "energetic action" and "strong attitude" to describe the American Consul's engagement on behalf of Armenians, the *Times* created a forceful image of "manliness," just as it had done with the Armenians of Sasun. In contrast, the German Consul appeared indifferent and uninvolved.

A similarly volatile article appeared five days later on January 23rd under the headline, "Burn Priests in Armenia," with the subheading, "Turks Murder Many Catholic Clergymen, Archbishop Writes." The article quoted an Armenian Catholic Archbishop in Rome who said, "indeed, the massacres in Armenia seem incredible, but they are true…. What the people know is inconceivable, but the facts are much more terrible. The barbarous Turks do not permit the real facts to be known."[8] By using the term "barbarous" to describe the Turks, the article associates the Turks with savagery, a trait confirmed by their use of fire to kill Christians. Clearly, the evil Turks existed outside the bounds of civilized society. The January 23 report may have served an additional purpose. By attributing the story to an Armenian Catholic Archbishop, the story demonstrated that Catholic Armenians as well as Gregorians and Protestants were being persecuted by the Turks, perhaps motivating American Catholics to contribute to ACASR.

The *Times'* regular depiction of the Turks as callously cruel was particularly evident in January 1916, in contrast to the *Herald*, which had begun using more restrained language about Turks, in anticipation that the Board might be operating in the future in a Turkey without Armenians, and that a more neutral stance might further the massive relief efforts planned by the missionary organization. The *Times*, however, continued to play up the sensational aspects of the news from Turkey. Neither a relief organization nor a missionary enterprise the newspaper could publish what it wished without regard to its own future in Turkey.

The *Times* thus continued to publish stories that publicized the Armenians' situation. In the short month of February 1916, it included eight articles on the same issue, many several columns long. On the first Sunday in February, it published, without attribution, a story from the *Herald*, in which the deportees' difficulties were described in detail. Included is an account about the deportation of a young Armenian woman whose physician husband was serving in the Turkish Army at the front. Although the *Times* had condensed the *Herald's* story from 58 to 28 lines, the story nevertheless contained enough detail to create a picture in the reader's mind about the plight facing this young woman. She was depicted as a young and courageous mother with a beatific smile, a woman who was fully aware of the fate facing her and her two little children. The story emphasized the point that despite her husband's service in the Turkish Army, she was not protected from deportation. The story also included descriptions of already deported Armenian mothers so crazed by their inability to feed their infants as they were being driven over the Taurus Mountains and the Syrian deserts that they threw their babies into rivers to make sure that the children would quickly die. The story quoted a threat made by the local Turkish commander that anyone who helped an Armenian in any way would be beaten and thrown into prison. It also quoted a German officer who described the scenes in the interior of Turkey as "the most terrible sights [he] ever saw in this life."[9]

This and other stories in the first part of February 1916 are full of evocative images that would certainly appeal to the readers' emotions. The characters in the February 6 story include the saintly mother, the cruel Turks, and the honest German officer who told the truth about what he had seen. The news report has a "good" versus "evil" theme that provided a perfect vehicle for eliciting emotional responses of the kind that could help fuel readers' desire to contribute. After a span of ninety years, the story still has emotional power.

The *Times* continued to publish these kinds of stories. On February 7, a news account appeared with the headline, "Tells of Great Plain Black With Refugees," with a subheading, "Agonies of Armenians Described by Dr. Richard Hill in Letter From Caucasus." Dr. Hill, a member of the Rockefeller Relief Commission, had gone to the Caucasus to assess the situation on the Persia-Turkey border. Hill dined with an unidentified person who had traveled by train through the Erivan Plain, who informed him about the condition of the refugees who had been on the march for weeks. Dr. Hill quoted his dining partner's description of the 250,000 refugees who were wandering aimlessly and listlessly. "Children were dying by the hundreds, sometimes the frenzied mothers would, in their helpless mad grief, fling their children from them over the roadside into the fields, so as not to see the dying agonies of their emaciated and starved babies."[10] He also saw "women found dead by the roadside and a baby trying to waken the mother by pulling at her face and demanding food. Of new-born babies left just as they were born, carelessly flung aside, the mother often dying shortly afterwards...."[11]

It is hard to judge the accuracy of this account, because the writer did not describe any landmarks such as nearby towns and cities, or what is meant by the Erivan Plain. One quarter of a million refugees in this particular setting is an enormous number of refugees, since the total estimates of Armenian refugees usually number around one million. At the same time, the details of this story mirror many of the details reported in earlier accounts. The image of mothers, unable to feed their children, so distraught they killed their children to end the children's suffering or simply because they were no longer able to bear the children's' crying for food, is particularly haunting. For the readers of the *Times*, living comfortable lives in the United States, these accounts must have evoked compassion and, for some, a desire to contribute to improve the situation of these refugees. While the story did not directly address the Turks' responsibility for the deportation of these women or the conditions they and their children were experiencing, the horrifying conditions that resulted from the Turkish decision to deport made such a connection unnecessary.

American concern for Armenians soon led the United States Senate to become involved in these questions when, in February 1916, it asked President Wilson "to set apart a day on which the public may contribute to the relief of distressed Armenians."[12] The Senate's request of President Wilson demonstrated the level of concern that officialdom in the United States had for the deported and persecuted Armenians. Oddly, the editors of the *Times* chose to put this story on page four rather than page one, where so much significant journalism on this subject had appeared and where the story would have attracted more attention. Nevertheless, the newspaper did inform its readers that official Washington was supportive of aid to Armenians.

The *Times*' next story during the month of February introduced the subject of the fundraising needed to ransom Armenian women and girls taken from caravans of deportees by mounted Turks or Kurds. The story, headlined "Ransoms Armenian Girls" and sub-headed "American Committee Asks Funds to be Paid To Turks," began with the now standard introduction describing ACASR as a committee "among the members of which are Cardinal Gibbons, Oscar S. Straus, Bishop Green, Charles R. Crane, and many other prominent Americans." Different members of ACASR would be named in subsequent stories to introduce them to the public. In addition, the mailing address of Treasurer Charles R. Crane typically ended these stories about Armenian refugees.[13]

The *Times* had previously reported that Turks or Kurds would approach a caravan of deportees on horseback, seize a beautiful Armenian girl or woman, and ride off with her. Thanks to the work of ACASR, many of these captives had been recovered, reported the *Times*. Now ACASR wanted whenever possible to locate those remaining in captivity, pay a ransom when demanded, and return the captives to their families or some other safe place. This story in the *Times* reminded readers that the problem was ongoing, that intervention by ACASR was still needed, and that readers had an opportunity to participate in these rescues vicariously through their financial contributions.[14]

This story portrays the Turkish and Kurdish captors negatively, the Armenians as innocent victims, and the missionaries as altruistic individuals willing to seek out the captors and pay money to regain the victims' freedom. Although this important story includes evocative images of rescue from slavery, perhaps only a few readers would have ever seen it because the *Times* printed it in Section VII of the Sunday edition of the paper, an inexplicable location.[15]

Most of the letters published by the *Times* came from Armenian supporters, but on February 22, the *Times* published a letter from Djevad Eyou, a Turk who objected to the American efforts to ameliorate the conditions of the deported Armenians. President Wilson had instructed the State Department to remonstrate with the Porte about the treatment of Armenians in Turkey, wrote Eyou. Such an attempt to interfere in the internal affairs of Turkey violated Turkey's sovereignty and also ignored American objections to similar interferences in the internal affairs of the United States.[16]

Armenian spokesman Arshag Mahdesian did not let the letter from Djevad Eyou go unanswered. In his response, Mahdesian asserted that Turkey had never been a civilized nation and could justifiably be denied unfettered control over her internal affairs, as exemplified by the capitulations to which the Turkish government itself had agreed.[17]

This response to Eyou's letter is puzzling. Eyou did not argue that Turkey was a civilized country, but only that the United States had no right to intervene in the internal affairs of another nation, a generally accepted principle of international law. Mahdesian ignored the issue posed by Eyou – Turkey's sovereignty – and used his letter as an opportunity to attack Turkey for its massacre of Armenians. Why the *Times* felt that this non-responsive letter from Mahdesian should be published is unclear. Its failure to exercise editorial discretion suggests a pro-Armenian bias.

A second article appeared on February 22 in "The Topics of The *Times*" section of the paper, with the headline, "Promising to Hang Some Turks." The article reported that after capturing the Ottoman citadel at Erzerum, the main bulwark against invasion of Turkey from the east, the Russians announced they would hold Turkish officials responsible for the "atrocious treatment" of the Armenian population. The article reported that the Russians expected to hang large numbers of those who had ordered or facilitated the Armenian massacres.[18] Although hesitating to support further killing during the terrible war years, the *Times* wrote that nothing short of that seemed capable of convincing the Turks that their behavior was intolerable.

While the instigators of these atrocities were not yet identified, said the *Times*, the Russian promise to ferret them out and inflict proper punishment was "satisfying news indeed." While Russia's own history showed that Russia was equally capable of oppressing "helpless peoples," the article said, Russia's current participation in the war demonstrated that it was a new Russia, and one that nowadays kept "better company."[19]

The editorial content of this news article illustrates the pro-Armenian, pro-Allied, bias of the *Times* at this point in the war. Yet the most significant part of this story is the *Times*' acceptance of Russia's role in determining the guilt or innocence of the Turks. As the paper pointed out, the Russians themselves had not treated their own minorities well. Yet because Russia had allied with England and France, the *Times* was willing to overlook Russia's past behavior and now found it an acceptable arbiter of the culpability of the Turks.

The *Times* also continued to give prominent coverage to Lord Bryce's statements about the treatment and condition of Armenians. "[N]o people in the world ... has suffered more," he said, while at the same time providing a different rationale for the Armenian massacres of the nineteenth century. Unlike past killing of Armenians out of religious hostility, Lord Bryce viewed the massacres of the war years as the Turks' efforts to thwart the emergence of any sense of ethnic independence by any of the non-Turkish peoples of Turkey. The massacres were a calculated political act to destroy the Armenian nation, and not an explosive religious movement.[20] While this story might not have had the same emotional "clout" as others, it did offer the *Times*' readers an alternative explanation of Turkey's treatment of the Armenians.

A second story quoting Rev. Richard Hill appeared on February 23. Hill's earlier statements on the Armenians' situation, printed on February 7, had described ACASR's operations in the Russian Caucasus and the support garnered from the Russian government. The *Times*' February 23 report, much like Mr. Hill's earlier account, described some of the actual relief activities undertaken by ACASR. An example was "quilt day," in which 400 quilts were given away to help refugees who had fled into the mountainous Caucasus in the cold of winter.[21] By quoting Hill at length, the *Times* gave extensive publicity to the evangelist's experiences in the region. His description of the concrete activities undertaken on the refugees' behalf doubtless helped ACASR contributors to see where their funds were going, and may have elicited additional contributions. Like every other story of this type, Treasurer Crane's address appeared at the end of the report.

During March 1916, the *Times* continued to run stories about Armenians. A story published March 2, captioned "Detail Armenians' Plight," described confirmed reports received from several German nurses that matched reports received from other less impartial sources. Upon visiting one of the deportation camps, a nurse described the burials of 580 Armenian dead in one day; she called the sights she saw "the outrages committed by the Turks on the Armenian population."[22] The scenes depicted in this story were more likely to be accepted by the *Times*' readers because the information came from German sources, which normally would have been expected to support Germany's ally, Turkey.

The *Times* of March 4th also discussed an address given by United States Ambassador Henry Morgenthau. At home on leave, Morgenthau informed American audiences about conditions inside the Ottoman Empire. At a luncheon in his honor given jointly by the Trustees of Robert College, Constantinople College, and Syrian Protestant College, all of which had Board connections, about one hundred "prominent men," including many who served as directors of ACASR, listened to Morgenthau speak about the need to support these American institutions in the Middle East.[23] The common interconnectedness of the attendees at this luncheon evinced the acceptance of ACASR's activities by men of social, business, and religious standing.

On the next day, March 5, the *Times* printed an account of a speech given by George Haven Putnam. At a meeting of the Stationers and Publishers' Board of Trade at the Hotel Astor, Putnam declared that it was the duty of the nations of the civilized world to " 'surround [Turkey], to stop its fury, and to drive it back to the kennel, where it can do no harm.' "[24] The *Times* chose to place this story on page two of the first section of the Sunday edition of the *Times*, thereby giving it maximum coverage, while displaying the *Times*' bias against Turkey.

The next few days in early March saw the *Times* publish four more articles on Armenians. In a story dispatched from Petrograd to a London newspaper, the *Times* described the Russian capture of Bitlis (near the west end of Lake Van) and their slaughter of all of the town's Turkish defenders, giving "no quarter" to the men held responsible for the massacre of the Armenians of Bitlis in May, 1915. The *Times* stated that the Russian troops had little compassion for their Turkish opponents because the invading soldiers had witnessed the genocidal crimes perpetrated by the Ottoman Empire's troops at Van, Moush, and many other places.[25] But the *Times* failed to question whether the slaughter of all of the Turkish troops without any kind of determination of individual culpability raised ethical issues about wartime behavior. Perhaps the Turks should have been treated as prisoners of war until the degree of responsibility for the slaughter of Armenian civilians was determined.

On March 8, 1916, the *Times* reported the good news that the Turkish Minister for Foreign Affairs had informed the American charge d'affaires in Constantinople that all deportations of Armenians had stopped, and that Protestant and Catholic Armenians could return to their homes. The American official added that American relief efforts were already aiding the surviving Armenians, and that such assistance was being administered without local official interference.[26] This story illustrates Turkish policy of dividing Armenians by giving certain exemptions and privileges to Catholic and Protestant Armenians that were denied the Gregorians, thereby splitting the Armenians politically at a time when they needed more than ever to be united. Since about ninety percent of the Armenians were Gregorians, this sop to Armenians carried little significance.

On March 9, the *Times* published a front page story about Russia's military progress on the Turkish front. When the Tsar's troops seized the forts at Erzerum, Turkey's main barrier to attacks from the East, they found only sixteen Armenians alive out of a population of 40,000. Local Turks, the article said, had reported that "a few days before the Russian capture of the fortress, all the Armenians in the town were driven out by the police in a westerly direction, where the Kurds, who had been forewarned, killed all of them."[27]

This story also included a thrilling account of the 10,000 "mountain Armenians" near the eastern Mediterranean coast who successfully resisted the Turks' orders to deport them.[28] This front page story of resistance and rescue, however, lost its impact by being combined with the dreary tale of the slaughter of Armenians of Erzerum.[29] Two days later, the *Times* featured the full-length story of the Musa Dagh rescue in the first section of its Sunday edition. Headlined "Beat Off 4,000 Turks," with the sub-heading "Armenian Refugees on Mount Moses Had Only 127 Rifles," the account described a dramatic rescue of a group of Armenian highlanders. Having learned about the horrific conditions of the deportations and the death of so many of the deportees before they reached their destinations, the Armenians of Musa Dagh chose to resist the government's order of deportation. With very few arms, and for forty days, they successfully resisted the repeated attacks of the 4,000 Turkish troops sent to rout them out. Coming to realize, however, that because of limited weapons they could not hold out indefinitely, they created a huge white flag with a red cross in the center. By displaying it on a hillside above the seacoast, the Armenians attracted the attention of a French cruiser, which evacuated them all to the safety of Port Said, Egypt.[30]

The Armenians depicted in this *Times*' story display energy, resourcefulness, courage, and initiative – traits that would appeal to the *Times*' American readers. The story has a mythical quality: the hardy Armenian mountain people successfully resisting the overwhelming power of the Turkish state, a triumph of good over evil. The story represented a "breath of fresh air" amidst the stories of indescribable cruelty wreaked on the typically defenseless, dispirited, sick, and dying deportees, and allows the reader to see Armenians in a new heroic light.

Turkish oppression of Armenians, the conditions of deportation, Russian military victories over their Turkish foes, and, most importantly, the beginning of relief activities, were among the stories featured by the *Times* during the first three months of 1916. The newspaper's mission meant that the articles appearing in the *Times* differed in approach, content, and tone from those appearing in the *Herald*. It did not, for example, provide stories about "the good Turk," because unlike the *Herald*, it did not need to curry the favor of Turkish officials so that relief workers and supplies might reach the interior of Turkey.

THE MISSIONARY HERALD

After the horrors of 1915, a January lament from the Board's editors was hardly surprising. Calling the war an abysmal folly, the Board asked its readers, "How can we say 'Happy New Year' when the world is so desolated and so defiled?"[31] Yet despite its despair about the war, the *Herald* continued its work of addressing the needs of Turkey's Armenians, whom Dr. Barton called in a Boston newspaper "a race superior to most of the peoples in the Near East."[32]

In some areas in Turkey, things remained surprisingly normal. Board Schools in Istanbul, Adana, Smyrna, Talas, Tarsus, as well as Anatolia College in Marsovan and the Marsovan Girls' School, opened in the fall of 1915 as usual and followed their standard procedures so far as possible.[33] Yet, warned the *Herald*, Turks had their eye on these American schools and wanted to rid the land of the "inconvenient Americans." Still the missionaries kept doing their best, reported the *Herald*, bravely safeguarding the Board's property, conducting schools, and dispensing relief funds.[34] The order of the tasks enumerated by the *Herald* is telling. Despite the death and destruction all around them, protecting the Board's property remained the paramount concern for some of the missionaries, as the Board saw it.

Early in the year, the *Herald* had pointed out that missionaries not only preached the Gospel but provided practical benefits to the United States as well. They promoted trade with the United States of such merchandise as sewing machines, kerosene, railroad cars, and tin shields for ships. In addition to fostering a demand for American goods, the missionaries in Asia Minor had battled diseases like cholera, typhus, and the bubonic plague. Thanks in part to missionary study of these ailments, epidemic diseases rarely struck the United States. Benefits from missionary activity therefore included better health as well as commercial advantages.[35]

The *Herald* also made clear not only the conditions in Turkey and the now-familiar horrors of the deportations, but also described for its readers the stress experienced by American missionaries when neither the missionaries nor friendly Turks were permitted to ameliorate the conditions facing the deportees.[36] Demonstrating a humanity not always apparent in its pages, the

Herald even expressed sympathy for those Armenians who had accepted conversion to Islam as a possible way of changing their fate.[37]

Despite the horrific events swirling around them, the Board's missionary community, as usual, expressed optimism about the future. Rather than bemoan the present crisis, the Board emphasized the new opportunities for evangelists in the post-war Near East. Well established by 1916, ACASR would soon be able to directly help some of the desperate refugees. Half of the Armenian people had survived, and nearly one hundred Board missionaries remained in Turkey to serve them. Indeed, two of the Board's more experienced missionaries were on their way to Tiflis in Russia to join ACASR's relief bureau newly established there. About 180,000 Armenian refugees inhabited the four vilayets closest to Tiflis, and these could be reached and helped.[38]

William W. Peet, the Board's treasurer in Istanbul, had by now developed a new source of funds. The *Herald* reported that "generous friends" in the Board's constituency who wanted to provide financial aid to the refugees were sending money directly to Peet, thereby creating a source of income independent of ACASR that Peet could use however he saw fit. Peet also tried to stimulate additional support by sending out a plea to the *Herald's* readers for "sacrificial giving."[39]

The *Herald* also had to address the picture created in its pages and in the secular press of the "fiendish" actions of Turks. Amidst the images of Turks that its stories had evoked, the *Herald* now began to take care to present a more evenhanded view of Turks, describing for its readers "good" Turks who had objected to their government's policies toward the Armenians. In Hadjin,[40] as it reported in its February issue, the Kurdish sheik Dersoon Effendi had come from a nearby village to witness the beginning of deportations from that city in the summer of 1915. Remaining only for an hour, and with tears streaming down his cheeks, he left to return home, saying he could not stand to witness such sights. He returned a second time that summer to say goodbye to his Armenian friend, Vartan Effendi, kissing each of Vartan's children and pressing them to his heart.[41]

Not only the Kurdish sheik but also the Mufti of Hadjin objected to the Armenian deportations. The Mufti had been close personal friends with one of the leading Protestant Armenians in Hadjin and had tried unsuccessfully to save him from deportation. Asked by the local ruler Alai Bey for the Mufti's approval of the measures taken against the Armenians, the Mufti said he could see no good in it.[42] Some of the village Aghas[43] in Hadjin predicted that such cruelty would not go without retribution and asked how the people of that village would manage without any artisans or shopkeepers to supply their needs. "These examples of kindness are faint gleams of light in the midst of four months of horrible darkness," wrote Edith Cold, a Board missionary at the Hadjin station who had returned to the United States.[44]

The *Herald* provided still other accounts of the actions of "good Turks." In Adabazar, a well-loved Armenian had served as President of the Board of Trustees of the Armenian girls' high school for almost thirty years but had become disabled with paralysis. When the deportation order came, Turkish friends who held him in high regard intervened to get an exemption for him and his family.[45]

Turks in other cities also objected to the deportations. Many of the rich, influential Turks of Erzerum objected to the deportations and went repeatedly to the government to try to get the orders changed. The Turkish officials, however, finally told them if any of them tried to hide or help Armenians, they would be hanged in front of their own front doors.[46]

In addition to these accounts pertaining to local conditions, the *Herald* reported that Ahmed Riza Bey, a senator in the national Parliament, had criticized the government for massacring Armenians and persecuting other Christians in Turkey, and for that he was arrested by the authorities, but subsequently released.[47]

These stories indicate that the decision to deport was not necessarily based on local conditions, and not always supported by local Turks and Kurds. To the contrary, the accounts suggest that Armenians had been welcome in many places and had formed significant bonds of friendships so that local Turks sometimes objected to deportations, even if they were powerless to affect the government's policies.

The Board appears to have had several reasons for publishing positive news stories about the "good Turks." First, as a result of graphic news stories about the Armenian Genocide appearing in American publications like the *Times*, the American public had read almost nothing but extremely negative stories about Turks and Kurds. The Board now had to counteract that negative imagery so that potential American financial donors could accept the principle that assistance must be provided to all the peoples of the Middle East who needed it, not just the persecuted Christian minorities. The stories from Hadjin that portrayed local officials, including the Mufti and a Kurdish sheik, as sympathetic to the Armenians' plight, served that purpose well. Second, it was nothing but fair and accurate reporting to provide information about Muslims who opposed their government's policies. Possibly, the Board's concept of Christian humanism, which it cited but did not define during the years covered by this book, may have led it to believe that all persons are capable of goodness regardless of their religion or ethnicity, and that it wanted the *Herald* to convey that message. Third, the refugee workers themselves needed to maintain a standard of impartiality so that they would not fall into the trap of wanting to help only the "worthy" refugees.

The kind of detachment the Board was demanding was no doubt difficult for some of the Board's staff. Many of the missionaries had witnessed events of terrible cruelty; others had spent their whole lives working with Armenians and were emotionally connected to them. Nevertheless, it was the Board's position that all refugees must be treated equally, regardless of personal feeling. It was only proper that all in need be helped. Fourth, ACASR needed governmental permission to import the foodstuffs and other supplies necessary to save refugees. Without such permission, ACASR's mission would fail. It was therefore essential that the missionaries not only treat all refugees alike, but that they be *perceived* to operate without partiality toward any group.

The even-handed approach adopted by the Board may also have related to the Board's underlying philosophy about its mission in Turkey. As indicated earlier, the Board's original mission was to evangelize the Turks. When unable to do this, the Board turned its proselytizing attentions to Armenians. If Turks and Kurds received assistance from the American missionaries and ACASR workers, they might be more willing to embrace Christianity, and the Board could actualize its original goals in Turkey. The news conveyed in the *Herald* made it clear that the Board planned to stay in Turkey without regard to whether any Armenians remained in the Empire. Dr. Ussher's fundraising efforts for a new hospital in Van (to be named for his deceased wife) and Dr. Raynolds' institution for the study of the Turkish language at the Hartford School of Missions illustrate this well.[48] The missionaries knew the Turks; they often had excellent relationships with them, and they hoped that the Turks would some day become Christians. Not surprisingly, therefore, the Board's staff looked towards a Turkey without Armenians to salvage something of their investment, both physical and spiritual, in Asia Minor.

Communication difficulties with some of its field staff still beset the Board. Letters from Turkey, the *Herald* reported, were few and far between, had to be brief, and were confined to unimportant matters; if not, they would not get past the censor without "severe mutilation." How were things, the *Herald* asked rhetorically, at Mardin, Harpoot, Aintab, Sivas, Marsovan, and all the other interior stations? The Board had no way of knowing.[49] News from Turkey came in fragments, highly censored, sometimes through travelers or doctors returning from the war zones, and sometimes from Board missionaries who had come out of the country.[50] This must have been an issue of serious concern for a mission board that had placed staff, including single women, in remote areas of Turkey only to find later that contact with them had been broken off.

The letters that got through to the Board from Turkey now dwelt on relief work and the satisfaction gained from providing it:

> ... the gratification that funds can be received, forwarded, and applied; the satisfaction of being able to do something in these times of interruption and overturning; ... of allaying somewhat the suffering; of actually saving lives and enabling destitute women and children to keep going through this cruel winter.[51]

While the cruel winter had made life almost impossible for the destitute women and children, thousands of "wretched and starving Armenians" at many mission centers, and in detention camps along the main highways of deportation, had been saved. Contributors to ACASR had the satisfaction of knowing that funds for the refugees could be given and received in the United States, forwarded to Turkey and Russia, and put to immediate use.[52] The *Herald* as always made sure that contributors to ACASR knew that their money was being properly used. It wrote:

> Every dollar meet[s] a desperate need and every dollar yield[s] its full hundred cents. The work has been a blessing to those who have done it, as it has furnished occupation for hands that might otherwise have been wrung with impotent grief; and it has saved and sustained the lives of a multitude of defenseless sufferers.[53]

But the situation in Turkey and Russia took a toll on the Board's missionary staff. In December 1915, the Board suffered a serious blow when three of its long-time physician missionaries died of typhus. Dr. Frederick Shepard, a highly respected physician whose energy was prodigious, had worked in Turkey for thirty-three years. The news about his death "caused a painful sinking of heart to those who realized what he had been for one-third of a century...."[54] He was described by a colleague as:

> strong and brave, ... a wise and ever ready counselor whose single purpose was the consecration of his splendid skill as a physician-surgeon to the services of his fellow man in the advancement of the Kingdom of Christ.[55]

Most recently, Dr. Shepard had served as medical director of the new Azariah Smith Hospital, where he had been treating "hundreds of miserable exiles, with no bedding and no food, all of them ... infected with typhus."[56]

Dr. Henry H. Atkinson, a medical missionary in Harpoot for fourteen years, had overseen the building of the large, well-equipped Annie Tracy Riggs hospital at Mezereh, near Harpoot. While treating deportees, Dr. Atkinson also contracted typhus and died on December 25, 1915.[57] In addition, Dr. Daniel Thom, a medical missionary in Mardin for forty-one years, died from typhus on December 6, 1915.[58] All three had provided medical care in Turkey for many years and had been repeatedly honored by the highest Turkish officials for their services.[59]

The Board viewed the three doctors and the final years of their careers as particularly useful for demonstrating Christian charity, in that their services were received, welcomed, and appreciated by both Muslims and Christians, a fact that might aid in securing a permanent place in Turkey for the Board. By providing services that were easily identified, altogether necessary, and made available to both Turk and Armenian without discrimination, the Board's physicians in Turkey protected the whole community from the scourge of disease. Their deaths from typhus were particularly ironic since all three had long battled the disease in others.[60]

APRIL - JUNE 1916

THE NEW YORK TIMES

On April 9, the *Times* headlined a story "Turks Renewing Armenian Evictions," giving it the sub-heading, "Relief Committee Gets Word That More Funds Are Needed at Once." Based on a dispatch from the State Department three weeks earlier, it told about recent deportations of Armenians who had resettled in their old homes, and it asked for increased funds to help this new cadre of deportees.[61]

In the April 9 article, the *Times* specified localities where refugees needed assistance, as described by workers on the scene. The American Consul at Aleppo had informed the American Embassy about the 500,000[62] refugees in the area of Aleppo, Damascus, and Zor (Der Zor). The article reported that existing relief measures were insufficient to bring the refugees through the winter, and that as much as one million dollars could be "very profitably employed."[63] From Tiflis, a cablegram from Consul Willoughby-Smith dated March 20 described repatriation efforts for refugees from Van that required hundreds of thousands of dollars. Willoughby-Smith's cablegram also included a detailed report from Rev. S. G. Wilson, one of the three ACASR workers in Erivan, about the conditions facing the refugees there. Such details as ages, gender, lack of clothing and bedding, and futile attempts to keep warm while huddled together under rags, created the kind of picture that was sure to influence the generosity of contributors to ACASR. The *Times*, as always, ended the three-column story, run in the first section of its Sunday edition, by naming some of the ACASR directors, and giving the address for ACASR's treasurer, Charles R. Crane.[64]

By April 1916, the Russians had recaptured Van, taken Erzerum and Bitlis, and were poised to seize Trebizond and other Turkish cities. The Russian capture of Erzerum was "nothing short of marvelous," wrote Richard Hill, an employee of ACASR stationed in Tiflis in a *Times* article on May 3 titled, "15,000 Massacred as Erzerum Fell."[65] Wading in snow waist deep, and pushing on in a blinding snowstorm, Russian soldiers scaled impossible heights, taking their guns apart and hauling them on their backs and by rope to the top of the heights surrounding Erzurum's forts. Dropping them down the icy cliffs, the troops reassembled them in the optimal location for attacking the forts, "where they brought terror and consternation" to Erzurum's Turkish defenders. Hill, who had gathered information about the capture of Erzerum from officials and Russian army officers who had returned to Tiflis, commented that the Russian troops showed as much valor as Napoleon's march over the Alps.[66]

After the capture, about one hundred Armenians reappeared after being in hiding, but the fate of the 15,000 Armenians deported from Erzurum in June of the previous year remained unknown. Some of the city's Armenians – those who had escaped to the Caucasus – were now planning to return to Erzerum to restart their lives.[67] Hill's praise of Russian soldiers illustrates the way information was passed on to the general public through the *Times*, making both the Russians and the Armenians appear more attractive to those who might support the Board's relief efforts by contributing funds to the ACASR.

The May 3 article includes a statement that 15,000 Armenians were killed by Turks at Mamakhatun prior to the evacuation of Erzerum by Ottoman troops. This account shows how difficult it is to determine the correct number of Armenians killed by Turks.[68] Some time earlier, news sources had reported that all of the Armenians of Erzerum had been killed or deported. This May 3 story speaks of Mamakhatun, but doesn't tell the reader whether the 15,000 represents the number of Armenians who were deported from Erzerum, and subsequently murdered at Mamakhatun, or whether this represented a new act of massacre.

When Russian capture seemed imminent, Taxim Bey, the Vali of Erzerum, who had aided the Armenians to the extent permitted by the government in Constantinople, went to the Board missionary, Rev. Stapleton, and asked him to approach the Russians with a proposal. If the Moslem population was not molested by the Russian troops, the Vali would do all he could to help the expatriated Armenians in Mesopotamia; "otherwise he would not answer for what might happen," stated the *Times*.[69] These statements are puzzling. No mention is made here of the threat to hang any Turks who helped the deported Armenians as they were preparing to leave, nor is it explained how the departing vali could assist deportees then in Mesopotamia.

Russian military progress in Eastern Turkey, described above, led many Armenian refugees then living in the Caucasus to consider returning to Turkey, wrote the *Times* in the same May 3 article. Yet the 200,000 Armenian survivors hanging on by their fingernails through the Caucasian winter could not just get up and return to their ruined homes, devastated fields, and destroyed businesses. Plows and other agricultural implements, tools of their trade, seeds, animals, and building materials would be needed to help them restart their lives. Women and children were advised to stay in the Caucasus while the men sorted things out in their old homes, now under Russian control. The *Times* concluded the May 3 article by naming the ACASR representatives in the Caucasus and publishing the amount of money already expended for the refugees of that region.[70]

Citing as its source a bulletin put out by the Board, the *Times* reported events just before the Russians captured Erzerum. Facing probable surrender to the advancing Russians, the Turks "perpetrated indescribable atrocities on the 20,000 Armenians who were then in the city," the paper said in a June 3 article.[71] Only 200 escaped, thirty of whom were sheltered by Board missionaries (the Stapletons) stationed in Erzurum. The Moslems came several times and demanded that the Armenian girls staying in the Stapletons' house be given over to them. Rev. Stapleton answered, according to the article, " 'You must kill me before you can touch them.' " A plot to set the Stapletons' house on fire was discovered, and the situation daily became more desperate until, at length, Stapleton said to his wife, " 'If the Russians do not arrive today, I feel sure that our time has come.' "

That night, before retreating, the Turks exploded their ammunition magazines in the forts above Erzerum. The shock of the explosions broke most of the windows in the Stapletons' house and all the windows in the nearby hospital. The Turkish troops fled, and local residents thereupon began looting. Indeed, the looters were approaching the American quarters when the Russian advance guard of Cossacks arrived and began to police the city. Later on, Russian officials called on the Stapletons and were entertained in their home. The Turks had sent most of their wounded away, but 200 who were unable to join the retreat remained confined in Erzurum's hospitals.

When Dr. Stapleton, a physician, and the Russian Red Cross physicians visited the hospitals, they found dead in almost every room. In a single, crowded room, the deceased and the living were mixed in together. Dr. Stapleton offered to take charge of the hospitals' patients herself, albeit with help from some of the Armenian girls whom she had been protecting. She reported that the patients were in terrible shape.[72]

After the depiction of these events, drawn from a Board bulletin, the June 3 article went on to describe another Board bulletin, which reported the Board expectation that the Russian occupation of Eastern Turkey would be permanent, and that Harpoot, Mardin and other portions of what was once the Eastern Turkey field would soon be reoccupied by the Russians.[73]

While the Board missionaries and the Russian army struggled with the situation in Eastern Turkey, fundraising at home continued at a feverish pace. Morgenthau, whose resignation of his ambassadorship was still awaiting President Wilson's acceptance, addressed a mass meeting in Carnegie Hall on May 14, 1916, seeking to raise $5,000,000 for the refugees.

Feeling relieved from the restrictions imposed upon him as a diplomat, he described the needs of the impoverished Armenians without mincing words and articulated a philosophy of giving that would affect international diplomacy. America can best bring about world peace, he said, if the warring nations understand that America is motivated by altruistic goals only.

> The only way to convince others of America's honesty of purpose ... [is] by aiding those on whom the curse of the war has fallen most heavily. ... [U]nless help is given to the Armenians, as well as to the Moslems in Turkey, there will be a fearful amount of starvation next Winter [sic]. If we are all brothers, and we are, have we a right to live on in the comfort and luxury of America and allow these people to starve?... I believe this country ought to assume the role of Big Brother to all the suffering now in the world.[74]

To add more emotional clout to his message, Morgenthau described a American missionary hospital in Turkey where a thousand people a day were being fed at a cost of three cents each. ACASR, he said, needed to raise $5,000,000 for the 1,500,000 refugees, amounting to only five cents from every American – the price of a movie ticket. Morgenthau added:

> America has gone crazy in selfishness. With humans dying by hundreds of thousands because they haven't a crust of bread, every church and college in the land is trying to raise money for extensions and endowments. It makes me sick. They can wait, but the starving cannot.[75]

Only four days later, ACASR conducted an interview with Morgenthau and reported the content of the interview to the *Times*, which the newspaper shared with its readers on May 20. Morgenthau repeated much of what he had said earlier at the mass meeting, but announced that he was now advocating a much larger fund of $500,000,000, or five dollars per American.[76] On May 23, the *Times* reported another address by Morgenthau in Chicago, in which the ex-ambassador again stated that at least $500,000,000 would be needed to rescue the Armenian refugees.[77]

The *Times* provided yet another article on the Armenians of Turkey in the second quarter of 1916. Titled "Turkey's Account With Civilization" and dated June 26, the story, authored by Vahan Cardashian, a noted Armenian spokesman and writer, attacked Morgenthau for asserting that Turkey was a vigorous body, quoting the Ambassador as saying that "in view of her [Turkey's] exploits during the present war, she can justly expect to enlarge, strengthen, and assert herself after the war." Cardashian, instead, anticipated the demise of the Ottoman Empire:

[D]ue to long periods of undisputed domination such as he enjoyed, and also by the infiltration of effete and degenerative types and elements, and his obstinate persistence to rule only by force, three principal reasons may be advanced in explanation for the abasement and breakdown of the Turk's power. Coming from Central Asia, he failed to learn from the civilizations of the nations conquered; he has always been in a minority within his own empire; and his religion is a barrier to social association of the conqueror and the conquered. Germany has an enormous national debt and will not be able to bail out Turkey at the end of the war. Consequently, Turkey should approach the Entente Allies to create some kind of settlement.[78]

The *Times* had regularly given press to all aspects of the Armenian situation. Now if not earlier, however, a more analytical and penetrating assessment of why Turkey had joined with the Central Powers and why it had decided to exterminate the Armenians could have been helpful to the *Times'* readers and to those seeking to determine how the United States should relate to Turkey in the future. Cardashian's provocative remarks did not address those issues.

THE MISSIONARY HERALD

Rumors abounded in Turkey that the country was in a desperate situation, wrote the *Herald*. Russia had defeated Turkey's armies in the eastern part of the country; the Egyptian campaign against the British had collapsed; Russia and England planned to join forces against Turkey in Mesopotamia; and Germany offered little help to her ally. But, warned the editors, it might be too soon to write Turkey off. As the "Sick Man of Europe," Ottoman Turkey had seemed on the verge of disintegration, yet it had "a wonderful history of escapes from doom."[79] The current emergency, said the *Herald*, had raised an opportunity to evaluate the Board's missionary enterprise in that country, to identify what Board properties remained and their condition, and to determine what aspects of the Board's work could be salvaged from this current emergency.[80]

In the April *Herald*, the Board cautioned its readers to avoid mixing relief concerns with political agendas. German friends in Adana, wrote the Board's missionary, Dr. Chambers, in a piece published in the next issue, had raised money in August and given it to the Armenian bishop of that area to help the deportees. To enable that to happen, a German woman of that city had appealed to the people in that area to come to the aid of Armenians and had obtained a significant amount of money. Then, having applied to the Turkish government for cloth to be made into underwear for Turkish troops, she had hired destitute Armenian women and paid them a living wage for the work they did under her supervision. This, the *Herald* pointed out, showed that wartime allegiances had little to do with addressing the unquestioned needs of Armenians for relief.[81] This was an important point for the Board to make, because one of the major tenets in its relief work was that assistance was to be given to all needy persons regardless of nationality or religion. It also demonstrated the success of the Board's own preferred method of relief – what it called "industrial relief" – so that recipients of relief could maintain their own work ethic, as well as their dignity.

The letter from Chambers in the April 1916 *Herald* also demonstrated the absence of partisanship in a report from sailors on the German ship *Emden* who had traveled through Turkey. The German sailors, Chambers said, "were outspoken in their denunciation of what they had seen as they passed through the regions where Armenians were under deportation orders."[82] This again demonstrated to the *Herald's* readers the Board's philosophy that humanitarianism had no ethnic base and that all human beings, regardless of nationality, including persons on active duty in Germany's navy, could care about injustice and distress caused to others.

As this report shows, the *Herald* vacillated between articles denouncing Turkish and German actions and accounts describing the concerns of German government officials and ordinary Germans about the excesses of its wartime ally. The sailors' story also may have sought to introduce to the *Herald's* readers the idea that cooperation with Germany after the war might be needed. If the Germans and Turks won the war, it would be easier for an American missionary enterprise to continue its work in Turkey if the *Herald* and other missionary publications had spoken appreciatively of Germany and "Turks who objected to the treatment of the Armenians."[83] At the same time, the Board had to be careful not to appear pro-German at a time when public opinion in the United States was turning against Germany more decisively.

In its April issue, as it did throughout this period, the *Herald* continued to express praise for Morgenthau, then home from Constantinople for two months' leave. Tirelessly working for twenty-seven months at what the Board called "the most difficult and exacting diplomatic post in connection with our own government or any other," Morgenthau had represented the interests not only of the United States but of nine other nations no longer maintaining embassies in Constantinople. Anxious to have some communication with Constantinople despite the rigid censorship in place, the missionaries typically wrote to him as "Uncle Henry," and, using that subterfuge, got at least some of their mail through to him. Morgenthau himself made no secret of his reliance on American missionaries in the interior of Turkey for information about the current situation there, or of his appreciation for the character, courage, ability, and work of American missionaries and institutions they had founded and represented. In response, the missionaries revered him as "another demonstration of the genius of our American society and government."[84]

While home, the Ambassador briefed the Board about the current situation in Turkey, including the viewpoints of the Turkish leaders and the policies currently in place. The Ambassador said that he had never seen such able men and women as the missionaries who stood up to the Turkish authorities. In his briefing, reported in the May issue, he called the Board's Treasurer in Turkey, W. W. Peet, the wisest man in Constantinople, and one of his most trusted advisors. Reassuring the Board about the safety of its staff in Turkey, he urged the Board not to abandon its mission in Turkey, because he saw the Board's work as helping to make Turkey a more modern country.[85]

The events surrounding the war had inspired yet another advance in missionary thinking. Belligerent nations, the *Herald's* editors said in their April issue, had mobilized millions of soldiers to fight their enemies in the war and had spent the equivalent of millions of dollars to equip their forces; the missions, in contrast, had been guilty of "thinking too small." "It is time," urged the Board, "for the Christian movement in the world to quicken its pace; to plan on an ampler scale; to issue a worthier challenge to its supporters."[86]

In its June issue, the *Herald* furnished its own version of the Russian takeover of Erzerum, which for the most part mirrored that of the *Times*. As already stated, the Turkish governor had asked Rev. Stapleton, a Board missionary stationed in Erzerum, to intercede with the Russians on behalf of the Muslim residents there. The vali sought protection for his Muslim subjects on the basis that Turkish civilians were not involved either in fighting the Russians or in deporting the Armenians. Mr. Stapleton agreed to do so and, while the Russians made no promises, none of the Turks was slaughtered or molested. Exercising their newly won control of the city, the Russians appointed a Turkish pasha – someone on the outs with the Committee of Union and Progress, the governing dictatorship of Turkey – as governor of the city. The Germans had left the city several months earlier. Only the German Consul remained in the city, and he left before the Russians arrived. The Russians took over a mission residence for use as the invaders' headquarters, and they also occupied the Stapleton's house. The Stapletons planned to return to the United States via Vladivostok, and to bring with them some of the Armenian girls who had worked in their home and hospital.[87] Everyone acted on the assumption that the Russians would remain in control of Erzerum.

The story by Dr. Stapleton, published by the *Herald* in its June issue, is much longer than the short, half-page articles typically published by the *Herald*. The missionary organ may have decided to publish her lengthy piece as a way of introducing its readers to the Russians, just as earlier it had introduced them and the Turks. Its readers had to get used to the idea that the Russians would now be exercising control over a significant amount of land in eastern Turkey, a long-time Board mission field. The subjects of the Board's missionary zeal would now include Russians, "nominal" Christians to the Board's way of thinking, and therefore ripe for conversion to what the Protestant Board considered a more genuine version of Christianity.

At the same time, the Board was not sure how such a change would affect its missionary enterprise in Turkey. In the past, Russia's Orthodox Christian clergy had been hostile to evangelical missionaries, and the Board's missionaries therefore thought it would be easier to deal with the Turks, with whom they had almost seventy five years' experience. Yet the Board expressed its usual optimism that Russia would be receptive to its missionary work in territories captured from Turkey.[88]

Since the Russians had captured a large part of the territory previously inhabited by Armenians, a return to the Armenians' former homes was now possible. In the article in the *Herald's* May issue, "Turkey by the Back Door," the Board counseled that repatriation of Armenians to their former homes had to be carried out carefully, because nothing of the refugees' former property would still be available to them. The besieged Christians would need relief restarting their lives until they became self-sufficient. Such relief would be provided by the Board's staff in Tiflis and Erivan.[89] In western Turkey, in Smyrna, Constantinople, and along the coasts of the Sea of Marmara, conditions remained especially bad. Famine and typhus had caused a high mortality rate among Turks and Armenians alike. Americans had sent money for relief to both the Red Cross and the Turkish Red Crescent, reported the *Herald*, again demonstrating that ACASR helped all those in need.[90]

At the same time, the Board struggled with the situation in Cilicia, at the eastern end of the Mediterranean in southeastern Turkey, and the inexplicability of Turkish activities in that area. The Turks, according to letters written in February by Board staff in Turkey but not received in Boston until April, had continued to interfere with the Board's use of its properties in the interior. In Aintab, the Turkish military authorities continued to maintain a guard around the missionary college, but neither the missionaries there nor the American Consul at Aleppo knew why. In Adana, although the American hospital previously closed by the Turks had been permitted to reopen, and although the missionary physician in charge, Dr. Haas, was allowed to manage the hospital without interference, the boys' school in Adana had been seized but not put to use.[91]

In its May issue, the *Herald* printed a report from the American Consul at Tiflis, F. Willoughby-Smith, who informed readers about the continued difficulty the Board and the United States were having in addressing the needs of all Armenian refugees who had fled to the Caucasus from their homes in Turkey. ACASR had sent three of the Board's experienced missionaries to the Caucasus: Rev. George Gracie of Urfa, who was on furlough in the United States when the war broke out; Rev. F. W. Macallum, recently of Bible House in Constantinople, the Board's publishing department; and Dr. Floyd Smith of Diyarbekir, who had been expelled from Turkey by the Turkish government for unknown reasons. The three men labored to set up refugee work in the Caucasus under the chairmanship of the Rev. Wilson, a Presbyterian minister who had spent many years in Persia. ACASR staff described the needs of the refugees as overwhelming: sanitary clothes and bedding were essential to keep people from freezing to death and from spreading typhus; sanitary housing facilities were required for 500-1,000 orphans, previously left to drift about on their own; and disinfecting centers were needed to clean and disinfect the refugees to stop the spread of typhus, from which thousands of refugees had already died. Somehow the committee had to feed, clothe, and keep in a sanitary condition more than 220,000 refugees in the Caucasus until they could return to their homes to rebuild them.[92]

The Russian government, the *Herald* reported in its May issue, played a notably pro-active and sympathetic role in caring for the refugees and providing for their needs, with Grand Duke Nicholas, Viceroy of the Caucasus, declaring that the work "of relief was very pleasing, and wishing [the committee] great success." The Russians also made rail transportation available to ship the committee's goods to locations where they were needed, for which the missionaries expressed considerable appreciation.[93]

The Board's missionaries were supported in their relief efforts by the Catholicos at Echmiadzin, the head of the Armenian Apostolic Church, who was caring for 7,000 refugees in Echmiadzin, Russia, by operating orphanages, a hospital, bakeries, and soup kitchens. In providing this help to the missionaries, the Catholicos expressed his appreciation for the work of the American relief committee.[94] In a war zone with a continually shifting border, the support received from both the Russian government and the head of the Armenian Church would be important to contributors to ACASR, so that they knew their benefactions would be welcome and useful.

The *Herald's* May report titled "Relief Work from Tiflis" also wrote about a delegation of Armenian doctors and nurses that had come from the United States to aid in the task of repatriating the refugees in the Caucasus to their former homes in Turkey. The delegation was headed by an Armenian American doctor. The son of the head of the Protestant Armenians of Turkey, he was already familiar to the missionaries, who were pleased to learn of his selection. The Armenian doctors and nurses were assigned to the Russian Red Cross and scheduled to work in Van under a governor chosen by the Russians. They were given responsibility for the two thousand refugees already repatriated to Van, and, wrote the *Herald*, an additional one thousand refugees who had returned to Bayazid (Dogubayazid), and five thousand to Diyadin, making a total of about 20,000 now in the Turkish provinces occupied by Russia. The 220,000 refugees in the Caucasus, described by the *Herald* as "human flotsam, rotted and at the mercy of every eventuality," needed just about everything.[95]

Despite Turkish assurances to the contrary, deportations continued in some areas. In Aintab, Central Turkey College had recently been closed and its teaching staff deported. The Board hospitals of Konia and Mersine had been shut down and remained closed on the pretext of some trivial violations of their municipal permit. Although the Adana hospital had been reopened as noted above, the terms of the reopening were not known. Several more missionaries were leaving Turkey for reasons not given, though there were "hints that their departure was wise," stated the *Herald*, without identifying the source of the "hints," whether it be Turks, other missionaries, or consular officials. Other missionaries in the interior would have liked to leave Turkey, but were unable to do so because passenger train service to and from Turkey's interior had been suspended. All trains had been converted to military use.[96]

Rev. Wilson, head of the ACASR operation in Tiflis, sent ACASR a lengthy report written in early March describing in detail the methods by which the delivery of clothing and bedding was made to refugees in Dilijan, Persia, which was then under Russian control. Thus far, ACASR had devoted itself to distributing clean clothing and bedding to Caucasus refugees whose names were provided by Willoughby-Smith. Notices were sent to refugee families that garments and blankets would be distributed on an appointed date. The families gathered in a storeroom, after which the name of the family would be called out, and a numbered coupon with its name and the ages of the children would be placed in the family's hands, with the stub with the same information retained. The family would then deliver the coupon to an officer at the guard's station, following which a comforter would be spread on the ground and garments for the different members of the family placed on it. Then the comforter would be gathered up into a bundle, which the refugee parents could carry away on their backs. Each day, Wilson moved the distribution to another refugee village, handing out whatever bedding and clothing they were able to provide. The people who received the distributed goods were highly appreciative, he reported.[97]

An article in the June issue of the *Herald* titled "Hardest on Children" told how poorly refugee children in the Caucasus were faring in relation to adult refugees. Adults outnumbered the children in the registered refugee population of 234,000; only 88,000 were school children under fifteen years of age. Wilson, director of the program in the Caucasus, attributed the unexpectedly small number of children to the children's natural inability to withstand the extreme rigors of the refugees' flight east in the wake of the Russian retreat from Van, and the weeks of "terrible suffering" and disease that followed until the relief program got started. Even now, wrote Wilson, the refugees must subsist, week after week, on bread and water paid for by the Russians, assistance that Wilson called "generous aid to the subjects of a foreign power." Since each refugee got either twenty ounces of flour or five cents per day from the Russian government, the relief efforts of the Russians seemed minuscule. In truth, Wilson wrote, that aid costs no less than $3,500,000 a year.[98]

Wilson had instituted typical programs of "industrial relief." In Erivan, ACASR supplied bookbinders, beekeepers, tailors, carpenters, cobblers, silversmiths, and artists with the tools they needed to ply their trades. To still others, ACASR provided raw sheepskins from which wool could be pulled and sold, along with the remaining hide. Wilson also sent letters to the United States to be forwarded to relatives of refugees who might be willing to help their uprooted relations now that the latter were settled.[99]

Despite all this emphasis on the practical aspects of refugee life, significant theoretical issues faced the Board. As the American public held increasingly negative views of Germany, the Board worried about what would happen to its staff and properties in Turkey if America were to declare war on Germany. Might America also declare war on Turkey? Wouldn't the Turks then seize American mission properties in Turkey and intern American nationals, including the Board's own staff? Perhaps, hoped the *Herald* in an article in its May issue entitled "Turkey's Desperate Plight," Turkey might come to realize that America was "really her truest and most unselfish friend" and refuse to be pulled by Germany into war with the United States.[100]

The Board's concern illustrates how missionary policy and American foreign policy interacted with each other during 1916. The kind of information the American public had been given about the inhumanity and barbarity of the Turks would have certainly motivated the American people to lump Turkey with the hated Germany, if a declaration of war were issued against the Central Powers. On reflection, however, the Board must have concluded that the possibility of internment of its staff in Turkey, Turkish seizure of its property and the possible demise of its critically important relief programs for refugees far outweighed any benefits that might flow from treating Turkey and Germany alike.

Whatever the political concerns of the Board, its desire to save the refugees inspired it to continue its vigorous fundraising activities in the United States. The Federal Council of Churches, a national body of Protestant and Orthodox denominations, approached President Wilson and requested that he invite all religious organizations to set aside Memorial Sunday, May 28, as a day of contributions to relief organizations in the United States. In a June article headlined, "The Federal Council Tackles a Big Job," the *Herald* exhorted its readers to participate: "the United States has not begun to give sacrificially or adequately for the relief of the war-swept lands."[101] Despite any misgivings it might have had, the Board chose to plow forward vigorously along the same paths it already followed.

JULY - SEPTEMBER 1916

THE NEW YORK TIMES

During the second half of 1916, the State Department continued its efforts on behalf of the Christians of Ottoman Turkey. Concerned about the fate of Armenian deportees in Syria, it directed its chargé d'affaires in Constantinople to inform the Turkish government that no response had been received from the State Department's three previous requests that neutral nations be permitted to feed the starving refugees. The *Times* reported this news in a July 7 article titled, "Washington to Press Turkey for Syrians." In that story, the *Times* reported that the State Department had informed the Turkish government that it understood that the entire Christian population of Syria was on the verge of extermination, and that 50,000 to 80,000 had already died. Despite this situation, according to the *Times*, the Turkish military continued to seize food supplies sent by the United States for distribution to refugees. The American people were anxious to assist the stricken in Syria, stated the Department. It asked the Turks to determine if its information was correct and to inform the State Department of its determination. Washington reminded the Turks that failure to respond despite repeated requests would severely strain relations between the United States and Turkey.[102] Obtaining the State Department's intervention on behalf of ACASR (and the Syrian civilians) demonstrates the level of support that ACASR could expect from American agencies such as the State Department, no doubt because of the prominence of the members of ACASR and their connections to the government.

The *Times* continued to publish letters it had received from Armenian sympathizers about conditions in Turkey. A long letter titled "For Armenian Refugees" from Mrs. Mary Hickson, published in the July 17 issue approved ACASR's efforts, as reported by Board missionary Gracey, to repatriate Armenian refugees from Syria to the "conquered districts of Turkey." To prepare for this, 800 houses and 500 small shops of the city of Van had to be either burnt down or gutted in order to refurbish them, their filthy and possibly disease-bearing condition threatening to contaminate the emaciated refugees. Oxen for current farmers and the resources for chicken and pig farming for others had to be provided to enable the refugees to return to self-sufficiency.

Hickson added:

> There is complete security from Turks and Kurds in these districts, and we may hope that in the not far distant future, ... these much-tried people may see their homes restored and smiling fields and gardens giving of their abundance, to atone in some small degree for the sorrows and bereavement and sufferings of the past.[103]

By printing this letter, the *Times* helped inform the American public of efforts to rehabilitate and repatriate the deported Armenians.

Four days later, a story headlined "Famine and Cholera in Turkey Revealed," with a sub-heading "Conclusions Drawn from Veiled Allusions in Post Card From an American Nurse," highlighted both the gravity of conditions in Turkey and the continuing difficulties the Board experienced in getting information from its staff in Turkey. An innocuous-appearing, holiday postcard from an American missionary nurse mentioned Bible verses from the Book of Job and the Psalms; it also mentioned Dr. Hamlin's famous mixture. After looking up the cited verses in the Bible that spoke of famine and disease, and then recognizing Dr. Hamlin's mixture as a medicine used to treat cholera victims, the Board's readers clearly considered the "veiled allusions – veiled to the censor, but clear to us," to mean that famine and cholera were then "raging" in that part of Turkey.[104]

The same article made brief mention of the Turks' seizure of the Board's mission compound in Marsovan and the deportation of the missionaries who lived there. Similar events, according to the news story, had occurred at Sivas, Kayseri (Talas), and Mardin; from the later city, five women missionaries were ordered to go to Aleppo, perhaps because Mardin lay in the path of the Russian force's westward advance from Van.

The *Times* expressed its concern about the heightened level of atrocities that were being practiced against Armenians now located in the "Mesopotamian and the Arabian" districts. The paper thought that the rationale for the continuing persecution of Armenians was the success of the Russian army that by now was occupying most of Turkish Armenia. The State Department had asked the new American Ambassador to the Porte, Abram I. Elkus, to take up the issue as soon as he arrived in Constantinople.[105] But the new Ambassador had other issues he needed to address with the Porte, in particular the Turkish military's takeover of the Board's mission station at Marsovan and the eviction of the American missionaries who were posted there.[106] (The *Times*' story was based on information provided in the August edition of the *Herald*.)[107]

The Turkish rationale for the Marsovan evictions and other similar actions was the Turks' mistaken belief that the United States and Germany were now at war. When that was proven to be untrue, stated the August 13th issue of the *Times*, the Turks changed the rationale for the seizure, alleging military necessity, even though the closest fighting had occurred no less than 150 miles away. The Board, reported the *Times*, complained that the Turkish actions were "poor requital for the relief work of our hospitals," noting that the missionary doctor at Sivas alone had treated 12,000 cases for the Turkish army.[108] The hardest part for the missionaries in both Marsovan and Talas was the seizure of Armenian girls and women who were cared for by the missionaries. The Talas girls were forced to become Muslims the day they were taken.[109]

The *Times* story of August 16 provided a day-by-day description of the days between May 10th when the missionaries were informed that they were to leave Marsovan the next day, and May 15 when they actually left. As soon as they were informed of their expulsion, the missionaries sent telegrams to the American Embassy and to Peet, both located in Constantinople, but the local official in charge of censorship told White privately that the missionaries' dispatches would not leave town. The missionaries were, however, able to get a message via a friendly traveler to Mr. Peters, the American consular agent at Samsun by Friday morning. Two days later Peters wired back that he had received their message. This was the only communication received by Marsovan missionaries from the outside throughout the whole ordeal, wrote the *Times*.[110]

On August 13, the *Times* provided a detailed description of the facilities of the Marsovan plant. The mission station included thirty-seven acres of land; a fine hospital and dispensary of three buildings; six large college and girls' school buildings; the foundations of two more buildings in the process of construction; a school for children with hearing loss; an extensive cabinet shop with woodworking and iron working; a flour mill; thirteen residences, and many smaller structures with furniture, appliances and equipment; a library of 10,000 books; a museum housing 7,000 objects; and the personal effects of six American families and five single persons. The property alone was valued at $500,000.[111] For missionaries with such a heightened sense of duty about protecting the Board's property, the surrender of this property and all of its carefully acquired accouterments, coupled with the kidnapping of Armenian girls, must have been wrenching.

President White's report conveyed the sense of outrage at the events that had transpired:

> They cut up our premises by barricading off certain parts, a proceeding which had no legal relation with sending away foreigners or equipping a hospital. ... They assumed the conduct and management of our schools, as if these were hostile institutions. They required every American to leave Marsovan, but not Miss Zbinden, who is a Swiss citizen, thus discriminating against American citizenship.[112]

The anger expressed in White's choice of language to describe what was happening to his college, staff, and charges suggests that the missionaries did not see themselves as aliens in a Muslim country, but rather as holders of privileges granted to them in perpetuity by the Ottoman Empire. The missionaries might have felt that the United States' lack of interest in seeking permanent territory in Turkey meant that America's role was totally beneficent and without blame. They may have looked at the imperialistic colonial policies, practices, and holdings of Britain, France, Germany, the Netherlands, Belgium, and Portugal and contrasted these with the policies and practices of the United States, a power they saw as working in Turkey for altruistic reasons only. Indeed, unlike Britain, France, and Russia, the United States had no secret wartime agreements to carve up the Ottoman Empire after the war. Given these circumstances, the missionaries' attitude about their role in the life of Turkey is not surprising.

The *Times*' publication of this lengthy story shows its dedication to publicizing the difficulties facing the missionaries. Since this story was not seeking to raise funds for relief, its motivation for this style of reporting may have simply been to report news that it found important. The subject of missionaries at that time was of great interest. Yet the story did give a foretaste of what missionary life and property would be like if the United States were to declare war on Turkey. The *Times* may have expected this account to help galvanize missionary supporters to fashion new ways of dealing with Turkey that would eliminate such seizures and evictions.

As well as its news reporting, the *Times* continued to print letters on Armenian issues. A letter cryptically signed, "A Student of Near Eastern Affairs," accused the American government of failing to protect Armenians as it should, both in the past and the present. Had the American government done its duty, claimed the letter writer, the Armenian tragedy would never have occurred. President Wilson had made two major mistakes, stated the correspondent. He had failed to adopt a firmer approach with Turkey because he feared a rupture in diplomatic relations, and he had believed that America's duty to intervene on behalf of "the bleeding and starving Christians" was met by imploring Constantinople to improve its treatment of the Christian minorities in its lands. Instead, the anonymous letter said, the United States should have registered a protest each and every time an act of "purposeless barbarity, no matter where and by whom, was committed." If this approach did not persuade the Turkish government to put a stop to its "feasting on the blood of the defenseless and the purity of the maiden and the matron alike," the president should have severed all diplomatic relations with Turkey. The "limited work of mercy" now carried on by the American consuls and American missionaries, the letter writer claimed, "could readily have been entrusted to Spanish, Swiss, and Swedish aid workers."[113]

This letter illustrates the ongoing debate in missionary and other circles about pressing the United States government to end diplomatic relations with Ottoman Turkey. While the letter writer saw no benefit from continuing to recognize Turkey diplomatically, others felt it was essential to avoid a break. Although Russia was open to ACASR's efforts, the latter organization's relief personnel had to take the trans-Siberian railway to get to Tiflis, its headquarters in the Caucasus, and supplies had to be purchased wherever they could be found. The work in Syria and Turkey, in contrast, could be readily provided through ports in the Mediterranean, allowing easier access for both ACASR workers and supplies. For this reason, the missionaries successfully pressed the State Department to continue United States diplomatic relations with Turkey.

THE MISSIONARY HERALD

The middle of the year 1916 saw the *Herald* exploring the implications of Russia's continuing drive into Turkey, and what that might mean for the Board's missionary programs. Should this rate of advance and capture of territory continue, mused the *Herald*, large parts of the interior of Turkey would be held by Russia. Russian governance of those parts of Turkey would help the Board keep in touch with its staff in Turkey, since the Russians would not censor its mail, they believed. A good example of the difficulties was demonstrated by a postcard that "drifted in" from Trebizond (Trabzon), still at that time in Turkish hands. Rather than reveal the date of April 19 on which he wrote it, the missionary writer, Dr. Lyndon S. Crawford, dated the post card "Lexington Day," a reference to Paul Revere, so that the censor would not recognize the date, but the Board staff would. On that postcard, Dr. Crawford wrote briefly that the Russians had arrived.[114] The Board would have to content itself with this brief notice about Trebizond until later.

The Board not only concerned itself with relief efforts, but also kept a close watch on political developments in the Near East. In particular, the *Herald* called attention to the "rebellion in Arabia" in which "[t]he long smoldering resentment of the fierce and bigoted followers of Islam in Arabia" were revolting against the "tyranny and trickery of Turkish rule." If the Arabs successfully broke away from Turkey, and if they united with other Muslims to overthrow Turkey's hold on the Caliphate, the result for the missionary enterprise could be "sharper antagonism of that portion of Islam to the Christian world," wrote the *Herald*.[115] The article, "Arabia's Revolt from Ottoman Rule," expressed the Board's conclusions that it felt comfortable with Turkey and that it was even gaining some influence on Islam, neither of which would be possible under the stricter Islam of an Arabian caliph.[116]

Beginning efforts to re-establish the Armenian community in Van, reported the *Herald*, had led Gracey and Macallum, ACASR's workers in the Caucasus, to return to that city to examine the conditions of the existing buildings and their potential for refurbishment. When the two men went to the American mission quarters to check its condition, they heard the pleasant sound of Russian church music. The Russians were holding church services in the still-intact church in the American compound! Of the total of fifteen mission buildings, only four still stood, including the church; the rest were beyond repair. Granted permission by the local Russian authorities to reclaim the American compound and do whatever they wanted to it, the ACASR staff located workers and hired them to start restoring the buildings.[117]

Mrs. Crawford, in a letter to the Board received June 5, described the Russian capture of Trebizond. When the Russians sailed into Trebizond harbor, she said, the Turks abandoned the town without resisting, and the Turkish governor of the city placed the governance of the city in the hands of the Greek bishop. A representative of the Greek primate, accompanied by the American Consul Heizer, visited the Russians and informed them that the Turks had fled without a fight. As a result of the peaceful transfer of authority, the Russians did not shell the city, and the city remained intact.

The occupiers immediately turned Trebizond into a Russian city with Russian money and soldiers, a Red Cross hospital, and a re-established telegraph line, the latter greatly appreciated by the missionaries. Five hundred Armenians – men, women, and children – descended into the city from nearby mountains where they had been hiding in dens and caves, and others left the homes of the Greeks, Armenians, and Muslims where they had been concealed. While relief funds were in short supply, reported Mrs Crawford, Armenians from Russia provided needed help to their returning countrymen.[118]

If the Board looked forward to the end of the war and the rebirth of its closed or partially closed schools in Turkey, others did not relish the prospect of the Board's return. The *Herald* in July published a note about an editorial in the Turkish journal *Hilal*. Quoting a German parliamentary deputy who argued that all missionary work was exploitative, *Hilal's* editors praised the new rules that required the mission schools to close – rules that they assumed, in error, were a necessary result of the abolition of the capitulations.[119] Such schools had allowed missionaries "to exercise great moral influence over the young men of the country" and to be "virtually in charge of the spiritual and intellectual guidance in our country," argued *Hilal*. Appreciative of the "backhanded compliment" that its schools were taking charge of the intellectual and spiritual guidance of the young, the *Herald* expressed its amazement that education and the offering of educational privileges to "the aspiring youth of Turkey" could be seen in any way as subversive. Ignoring *Hilal's* critique of the Board's programs, the *Herald* maintained that the future will be "even brighter and more promising for American and Christian education in Turkey."[120]

In the past, the Board had estimated that about one million Armenians had been murdered or deported, or had fled into the Caucasus to escape Turkish pogroms. Even if a significant segment of the remaining Armenians were repatriated, that remnant had to be far smaller than the number of pre-Genocide Armenians living in Turkey, suggesting that the number of pupils in the Board's schools would be significantly reduced. Nor, the Board concluded, was it likely that the Turks would be more receptive to education in Christian schools, as Turkish families generally had declined to allow their children to attend Board schools in the past. Although unstated by the *Herald*, the missionaries possibly hoped that the Entente Powers would win the war and introduce a restructuring of Turkish society in which Christian education would then become more attractive to Turkish parents.

As the first half of 1916 drew to a close, the missionaries continued to be faced with the needs of the deported Armenian refugees. A great deal more money was needed. At a center near Aleppo, for example, 50,000 Armenians had congregated and the "misery is indescribable."[121] At the same time, the Board was expanding its missionary base in the Caucasus. On July 15, five missionaries from the Board – Dr. George C. Raynolds, Rev. and Mrs. Yarrow, Rev. and Mrs. Maynard, plus the Yarrow and Maynard children – sailed from New York on their way to Tiflis to join the existing Board staff in the Caucasus. The three men planned to work in Van and the other mission stations now part of the Russian Empire. The *Herald*, expressing its usual optimism, proclaimed that "all the missionaries' eyes are toward the future [and] are already forgetting the dark days behind them in anticipation of the fresh opportunities ahead."[122]

The August issue of the *Herald* told about the missionaries headed for the Caucasus, but also about expulsion of the missionaries working in Marsovan. The story about the eviction from Marsovan had appeared in the *Times* on August 13.[123] The *Herald's* account of the expulsion from Marsovan was virtually identical to that published in the *Times*, except for one short insignificant paragraph.[124] The *Times* had acknowledged that it took its story from the *Herald*, thus demonstrating the role of both papers in publicizing news about the missionary enterprise in Turkey, and their mutually supportive practices.

As soon as the ejected Marsovan missionaries had arrived in Constantinople on the 24th of May, they immediately began trying to obtain approval for their return to Marsovan "to recover control at least of portions of the property and to safeguard the American Board's interest there." Having obtained permission to return, by August 4 they were safely back in Marsovan. In its September issue, the *Herald* wondered what the missionaries had found upon their return. Were the buildings intact? What was the condition of the missionary residences? Their return, the *Herald* declared, "will mean much for the saving of the work as well as the plant that some of the staff are once more on the ground."[125]

The September issue also informed readers of the expulsion of almost all of the missionaries from Sivas. On Monday, May 8, the "Merkez" commander of Sivas came to the mission station and ordered the missionaries to leave immediately. The Turkish commander explained that the military needed the buildings for the war effort, that the orphans in their charge would be transferred to the Turkish orphanage, and now that the missionaries would be permitted to take with them their servants but none of the mission's children. Protests to the vali were futile, and the Sivas missionaries left on May 14 reaching Constantinople on May 25 without the mission's children or their own servants, the earlier permission to take their servants having been rescinded. Among the missionaries stationed in Sivas, two of them, Miss Graffam and Miss Fowle, were permitted to remain in the city; no reason was offered by the *Herald*.[126]

As the second half of 1916 unfolded, the destruction of the Armenian people continued unabated. In September, the *Herald* announced that its hopes that the worst of the Armenian horrors had ended were unfounded. Instead, word had been received through "high diplomatic authority (not American)" that deportations were continuing, and, quoting a report from ACASR, the magazine wrote:

> [t]housands of deported Armenians were seen under tents in the open, in caravans on the march, descending the river in boats, and in all phases of their miserable life. In only a few places does government issue any rations, and those quite insufficient. People therefore themselves are forced to satisfy their hunger with food begged in that scanty land or found in the parched fields. They were seen eating grass, herbs, and locusts, and in desperate cases dead animals and human bodies are reported to have been eaten. Naturally the death rate from starvation and sickness is very high and increased by brutal treatment of the authorities, whose bearing toward exiles as they are being driven back and forth over the desert is not unlike that of slave drivers.
>
> There appears, in short, a steady policy to exterminate these people, but to deny charge of massacre. Their destruction from so-called natural causes seems decided upon.[127]

By publishing an account like this amidst the *Herald's* articles about the everyday activities of its mission staff, the Board reminded its readers that the campaign to destroy the Armenian people of Ottoman Turkey had not ended. Once the *Herald's* readers understood the crises facing the deported

Armenians, the Board believed, they would not only be motivated to contribute to ACASR themselves, but might also join in the fund raising so essential to keeping the remainder of Armenians alive.

OCTOBER - DECEMBER 1916

THE NEW YORK TIMES

As the end of the year 1916 approached, the *Times* furnished its readers with a shocking feature story on the Armenian Genocide. For the first time, its readers could gain a sense of the continuing horrors being inflicted on the Armenian people, not in the bits and pieces gleaned from regular newspaper reading but in a comprehensive account, spread over three pages of the second section of the Sunday edition, and coming from an impeccable source, the British peer, Viscount Bryce.

The design of this eye-catching and comprehensive news story would grab the attention of even the most casual reader who did no more than glance at the second section of the paper. Large letters at the top of page one of the second section of the *Times* steered readers to the next page with the words, "Lord Bryce Tells of Armenian Atrocities."[128] A reader turning to page two would see an eight column story taking up all of page two and flowing on to pages three and four. Introducing the story and running across all eight columns of page two was a headline in six-inch-high block letters that read, "Lord Bryce's Report on Armenian Atrocities: An Appalling Catalogue of Outrage and Massacre." Underneath that headline the *Times* placed an attention-grabbing, multi-line sub-heading, also running across the whole page, that read –

> Record of the Exhaustive Investigation Conducted by the ex-British Ambassador to This Country to be Officially Published by His Government, Advance Sheets of Which Have Just Reached *The New York Times*, Tells of the Deportation and Murder by the Turks of Hundreds of Thousands of Men, Women, and Children in an Attempt to Exterminate Entire Armenian Nation.[129]

The details provided in Lord Bryce's report defy belief. By reassuring the *Times'* readers that the report had been issued by a British peer, and that the report would be published as an official publication of the British government – a "white paper" – this almost unbelievable story would have received optimum credibility. Just before the *Times* published this story, Lord Bryce sent a cablegram to Rev. James Barton, Chairman of ACASR, in which he described his report on Armenia and the "awful conditions there." The *Times* set the stage for Bryce's report by quoting the entire text of Bryce's cablegram:

> London, Oct. 4.–All the civilized nations able to assist the Armenians today should know that the need is still extremely urgent. Several hundred thousand exiles who survived the horrors of deportation are now perishing of exposure and starvation in the Arabian desert. Latest reports of neutral eyewitnesses describe terrible conditions. Sick people are throwing themselves into graves, begging grave diggers to bury them: women are going mad and eating grass and carrion; parents are putting children out of their misery, digging their own graves and awaiting death. The future of the Armenian nation depends on saving the refugees in Russia, but this requires worldwide assistance for feeding, clothing, housing and repatriation. A book telling the whole story is just appearing here with a fuller statement by me. I feel sure American generosity will again respond to the call of humanity.[130]

1. The *Times*' Introduction

The text of Lord Bryce's cable was followed by an introduction, written by the *Times*, explaining the origins of Bryce's book. The mass of documentary evidence, the newspaper said, was so voluminous that it made up a six-hundred-page volume. To obtain the book's 150 documents, Bryce had written letters to "anyone who could throw light on Armenian conditions." Those who responded included American missionaries, who he knew had long been a presence in Turkey, German nationals who were working in Turkey in philanthropic activities and whose reports could not be dismissed as war time propaganda concocted by the Allies, and nationals of neutral countries living in Turkey and often eyewitnesses to the events about which they wrote.[131]

The bulk of the evidence in Bryce's book, wrote the *Times*, came from eyewitnesses – an indicia of reliability– but the identities and sometimes the location of the eyewitnesses, still in areas controlled by Turkey, had to remain temporarily confidential to protect them from Turkish reprisals. The documents formed a record of "horror, callous cruelty, and fiendish massacre far more revolting than Lord Bryce's report on German atrocities in Belgium which shocked the world a short time ago," stated the paper.[132]

Lord Bryce shared the advance sheets of the book with a number of prominent persons including Lord Grey, the Foreign Secretary of Britain, Moorfield Storey, the former President of the American Bar Association, and Professor Gilbert Murray of Oxford. Lord Grey described the book as "a terrible mass of evidence," yet urged that it be published not only to inform the public about these events "but as a mine of information for historians of the future." Storey, an attorney, offered his opinion that the evidence presented in the book had been obtained in a manner consistent with standard evidentiary procedures and therefore could be relied upon. [133]

By linking the account of Armenian suffering with Germany's record in Belgium, by using terminology like "fiendish massacre" and "callous cruelty" in its introduction, and by citing official British support for the report itself, the *Times* appears to have tried to kindle the interest of its readers in ways that would have compelled them to read the story.

2. Lord Bryce's Preface

Lord Bryce's preface opened by describing his reasons for compiling and publishing the documents. Originally, he wrote, little information about the events of summer 1915 had been reported to the outside world. Gradually, despite rigorous censorship by the government, more information was leaking out; when the emerging data was analyzed, it had become obvious to him and his editor Arnold Toynbee that Ottoman Turkey's troops were exterminating the country's Armenian subjects. Once he had come to that conclusion, he wrote, he was obliged to bring these facts to the attention of the world, so that others would understand what was occurring inside Turkey.[134]

The book focused on the massacre and deportation of Armenian and other Eastern Christians living in Asia Minor and Northwestern Persia, as documented so far in written materials that could be accumulated. Bryce also wanted to help the "civilized nations" of Europe determine what was to be done with Turkish territory at the end of the war. The goal of the book, Bryce said, was to ferret out objective facts without regard to religion, political affiliation, ethnicity, or the horror of the crimes.[135]

Reiterating statements made by the *Times* in its introduction, Bryce stressed that almost all of the evidence came from eyewitnesses, including those who wrote about what they had observed and those who described what they had seen to others who in turn recorded their statements. All of the eyewitness statements were written contemporaneously with the events that occurred. If the same evidence was provided by witnesses who had no contact with each other, Bryce deemed that testimony valid. Despite some instances of errors in detail, or of exaggerated accounts of experiences, as might have been the case with "native" reporters, the vast majority of the evidence was so overwhelmingly consistent, stated Bryce, that any "inconsistencies were insignificant."[136]

Bryce pointed out that the evidence was cumulative. Each piece of evidence verified other evidence that independently described the same kinds of events. Moreover, testimony about the most horrific events came from the most trustworthy neutral observers. No affirmations of the worst of the cruelties came from "native" witnesses alone. When asked if these allegations could really be true, Bryce asserted that the history of the Ottoman Empire had shown that similar events had occurred in the recent past, as in the 1895 and 1896 massacres of Greeks, Bulgarians, and Armenians. The latest crimes involved the same kinds of cruelties that had been inflicted in the past, but on a grander scale, he maintained. At the same time, Bryce conceded that his way of validating evidence based on independent but similar descriptions of events might have flaws. He also acknowledged that the evidence presented in his book could not have the level of credibility of judicial evidence presented in a court of law, because no possibility existed of cross-examining witnesses.[137]

Bryce gave credit to those Turkish officials who had objected to the massacres and deportations and who, as a result, were subsequently dismissed from their posts. Also mentioned were the pious and compassionate Muslims who tried to save the lives of, or mitigate the miseries of, their Christian neighbors. He called such events "points of light in the gloom."[138]

In concluding his preface, Bryce stated that European travelers had frequently remarked that they found the Turkish peasants to be honest and friendly, that British soldiers had found the Turks to be fair fighters, and that Bryce himself had encountered Turkish officials who were persons of honesty and good will. Nevertheless, he declared, the last two or three centuries of Turkish interaction with the West has been "an almost unbroken record of corruption, of injustice, and of oppression which often rises into hideous cruelty." The general pattern of deportation of the population of Erzerum, Kayseri, Diyarbekir, Urfa, Trebizond, Sivas, Harpoot and Van had scattered about one million Armenian deportees throughout the Near East, from the southern outskirts of Aleppo to Mosul and Baghdad; it was a scheme, Bryce concluded, not for relocating the Armenians but for "exterminating the Armenian nation wholesale without any fuss."[139]

3. The Documents

The three-page article is peppered with an array of carefully honed descriptive sub-headings above individual, stand-alone, news stories. This style of presentation may have been needed because the stories were often repetitive, a result of the same kind of abuse being inflicted on Armenians in many different regions of Turkey. In addition, the *Times* already had printed many of the stories during 1915 and the earlier months of 1916, and the topics in the feature therefore had already been addressed.

On page two, headings over the news stories included words and phrases that described the character of the subject matter featured in the particular story – for instance, "Thousands of Corpses Line the Roads," "Frightful Massacres in Mush District," "Harput 'Cemetery of the Armenians,' " and "Awful Story of Two Red Cross Nurses."[140]

At the top of page three a major heading appeared similar to the one on page two. Like the other, it extended across all eight columns in large block capital letters. The descriptive sub-headings in the article on page three included "Futile Efforts to Save Children," "Thousand Ruthlessly Cut Down," "Work of Heroic Americans at Van," and "Armenians of Mush Wiped out."[141]

The heading at the top of page four ran across six instead of eight columns, but its message – "Lord Bryce's Report on Armenian Atrocities" – was similar. The individual sub-headings read, "Savage Treatment of Women Prisoners," "Woman Saw Two Priests Murdered," "Slaughter of Armenians of Trebizond," and "Girl Refused to Abjure Christianity."[142]

These stories provided detailed accounts of horrific tortures and death, such as horseshoeing people, burning adults and children alive, establishing a brothel with good looking Armenian girls and women to which Turkish men were admitted free, and administering the bastinado for as many as 800 strokes, so that the battered foot had to be amputated.[143]

The *Times*' readers, which included the power-elites of New York and other large cities in northeastern United States, could not have avoided seeing stories of Turkish torture, murder, and deportation of Turkey's Armenian citizens presented in such detail; they had to have been shocked at what they read. Whatever reservations they might have had about the Near East in general, and Armenians in particular, no one could deny that the behavior depicted in the article was so far beyond the pale of civilized society that little else could compare.[144] When ACASR urged individual members of the American public to donate their wealth and energy to help save the Armenians of Turkey from extermination, the *Times* story must have ensured that prospective donors would truly understand the urgent need for aggressive, large-scale relief intervention and assistance, and that their contributions could provide it.

In late October, the *Times* published a story that gave voice to the Turkish perspective on the deportations of the Armenians. In an interview held in Vienna with an AP representative, Halil Bey, Turkish Minister of Foreign Affairs, alleged that the Armenians had none but themselves to blame for the "drastic measures" the Turks were being forced to take. The Turks, he said, were willing to give Armenians an equal share in the government and had done so, resulting in a large number of Armenians in the Chamber of Deputies and several senators as well. All people want self-government, he explained, but the Armenians wanted political independence in localities where they were not a majority. To help achieve independence, the Armenians had formed a network of rebels throughout the country, and had brought into Turkey bombs, rifles, ammunition, and money. When the Russians invaded Asia Minor, the Armenians came to the Russians' support. He added, " 'the Armenians' organization made it impossible to confine the steps taken against the Armenians to a single locality in rebellion, because the [Armenian] organization was so perfect that only a sweeping measure at the first hint of an uprising could meet the situation." Halil Bey also offered his opinion that Germany could not be beaten, and that a successful harvest that summer had guaranteed a plentiful supply of food for Turkey.[145]

Two letters refuting Halil's defense of Turkey's actions soon appeared in the *Times*. One, by R. N. Serabian, characterized Halil Bey's statements as an attempt "to exculpate himself from a culpable act." Calling Halil's statements "ridiculous and erroneous," Serabian argued that the Turks had already conscripted all of the Armenian men of military age into the Turkish Army by the time Turkey entered the First World War. All that remained in the towns were women, children, and old men, who hardly constituted a real military threat to Turkey's government. Moreover, Serabian asked, if Halil's argument about Armenian activists were accurate, did that really justify exterminating or deporting all the remaining Armenians?[146]

Arshag Mahdesian, a frequent letter writer to the *Times*, also responded to Halil Bey's allegations. He asserted that at the time Turkey decided to enter the war, the Ottoman government asked a political party of Turkish Armenians (the "Dashnaks") to try to persuade their fellow Armenians in Russia to join with Turkish forces when the latter troops invaded Russia. The Dashnaks agreed to do their duty to serve loyally in the Turkish army, Mahdesian wrote, but refused to try to induce Russian Armenians to rebel against their own government. To the Turkish claim that Armenians were serving in the Russian army, Mahdesian pointed out that most of the Armenians serving in the Russian army were Russian citizens, or had come there from the United States to fight the Turks. Mahdesian quoted Hussein Jahid Bey, a leader of the Young Turks, who had written during the Balkan War[147] that the Armenians would have never turned against the Turks had Turkey not shown the Armenians "the club, the sword, and fire." If Armenians had indeed revolted, said Jahid Bey, then punish the guilty, not the whole nation.[148]

The *Times*' publication of these letters by Armenians objecting to the information presented by Halil suggested that it was willing to give voice to Armenian commentators whenever they submitted a letter for publication. While Halil's arguments about the culpability of Armenians and Serabian's and Mahdesian's responses may have appealed to those trying to rationally weigh the arguments of both sides, the more important story presented by the *Times* dealt with the fate of those Armenians still alive. In light of the kind of information the public had received about the Armenians, it is unlikely that the *Times* was concerned about the relative guilt of the parties. All Americans could join together to feed, clothe, and shelter the surviving Armenians, regardless of who or what had caused their suffering.

In October, the *Times* briefly mentioned the pastoral letter written by Cardinal Mercier, Primate of Belgium, denouncing Turkish atrocities against Armenians. Receipt of the letter by Catholic headquarters in London had been delayed because it had been written in Belgium behind German lines. The letter asked that prayers be said for various segments of Belgian society, and it also addressed the larger topic, that of the Armenians. "Mussulman fanaticism has put to death thousands upon thousands in the course of the present war and made slaves of their wives and daughters," the Belgian Primate wrote.[149] Using the term "Mussulman fanaticism" to describe the impetus behind the slaughter of Armenians contributed to the overall negative image of the Turks as beyond the pale of the civilized world, while referring to the enslavement of Armenian wives and daughters suggested a form of sexual slavery, much like the traditional portrayal of a Turkish sultan's seraglio. Regardless of readers' interpretation of this statement, support for Armenians by a European Catholic prelate had to help raise funds for ACASR because it demonstrated that Catholic Christians, as well as Protestants, cared about the welfare of Armenians.

On December 30th, the *Times* published a story from ACASR about the desperate need for food in Turkey. The new American Ambassador at Constantinople, Abram I. Elkus, had received word that the temporary suspension of relief funds for food had caused great distress in Aleppo, where fifty thousand Armenian deportees were starving and helpless; in Aintab where Armenians who escaped from the desert had landed; and in the Anatolian cities of Harpoot, Konia, and Sasun. The purveyors of American relief for the cities of Constantinople, Smyrna, and Brousa (Bursa) in western Turkey badly needed foodstuffs and money as well.[150]

The presence of a new American Ambassador to Turkey helped reassure the missionary community that the State Department was listening to their concerns. Yet life in Constantinople continued to be difficult for the missionaries as well as others. Fuel supplies were diminishing, and it was not clear from what sources replacement would come. In the field, Board missionaries at stations in Harpoot, Sivas, Aintab, Marash, Aleppo, Tarsus, Adana, Konia, Brusa, and Smyrna urged the Board to increase appropriations for relief work for the coming winter. Ambassador Elkus sent a telegram informing ACASR about the terrible suffering of the 50,000 deportees in Aleppo caused by the Board's decision to temporarily halt appropriations. Many refugees had escaped from the desert and had made their way to Aintab; Missionary Merrill needed 8,400 Turkish pounds a month; Missionaries Riggs and Cushman each asked for 3,000 Turkish pounds a month for Harpoot, Konia, and Sasun. The *Times*' story closed with a statement describing the missionaries who, despite the ongoing war, massacres, and deportations, had remained in Turkey to aid in needed relief work.[151] This story, published only five days after Christmas, reminded the American public of the desperate conditions facing the people of the Near East, especially the Armenians.

THE MISSIONARY HERALD

The opportunity for Americans to help the desperate Armenians was made easier in the fall of 1916 when President Wilson issued a proclamation establishing Saturday and Sunday, October 21 and 22, as two national days for giving to Armenian relief. Those who observed the Jewish Sabbath, as well as those who kept the Christian Lord's Day, were asked to do whatever they could "to lighten the suffering of the races whom the Turks have frightfully oppressed."[152] The Board waited eagerly to find out what the response to these special days of fund raising had been, fully aware that it was one thing to solicit contributions as a one-time gift, but quite another to inspire regular, sustained giving. Indeed, only the latter kind of philanthropy would raise the vast amount of funds needed to save the peoples of the Near East. What an amazing situation has developed, stated the *Herald*, when the welfare of the Armenians, an "ancient and sturdy race," depended on the beneficence of another people on the other side of the world.[153]

The *Herald's* editorial in the November issue pointed out that for the previous year and a half, each of its issues had carried information "about the Armenian atrocities." The journal, it said, published only a fraction of the reports it received, deeming many of the stories too "harrowing," and fearing that its readers would tire of the material and think the Board had been "getting hysterical upon the subject." But the case had not been overstated, the *Herald's* readers were assured. The *Herald* quoted a cable received from Viscount Bryce informing the Board of his recently published book and describing some of the happenings reported in the book. Bryce pointed out that several hundred thousand exiled Armenians were now perishing from exposure and starvation in the Syrian deserts. Sick people were throwing themselves into graves and begging grave diggers to bury them; women were going mad, eating grass and carrion; and parents were killing their children to end their suffering. All of this and much more, wrote the *Herald*, had been included in Bryce's book on the Armenian atrocities.[154] The *Herald* expressed its hope that the Armenian relief days had produced enough funds to ease the Armenians' sufferings.

The November *Herald* also described existing relief efforts in Constantinople, which by that date were helping over two thousand people. All kinds of relief methods were employed, including the establishment of soup kitchens, food distribution networks, medical assistance programs, employment offices, schools for poor children, and orphanages. Some of these programs were operated by the Board's mission staff, and others were run by competent Europeans, Turks, and Armenians.[155] Yet the Board remained concerned, it said, that it had heard little from its stations in Sivas and Harpoot, and only an occasional word from Urfa, Aintab, Marash, and Adana; the Turks' political attacks on the Armenian Patriarch made the Board exceedingly uneasy.[156]

Despite the Board's concerns about the welfare of its staff, the *Herald* tried to keep the focus on Armenians rather than its own personnel, property, and programs. A short but wrenching piece of three vignettes about the suffering of the children in the south and east of Aleppo personalized the refugees for the journal's readers. A little boy who had not eaten in two days said to his mother, "We have a stove and a cooking pot, but why don't you cook us something to eat." Another child asked his mother, "Will I ever be able to eat as much as I like?" A little boy, sleepless from hunger, cried out for bread. The Arab in whose house they were staying heard the child and gave him some bread, and the child was about to eat it, but then said, "If I eat it today, I will be hungry tomorrow," and, holding the piece of bread close by, fell asleep, comforted by the presence of the bread.[157] The imagery created by stories of hungry children probably had far more power than matter-of-fact discussions of relief programs in Constantinople.

Despite the ongoing trials of Armenians, the missionaries no longer had to fear for their own safety. The Turkish government in Constantinople had issued orders to its interior staff that American missionaries were to be specially protected. This had to be a relief to a Board that had long struggled with the question of danger to its missionaries, especially to women staffing mission stations alone, without help from male colleagues. The Board attributed this change of heart to the goodness of the missionaries, who were living quietly, doing the best they could despite severe shortages of food and other essentials, trying to keep the lines of communication with the Turks open, and continuing to try to relieve the suffering around them in forty-one different places in Turkey.[158]

Also of concern to the Board was the role of Islam and the possibility of change that might result from the end of the war. Foreign Secretary Barton asserted that "[d]uring the year there has been marked evidence of the disintegration of Islam as a centralized religion." Barton based this evaluation on three facts: less than one quarter of Turkey's Muslims supported the government's treatment of its Christian minorities; the Muslims of other parts of the failing Ottoman Empire had failed to respond to the Ottoman Sultan's cry for a holy war; and the Sherif of Mecca had launched a revolt against the Turks. It was impossible to know what would come of this, cautioned Barton, but it appeared to offer mission opportunities in the larger Islamic world and especially opportunities to minister to the Turks.[159]

Some of Barton's analysis revealed wishful thinking. First, while Barton's assertion that only one-quarter of the Muslims of Turkey supported the murder and deportation of Armenians may have been true, none of the reports in either the *Herald* or the *Times* offer corroboration. Second, transfer of the Caliphate to another might constrain missionary work more rather than less. Turkey had permitted missionary activity in part because of pressure from European states having a presence in Turkey's economic life. Third, other Muslim countries not subject to that pressure might not allow foreigners to conduct missionary activities within their lands at all. The revolt of the Arabs against their Ottoman masters would not necessarily mean that mission activity would now be possible in territory occupied by the Sherif of Mecca. Fourth, a radical shift in the composition of the Ottoman Empire would not automatically lead to openness to Western ways and thinking. A more uniform Turkey might embrace a stricter form of Islam than that practiced during the war years.

In December 1916, the *Herald* announced a radical change in Turkish military policy. The Committee of Union and Progress (CUP), the ruling party of the country, announced at a September conference that although the government's deportations of Armenians had been justified, the need to exile the Armenians from their homes no longer existed. But in the same issue, the *Herald* cited consular reports of a terrible massacre by Turks of Armenians in the desert town of Der Zor, to which large numbers of Armenians had been deported. The *Herald* hoped that the massacre at Der Zor was the "last act in the tragic drama that for nearly a year and a half has horrified the world." Nevertheless, it stated, the task of "saving the remnant" of the Armenian people called for even greater American generosity. The United States and other neutral countries needed to maintain pressure on the Turks to allow neutral relief organizations to enter Turkey and help the refugees. The *Herald* added that activity of that kind might also help deter the Turks from waging still more attacks on Armenians and other Christian peoples, particularly

Greeks. This was not the time to slacken efforts to assist the refugees. To the contrary, the *Herald* stressed, a radical increase in giving was needed.[160]

At the end of 1916, the Board remained optimistic that its mission work in Turkey would expand after the war. The *Herald* published several communications from its missionaries in the field, including Rev. Arthur C. Ryan of Constantinople, Dr. Clarence D. Ussher of Van, and Rev. Robert Stapleton of Erzerum. Ryan expressed the Board's position toward Armenians the most forthrightly. He wrote of the need to save Armenians both for humanitarian reasons, so that "these people, individually and collectively, might be saved from an untimely and cruel death," but also for "the sake of Christianity in the Near East." Without the Armenians, Ryan stated, missionary work in the Near East would be difficult and progress at a snail's pace. "If for no other reason, we must hasten to save the Armenians in Turkey so that they may help to save our missions and the Moslems who are still persecuting them."[161] This surprisingly frank statement reflected the Board's long-standing position that revitalizing Armenian Christianity into a "more enlightened" evangelical Christianity would lead to the conversion of Muslims.

Ussher, back in Van, now occupied by Russian troops, wrote about the role of the Orthodox Church in Russian life, noting that the government had only recently repealed the death sentence imposed on those Russians who renounced it. He viewed both Van and Erzerum, also under Russian rule, as strategic points of approach the Turks. Ussher, who envisioned Van as the greatest Armenian center in the world, wrote, "[t]he spiritual life of an Armenia purged and purified by the fires of the past two years will be a potent factor in leavening the churches in Russia." The missionaries, urged Ussher, might work not only for the uplift of the Armenians and Russians, but also for the one million Muslims now under Russian control. Ussher recognized that the opportunity presented might not be long lasting and he exhorted Board supporters to seize this opportunity before it expired.[162]

Stapleton, who saw the Russian occupation of Erzerum as permanent, was especially pleased that the Turks who lived in the Russian-occupied area now saw the missionaries in a new light, as helpers who could provide schools and medical services. Now that the obstructionist Turkish government was gone, he wrote, "we are hoping for a better and a brighter day for him [the Turk] and a great advance in the Kingdom of Christ."[163]

While the use of the Armenians as a "lure"[164] to catch the Turks had long been standard Board policy, the benefits of the war in opening up some new areas for Christian missions had not yet been stated so baldly and so casually. Stapleton's idea that the Russians would retain the captured territory indefinitely reflected a lack of understanding of the kind of negotiations that occur at the end of a war when international boundaries can readily change. To conclude that Russia would retain captured Turkish territory that was far from its pre-war border with Turkey was naive.[165] Ussher's understanding, that this opportunity was of limited duration proved a better cut on the political situation in Russian-occupied Turkey.

As the Board contemplated the advance of Christian missions in the Near East, the current Christians in the Near East, the Armenians, were still dying of exposure, disease, and starvation. The year can be best characterized by a quotation from a book written by Rev. Nesbitt Chambers of Adana.

> Today the field of Armenia, drenched with the best blood of her sons and daughters and agonizing in what, if succor is withheld, may become her death throes, is offered for redemption. Shall not American Christian benevolence, led by the constituency of the American Board, redeem the field, weighing out the silver and sealing the writing? Do you not hear that agonizing cry from the desert sweeping over the Syrian mountains and across the seas and oceans; that piteous wail of a nation in distress?[166]

End Notes to The Year 1916

1. "Turkey's Past and Future," *New York Times*, 3 January 1916, 12.
2. Ibid.
3. "Submarines and Armenia," *New York Times*, 26 January 1916, 10. Although viewing Germany as the instigator of the Armenian genocide conflicts with America's view of the "terrible Turk," seems farfetched, Mahdesian, a prominent American Armenian, seriously advanced this theory.
4. "Submarines and Armenia," *New York Times*, 26 January 1916, 10.
5. Mountainous region north of Bitlis and west of Moush.
6. "500 Armenians Slain Under Turkish Order," *New York Times*, 15 January 1916, 2. This story is puzzling, because the *Times* story of November 27, 1915, described massacres that may also have occurred at Sasun.
7. "Saved by American Consul," *New York Times*, 18 January 1916, 4.
8. "Burn Priests in Armenia," *New York Times*, 23 January 1916, II, 2.
9. "Saw Armenians Go Starving to Exile," *New York Times*, 6 February 1916, II, 9.
10. "Tells of Great Plain Black with Refugees," *New York Times*, 7 February 1916, 3.
11. Ibid.
12. "Favors Day for Armenian Relief," *New York Times*, 10 February 1916, 4.
13. "Ransoms Armenian Girls," *New York Times*, 13 February 1916, VII, 6.
14. Ibid.
15. I attended a conference in 1989 in Sacramento at which a poet read a poem about his Armenian grandmother who went to church every day, always asking God for forgiveness, but apparently not feeling forgiven. The grandmother had been in a deportee caravan, and had worn a little red scarf. A Kurd on horseback came to the caravan, noticed her, and said "tomorrow I am going to come for you, red scarf." During that evening, another girl admired the scarf, and the grandmother gave it to her. The next day the Kurd returned, seized the girl wearing the red scarf, and took off with her.
16. "Turkey's Business," *New York Times*, 22 February 1916, 10.
17. "Dealing with Turkey," *New York Times*, 26 February 1916, 8.
18. "Promising to Hang Some Turks," *New York Times*, 22 February 1916, 10.
19. Ibid.
20. "Bryce Trusts America," *New York Times*, 23 February 1916, 3.
21. "Asks Fund to Save Million Armenians," *New York Times*, 27 February 1916, I, 14.
22. "Detail Armenians' Plight," *New York Times*, 2 March 1916, 4.
23. "Luncheon to Morgenthau," *New York Times*, 4 March 1916, 18.
24. "Plea for the Armenians," *New York Times*, 5 March 1916, I, 2.
25. "Russians Slaughter Turkish Third Army," *New York Times*, 6 March 1916, 3. Mrs. Yarrow, working with her husband for ACASR in the Russian Caucasus described the same event in an article published in the *Herald*.
26. "Armenians Get Relief," *New York Times*, 8 March 1916, 22.

27. "Russians Seize Port of Rizeh," *New York Times*, 9 March 1916, 1.

28. Ibid. This dramatic story was the subject of a highly popular novel, *The Forty Days of Musa Dagh*, by Franz Werfel, an Austrian Jew who himself was to flee extermination by the Nazis. Werfel died in exile in Los Angeles.

29 Musa Dagh of Jebel Mousa (Mount Moses) was mountainous region west of Aleppo.

30. "Beat Off 4,000 Turks," *New York Times*, 12 March 1916, I, 3.

31. "A Happy New Year!," *Missionary Herald* CXII (January 1916), 3-4.

32. "The Armenian People," *Missionary Herald* CXII (January 1916), 22.

33. "The School Situation," *Missionary Herald* 112 (January 1915), 30.

34. Ibid.

35. "Missions and Business," *Missionary Herald* CXII (February 1916), 25-26.

36. "Turkey," *Missionary Herald* CXII (January 1916), 27-31.

37. "Desperate Choices," *Missionary Herald* CXII (January 1916), 27-31.

38. "Saving the Remnant," *Missionary Herald* CXII (February 1916), 53.

39. "You Can Help Save Thousands of Lives," *Missionary Herald* CXII (February 1916), 103.

40. A major Armenian settlement, north of Sis, now renamed Sayimbeyli.

41. "The Attitude of the Turks," *Missionary Herald* CXII (February 1916), 73.

42. Ibid., 72-73.

43. An "aga" or "agha" is a Turkish landowner-chief of the Ottoman Empire.

44. "The Attitude of the Turks," *Missionary Herald* CXII (February 1916), 72-73.

45. "A Friend in Adapazar Gone," *Missionary Herald* CXII (March 1916), 109.

46. "Shut Up in Erzroom," *Missionary Herald* CXII (June 1916), 266.

47. "Turkish Critics of Turkish Affairs," *Missionary Herald* CXII (January 1916), 4.

48. "The Mission Stations," *Missionary Herald* CXII (March 1916), 129-131.

49. "A Dark Land of Silence," *Missionary Herald* CXII (February 1916), 53.

50. "Turkey: From the Front," *Missionary Herald* CXII (March 1916), 128.

51. "Relief Work a Double Blessing," *Missionary Herald* CXII (March 1916), 106.

52. Ibid.

53. Ibid.

54. "Dr. Shepard, of Aintab," *Missionary Herald* CXII, (March 1916), 115.

55. Ibid.

56. Ibid., 116; Alice Shepard Riggs, *Shepard of Aintab*, with new forward by Constance Shepard Jolly (Princeton: Gomidas Books, 2001), 126. (Constance Shepard Jolly is Dr. Shepard's granddaughter.) Dr. Shepard's son, Lorrin Shepard, also served as medical director of the hospital, as did Dr. Shepard's grandson, Barclay Shepard, who has recently retired from that post at age eighty-four. The current medical director is a Turk. The Turks still call the hospital "the American hospital."

57. "Two Devoted Physicians," *Missionary Herald* CSII (February 1916), 70. For a detailed first had accout of the activities of the Atkinsons, see Tacy Atkinson, *The

German, the Turk and the Devil Made a Triple Alliance: Harpoot Diaries, 1908-1917, (Princeton and London: Gomidas Institute, 2000).

58. Ibid.,69.
59. Ibid., 69-70; "Dr. Shepard, of Aintab," *Missionary Herald* CXII (March 1916), 115-116.
60. Turks Renewing Armenian Evictions," *New York Times*, 9 April 1916, I, 14.
61. Ibid.
62. It is impossible to reconcile the different numbers of refugees cited in different accounts of the Genocide.
63. "Turks Renewing Armenian Evictions," *New York Times*, 9 April 1916, I, 14.
64. Ibid.
65. "15,000 Massacred as Erzerum Fell," *New York Times*, 3 May 1916, 13.
66. Ibid.
67. Ibid.
68. Ibid.
69. Ibid.
70. Ibid.
71. "Erzerum Armenians Slain," *New York Times*, 3 June 1916, 5.
72. Ibid.
73. Ibid.
74. "Morgenthau Urges Aid for Armenians," *New York Times*, 15 May 1916, 3.
75. Ibid., 9.
76. Ibid., 11.
77. "Urges $500,000,000 as a Relief Fund," *New York Times*, 23 May 1916, 6.
78. Vahan Cardashian, "Turkey's Account with Civilization," *New York Times*, 26 June 1916, 12.
79. "Crisis in Turkey," *Missionary Herald* CXII ((April 1916), 153-154.
80. Ibid.
81. "Germans Who Deplore the Deportations," *Missionary Herald* CXII (April 1916), 189.
82. Ibid.
83. Ibid.
84. "The Adaptable American," *Missionary Herald* CXII (April 1916), 155-156.
85. "Ambassador Morgenthau Visits the American Board," *Missionary Herald* CXII (May 1916), 201.
86. "A Campaign for Millions," *Missionary Herald* CXII (April 1916), 157.
87. "Shut Up in Erzroom," *Missionary Herald* CXII (June 1916), 266-267.
88. "The Russian Field," *Missionary Herald* CXII (April 1916), 153.
89. "Turkey by the Back Door," *Missionary Herald* CXII (May 1916), 200.
90. "Turkey's Desperate Plight," *Missionary Herald* CXII (May 1916), 198.

91. "Side Lights from Several Stations," *Missionary Herald* CXII (May 1916), 220.
92. "Relief Work from Tiflis," *Missionary Herald* CXII (May 1916), 222-224.
93. "The Grand Duke and the Katholicos," *Missionary Herald* CXII (May 1916), 224.
94. Ibid.
95. "Relief Work from Tiflis," *Missionary Herald* CXII (May 1916), 223-224.
96. "Turkey's Desperate Plight," *Missionary Herald* CXII (May 1916), 198.
97. "On the Plain of Mt. Ararat," *Missionary Herald* CXII (June 1916), 275-276.
98. "Hardest on Children," *Missionary Herald* CXII (June 1916), 276.
99. "Starting Lines of Industry," *Missionary Herald* CXII (June 1916), 276.
100. "Turkey's Desperate Plight," *Missionary Herald* CXII (May 1916), 198.
101. "The Federal Council Tackles a Big Job," *Missionary Herald* CXII (June 1916), 248.
102. "Washington to Press Turkey for Syrians," *New York Times*, 7 July 1916, 3.
103. "For Armenian Refugees," *New York Times*, 17 July 1916, 10. The letter to the editor of the *Times* from Mrs. May Hickson does not explain what her relationship is to the "Mr. Gracey" from whose letter Mrs. Hickson drew the information for her letter to the *Times*.
104. "Famine and Cholera in Turkey Revealed," *New York Times*, 21 July 1916, 10. This technique of communication had also been employed by other missionaries.
105. "American May Renew Protest to Turkey," *New York Times*, 30 July 1916, I, 2.
106. "Trouble with US Expected in Turkey," *New York Times*, 13 August 1916, I, 8.
107. "The Story of the Marsovan Eviction," *Missionary Herald* CXII (August 1916), 354-358.
108. "Famine and Cholera in Turkey Revealed," *New York Times*, 21 July 1916, 10.
109. "Seize American Property," *New York Times*, 5 August 1916, 3.
110. "Trouble with US Expected in Turkey," *New York Times*, 13 August 1916, I, 8.
111. Ibid.
112. Ibid.
113. "For a Protest to Turkey," *New York Times*, 22 September 1916, 6.
114. "A Message from Trebizond," *Missionary Herald* CXII (July 1916), 324.
115. "Arabia's Revolt from Ottoman Rule," *Missionary Herald* CXII (September 1916), 395.
116. Ibid.
117. "What's Standing in Van," *Missionary Herald* CXII (July 1916), 327.
118. "A Message from Trebizond," *Missionary Herald* CXII (July 1916), 325-326.
119. The abolition of the capitulations did not require the mission schools to close.
120. "An Illuminating Editorial," *Missionary Herald* CXII (July 1915), 303.
121. "Is the Storm Passing?" *Missionary Herald* CXII (July 1916), 302-303. The term "concentration camp" was not used by either the *Herald* or the *Times* to describe these government-created and administered involuntary congregations of human beings.
122. "Turkey Missionaries Returning to Their Fields," *Missionary Herald* CXII (August 1916), 353.

123. "Trouble with US Expected in Turkey," *New York Times*, 13 August 1916, 1916, I, 8.

124. "The Story of the Marsovan Eviction," *Missionary Herald* CXII (August 1916), 354-358.

125. "Missionaries Return to Marsovan," *Missionary Herald* CXII (September 1916), 389-390.

126. "Expelled from Sivas," *Missionary Herald* CXII (September 1916), 417-418.

127. "Still Crushing the Armenians," *Missionary Herald* CXII (September 1916), 390.

128. "Lord Bryce's Report on Armenian Atrocities, An Appalling Catalogue of Outrage and Massacre," *New York Times*, 8 October 1916, II, 2-4.

129. Ibid., II, 2.

130. Ibid.

131. Ibid.

132. Ibid.

133. Ibid.

134. Ibid.

135. Ibid.

136. Ibid.

137. Ibid.

138. Ibid.

139. Ibid.

140. Ibid.

141. Ibid., II, 3.

142. Ibid., II, 4.

143. Ibid.

144. Unfortunately, the record of man's inhumanity in the rest of the twentieth century would make the tortures of the Armenians seem almost commonplace.

145. "Blames Armenians for All Their Woes," *New York Times*, 28 October 1916, 9.

146. R. N. Serabian, "A Reply to Halil Bey," *New York Times*, 9 November 1916, p.12.

147. It is not clear to which Balkan War Jahid Bey was referring. The First Balkan War, in which Turkey was quickly defeated, occurred in 1912.

148. "Armenians Not to Blame," *New York Times*, 10 December 1916, II, 4.

149. "Mercier Pastoral Decries Pacifism," *New York Times*, 15 November 1916, 2.

150. "Armenians Need Aid," *New York Times*, 30 December 1916, 2.

151. Ibid.

152. "A Relief Saturday and Sunday," *Missionary Herald* CXIII (October 1916), 441-442.

153. "The Armenian Emergency," *Missionary Herald* CXIII (November 1916), 484-485.

154. Ibid.

155. "Present Relief Work," *Missionary Herald* CXII (November 1916), 498-499.

156. Ibid., 498-500.

157. "The Cry of the Children," *Missionary Herald* CXII (November 1916), 500.

158. "Turkey Missionaries Returning," *Missionary Herald* CXIII (October 1916), 442.

159. "Work Conditions," *Missionary Herald* CXIII (November 1916), 516.

160. "A Welcome Rumor," *Missionary Herald* CXIII (December 1916), 541.

161. "Turkey's Threefold Challenge," *Missionary Herald* CXIII (December 1916), 549-550.

162. "Under Russian Rule," *Missionary Herald* CXIII (December 1916), 550.

163. "Erzroom Station under the Russian Flag," *Missionary Herald* CXIII (December 1916), 550.

164. I am indebted to Suzanne Moranian's dissertation for the use of the term "lure" to describe the relationship between the missionaries and the Armenians. See Suzanne Elizabeth Moranian, "The American Missionaries and the Armenian Question: 1915-1927" (Ph.D. diss., University of Wisconsin, 1994),

165. The Russians had only been in possession of the vilayet of Ardahan and Kars since 1878.

166. "Redeeming a Battlefield," *Missionary Herald*, CXII (December 1916), 549.

Chapter 5

THE YEAR 1917

As the United States entered the war against Germany, the situation of the Armenian exiles continued to deteriorate.

JANUARY - MARCH 1917

THE NEW YORK TIMES

On the first day of the year, the *Times* published a devastating report about the condition of Armenians.[1] The headline of the story read: "Found Armenians Starving in Camps." A reliable eyewitness, a citizen of a neutral country, of character and standing, stated the *Times*, had recently visited some camps for deported Armenians in the Euphrates Valley and in northern Arabia. He sent a report to ACASR telling what he had seen; ACASR chose to make his report public through the *Times*. Nothing could describe the horror he had experienced as he traveled along the Armenian encampments scattered along the Euphrates, he wrote, especially those on the right bank of the river between Meskene[2] and Der Zor.[3] "Encampments" was not the proper name for these gatherings of people, dragged from their homes, robbed of their property either at home, upon departure, or en route, and now penned up in the open like cattle, he stated. In the camps he visited, they had no shelter, practically no clothing, and were fed irregularly with insufficient food. More than 60,000[4] Armenians have already died, he wrote; those surviving can not last much longer if they do not receive adequate food and shelter.[5] The *Times*, the most prominent and widely read newspaper in the United States, published this story in the first section of the paper on the first day of the new year, suggesting a profound commitment to securing aid for Armenians. Armenian sympathizers hoped the story's headline would catch the attention not only of those already committed to aiding Armenians, but also of those who had not yet understood the gravity of their situation. The headline also helped solidify the slogan, "Remember the Starving Armenians," a saying that became a part of American lore, sometimes used by parents to admonish their children to eat their food.

Soon a new situation faced ACASR. Germany had just sent a note to the United States, informing the American government once again that neutral countries' shipping would be subject to German submarine attack. Despite rumors to the contrary, reported the *Times*, two United States naval vessels, the cruiser *Des Moines* and the collier *Caesar*, remained anchored in Alexandria, a British port. The ships had been unable to sail to Beirut and Jaffa to pick up the one thousand Americans waiting there, who hoped to be repatriated as soon as possible.[6] The possible resumption of submarine warfare compelled these citizens of the United States to remain in the Ottoman Empire where the State Department deemed them safer than on the high seas.[7] Sensing perhaps the probability of war with Germany, the ever active Morgenthau and his ACASR colleagues, Cleveland H. Dodge,[8] Crane, Barton, Dutton, and White, queried the State Department about problems with Turkey that might arise from Germany's new pronouncement about shipping. On behalf of ACASR, Morgenthau issued a statement saying that the committee did not expect any change in Turkey's attitude toward relief activities. Of all the nations, he wrote, America had been Turkey's truest and most disinterested friend; Turkey was not likely to cease her cordial relations with the United States. Moreover, stated the Ambassador, German, Swiss, and Swedish missionaries remained in Turkey and represented the most selfless and effective dispensers of relief.[9]

Lord Bryce also continued to lobby for Armenians. In a cablegram to ACASR made public by the Committee, Bryce informed the Committee that many thousands of the 700,000-800,000 Armenians who had perished in the recent massacres had done so as Christian martyrs. Had they been willing to embrace Islam, they could have saved themselves, he said.[10] By casting the Armenians as Christian martyrs, Bryce likely gained additional support from the American public, which at that time was largely made up of Protestant and Catholic Christians.

THE MISSIONARY HERALD

The *Herald's* main emphases in the first part of 1917 continued to be the overwhelming need for relief funds, the methods used by ACASR to raise the needed monies, and the uses to which the donations had been put. The *Herald* reminded its readers about the role played by members of the United States diplomatic corps in distributing relief supplies, suggesting that ACASR received support from the highest levels of the American government.

Regardless of official endorsement, ACASR still had to raise large sums of money in the United States. To do this, it organized a network of auxiliary committees throughout the United States. These affiliates collected contributions, deposited them in local banks where the funds were held in trust, and then forwarded them to Crane, ACASR's treasurer in New York City. As a result of this scheme, a continuous stream of contributions for the refugees poured into Crane's office. Wealthy members of ACASR, in addition to making significant individual contributions to relief activities, continued to bear all of the administrative costs for operation of ACASR's New York City office.[11] Since relief workers did not collect salaries from ACASR, all of the funds collected went directly for relief work, a fact that no doubt encouraged donors to give more generously.

The *Herald* provided a brief summary of ACASR's contributions to Armenian relief in its January issue. The first remittance to Constantinople had been made on October 25, 1915. By December 6, 1916, ACASR had collected and distributed a total of $2,399,406.34, including a gift of $530,000 from the Rockefeller Foundation. The Committee maintained that it would need an equal sum of money during the next eight months in order to keep the more than 500,000 refugees alive. Whenever possible, it hoped to aid any surviving Armenians to return to their own homes.[12]

At the same time, the *Herald* made sure to keep its readers informed about the acute stress facing its staff in Turkey, including the horrific problems they faced as they dealt with the day-to-day operations of their mission stations. One such story described the work of two single women who worked alone at the Board's mission post in Sivas. News from these mission stations reached the Board's headquarters very slowly, if at all. A letter from Miss Mary C. Fowle of Sivas dated July 6, 1916, arrived at the Board's headquarters in January, 1917. In her letter, Fowle described the situation facing her and her colleague, Mary Louise Graffam, in the summer of 1916. She noted that after Turkish officials in Sivas had imprisoned some 2,000-3,000 men, they decided to release the Greeks, Russians, and Muslims, and some Armenians who were skilled artisans and therefore essential to the community. The released Armenians men – all carpenters, masons, tailors, and other types of craftsmen – were then pressured to convert to Islam. The majority did so. But the intense pressure felt by the men who had abandoned their faith, wrote Fowle, proved more terrible than the physical suffering and fear that had occurred during 1915.

Those Armenians remaining in prison were next informed that they were going to be sent to the southeast of Turkey, to Bozanti,[13] to work on the German railroad [the Berlin to Baghdad railroad]. Assured by the German Consul in Sivas that the men would be safe, Fowle and Graffam urged the men to go, telling them that the days of massacres were over. They would be far better off in Bozanti than in this hell at Sivas, the missionaries said. The men went off in groups of two to three hundred per day; the first group, accompanied by a small Turkish escort, reached Caesarea safely.[14] Soon after, however, word reached the women that all the men who had left Sivas had been killed, taken from the group two by two and turned over to local villagers, who murdered them with axes, pikes, saws, or any other tools that they had. A couple of men escaped and notified the missionaries about what had occurred. However, those who had converted and had remained in Sivas continued to be safe, despite the emotional strain of becoming Muslims.

With typical missionary optimism, Fowle saw some good coming out of all this. If the converted men could survive until the war was over, and then return to their faith, their Christianity would be stronger, and no longer a mere matter of form. She posed a rhetorical question: "[U]nder the same temptation, I wonder whether we could resist as long and faithfully as they!"[15] The *Herald* did not indicate what Fowle felt about having been used by the Turks to dupe Armenians, or whether the German Consul had been misinformed or was part of the deception. On November 24, 1916, a few months after Fowle wrote this letter, she succumbed to typhus, leaving Graffam[16] as the sole missionary at Sivas. This account demonstrated well the hazards of missionary life and the role played by missionaries as "go-betweens" for Turks and Armenians.

One of the main questions perplexing the Committee involved the size of the refugee population. Peet estimated that except for Syria, the uprooted refugee population in Turkey and the Caucasus consisted of about 300,000 Armenians and 200,000 Turks and Greeks, totaling 500,000, mostly women and children.[17]

While the plight of Armenians was well known, needy Turkish families also struggled to survive in Brousa (Boursa), Konia, Tarsus, and Marash. The war and its consequences had caused these families to lose their breadwinners, reducing the families to dependent status; their needs could not be ignored. Peet, reflecting the missionary partiality shown to the Christian minorities of Turkey, stated that while the Turkish refugees were not so deserving as the

Christian races, the missionaries should not be indifferent to their needs. Besides, by assisting them, the missionaries would lessen opposition and increase the opportunities for ministering to the more needy Christian groups. Nonetheless, the latter depended far more upon the benevolence of the evangelists.[18] Peet, therefore, advocated aid to the Muslims not only to provide sustenance for them, but also as a means of reducing opposition to assistance for the Christian minorities.

This shows a somewhat "crafty" spirit on Peet's part, but his approach may have been the best way to ensure that the aid reached Ottoman Christians. While the Board's partiality to the Christian minorities was understandable, the open publication in the *Herald* of that bias was probably unwise. The *Herald's* editors apparently did not expect any Turks to read its monthly publication.

Help, however, was not always easy to provide. Despite the availability of relief funds, several impediments made finding foodstuffs to feed the refugees difficult. First, the refugees thronging into the cities had been forced to abandon their fields and could no longer till them. Second, any male able to work in the fields ran the risk of being seen and consequently drafted into the Ottoman Army. Third, the demands of the Army for provisions for its troops often exhausted the local food supply.[19]

The lack of foodstuffs made saving the refugees that much more difficult, and added to the strain experienced by the missionaries. The missionaries saw the refugees as innocent, unoffending people who had been caught up in the maelstrom of war. As a result of cruel circumstances the uprooted were now destitute. But ACASR, without sufficient funds or food to assist everyone who needed help, had to make the heartrending choice to help some refugees and not others.[20]

At the same time that the missionaries struggled to help the hordes of refugees, the *Herald* feared the consequences of the United States entering the First World War on the side of the Triple Entente, thereby rupturing its relationship with Germany's ally, Turkey. Would the Turks then seize all of the Board's buildings and expel or intern the American missionaries? That would be a most illogical and reckless course for Turkey, stated the *Herald*. The Turks, the *Herald* claimed, recognize that the United States has been her truest and most unselfish friend, one that has never sought to exploit her, to secure any of her territory, or to use her to advance American political or commercial aims. Moreover, it added, Turkey will need America at the end of the war to help her rebuild.[21]

Although these statements reiterated the Board's long held conviction that the United States' benevolence towards Turkey was entirely altruistic, Washington's firm support for the Board's "missionary agenda" itself revealed policies that were hardly disinterested. Only when compared to the cupidity of the Entente Powers did the United States involvement in Turkey seem magnanimous. The Sykes-Picot Agreement, for example, which laid out the Entente's plan for the partition of the Near East, called for Britain to control Palestine and Iraq; France to govern Syria, including Lebanon; and Russia to seize the Dardanelles. Yet the missionary plans to expand in Turkey in order to convert the Muslims must have envisioned a vastly increased presence, one that would have radically altered Turkey. From the Turkish point of view, the Board's missionary enterprise augured a profound and disruptive presence in Turkey at a time when the Ottoman government sought to eliminate its minorities and create a unified Islamic state. Consequently, the Board's plans may have embodied an imperialism of a different sort from that of the Entente powers.

By 1917, the *Herald* could inform its readers about specific relief programs, such as the attempt of ACASR to help the needy in Syria. To support this project, President Wilson and the State Department, with the support of both Houses of Congress, had authorized the United States Navy to furnish ACASR with a Navy collier, the *Caesar,* and the necessary crew to convey needed medical and food supplies to the refugees in northern Syria. The French government also had agreed to allow the *Caesar* through its blockade of the Syrian coast; and the Turkish government had granted landing rights and permission to transfer the cargo to the Red Cross agents responsible for its distribution to the refugees.[22] The ease with which ACASR secured these approvals demonstrates the degree of its political support by the State Department and Congress.

The *Herald* continued to describe for its readers its relief programs in the Caucasus. Relief worker Raynolds stated that the work earned some money, but it also provided the refugees the satisfaction of creating something with their hands and minds. Many more women and children applied for these jobs than there were openings.[23] Raynolds asked the *Herald's* readers to identify with the refugees' plight. Can you imagine, he wrote, what it means for these people to be forcibly evicted from their homes, with the loss of all that their homes contained, and to be cast adrift among strangers, with no way of providing for daily needs, with nothing to occupy hands and minds, and with no definite hope for the future?[24]

APRIL - JUNE 1917

THE NEW YORK TIMES

The heightened tension between Germany and the United States led the United States to declare war against Germany on April 6, 1917. The *Times* reported ACASR's immediate notice to its supporters that the break with Germany should not affect the provision of aid to Armenians and Syrians. Neutral agencies would continue to help, the *Times* said, and many of the areas needing relief fall under Russian or British control. Because few goods were provided by ship, relief programs should not be affected by the war with Germany. The relief workers on site used cash to buy the needed supply of goods.[25] So far $3,000,000 had been transferred to Constantinople for relief purposes in "Asiatic" (eastern) Turkey; $10,000,000 more will be needed to do the necessary relief work with Armenians and Syrians, stated the *Times*.

The *Times* continually informed the public about the ongoing needs of the refugees. Under the headline "Ask $100,000 for Armenians," the *Times* pointed out an immediate need of funds for the coming month because ACASR had overdrawn its accounts by $40,000.[26] To prevent Americans from losing sight of the ongoing situation in the Levant, the *Times* frequently included brief stories about deteriorating conditions in the Caucasus. Although local committees had furnished small quantities of clothing, the refugees were in critical condition, naked and physically exhausted. They eagerly awaited the warm garments to be provided by ACASR's workers that would ameliorate their plight, compounded by bad housing, most of it cold, damp, and uncomfortable.[27]

ACASR counted on Morgenthau's charisma to explain to the American public that large sums of money were *not* languishing in the Committee's bank accounts because the war made it impossible to transfer sums to Turkey. Under the heading "Fund Overdrawn $40,000, says Morgenthau," the *Times* on May 28 repeated Morgenthau's statements previously published in which he explained three different ways ACASR could get the funds to the refugee population.[28] It would be hard for any news-reading American to be unaware of both the extent of the need, and the means for meeting that need.

ACASR, moreover, finally obtained support from Theodore Roosevelt, who expressed his sympathy for the refugees living under the "Turkish yoke." A letter from him was read at a meeting for businessmen organized by ACASR, in which he expressed his appreciation for the difficult task of obtaining aid for the refugees and hoped that every American's heart would beat with fervent indignation at the plight of the defenseless women and orphaned children of the Turkish Empire who had suffered such bitter wrong.[29]

THE MISSIONARY HERALD

In addition to reassuring its readers that their contributions did not go for administrative costs, the *Herald* regularly noted that the missionaries who participated in distribution of relief funds were extremely careful with expenditure. The funds for refugees, the *Herald* stated, were dispersed with absolute care and devotion. There has never been a relief organization that dispensed aid more economically and efficiently, boasted the Board.[30] The Board also proudly informed its contributors that because of their donations :

> [h]undreds of thousands of lives have been saved, including 10,000 orphans in one center alone. Homeless, destitute, and starving humanity, in incredible numbers, has been caught at the brink of death and kept alive. A superb work of rescue has been accomplished by American generosity at home and by American devotion where these refugees are stranded.[31]

By continually emphasizing the frugality of the relief enterprise, the free services of diplomatic and missionary employees, the beneficence of the donors, but also the hundreds of thousands of persons whose lives had been spared, the *Herald* doubtlessly helped to convince financial contributors of their vital role. The *Herald* also must have assured these humanitarians that their future contributions would be just as important in saving the lives of the remaining refugees of the Near East, who continued to face famine and disease and were still struggling to survive.

By April 1917, reported the *Herald*, $2,733,515.28 had been raised.[32] Despite its recitation of all that had been accomplished for the refugees, the *Herald* carefully pointed out that the need kept increasing, as streams of new refugees arrived at the Syrian camps, came out of their hiding places in Turkey, or returned from their exile in the desert to their homes.[33] Countless more homeless victims would likely find their way to the various sanctuaries in Asia Minor.

ACASR radically upgraded Peet's March 1917 estimate of the number of refugees just one month later. In an article called "Seeing it Through," the *Herald* published new refugee figures: it now projected refugee numbers to be 500,000 Armenians in Turkey and 250,000 in Russia; 250,000 Greeks in Turkey; 1,000,000 Syrians and Assyrians in Syria and Palestine; and 50,000 Assyrians in Persia. The missionary magazine added, "[U]ncounted multitudes [exist] on every side, all in desperate case, and needing aid if they are to be kept alive until they can get started again on the road of self-help." The need, stated the *Herald*, kept increasing.[34] Even so, the *Herald's* figures could not have been accurate because they did not account for the deported Armenians in Syria and the needy Turkish refugees displaced by the war. The shifting estimates of the number of refugees demonstrated ACASR's difficulty in allocating aid workers and relief supplies based only on speculation of the number of refugees in each locale.

The Board also addressed the issue of what country was best suited to meet the needs of the refugees. Other nations had their own internal refugee populations and were struggling to assist them. But the United States, a moral and generous nation with no refugees of its own, had undertaken to save the less fortunate who were suffering from Turkey's policy of war and extermination, asserted the *Herald*.[35] "A superb work of rescue has been accomplished by American generosity at home and by American devotion where these refugees are stranded," wrote the *Herald*.[36] The Board continued to see the United States and itself as disinterested neutrals despite their own goals for Turkey in the future. At a time when European colonialism of the traditional sort remained widespread, the Board did not recognize the more subtle variety of colonialism that it and Washington practiced in Turkey.

As part of its sophisticated fund raising, ACASR decided that it should double its publicity and soliciting work, all done by volunteers and without the use of contributed funds, it was careful to inform its supporters. It described a new program inaugurated by one of its regional bodies, the New England Committee, in which pledges of $100 a month for a period of months were secured. Such contributions would keep 100,000 starving refugees alive, stated the *Herald*.[37] The pledges might come from individual donors who were able to give $100 per month, or from persons who banded together in a group to make up the monthly amount. Making sure not to offend its more limited donors, the *Herald* stressed that contributions of any size were always welcome.[38]

The main job for the missionaries involved developing relief programs that would keep the refugees alive. True to their Protestant ideology, they devised several endeavors toward that end, believing, not without cause, that work should not only yield a needed product, but also help refugees maintain their self-respect. In addition to the industrial relief previously discussed in the *Herald*, ACASR organized other labor programs for the refugees in Erivan that maximized hand work but required the least amount of capital, so that the largest number of individuals could be employed.

In the Erivan scheme missionaries purchased crude wool and took it to the river to be washed. They employed men to stand barefooted in the water all day (sometimes in freezing weather) and pound the wool, after which it was dried out in the open. Although they only paid sixty cents per day for the hard, disagreeable work, one hundred job seekers applied for every opening.

In sunny weather, the wool required two days to dry, after which it was taken to the carding factory where 200 women opened the wool and carded it on a nest of needles. For this they were paid twenty-five to thirty-five cents a day. After carding, women spun the wool and knitted it into socks. This enterprise employed about one thousand women who were given enough work to earn about sixty-five cents a week. These jobs were also highly sought after, with another thousand women applying and being turned away in despair. The missionaries hoped to raise spinning and knitting wages to one dollar a week, but so far had lacked the funds to do that. The refugee workers gave the byproduct of this process, the wool that was too coarse to be spun, to other women to make into heavy comforters that would last for a long time and would keep refugee families warm during the fierce Caucasus winters.[39]

Gracey, a relief worker in the Caucasus, sent reports to the Board. As part of his job, he toured the region to evaluate the needs of the refugees. He wrote an account published in the May issue of the *Herald* about the condition of the impoverished refugees that he encountered. Some, he said, had been held captive and treated as slaves by Kurds. Because of the conditions of captivity – little clothing and food and constant fear and dread – the refugees had a wild, hunted look and an emaciated appearance. But, said Gracey, they deeply appreciated their present liberty, procured by the gallantry of the Russians and the ransoms paid by ACASR, at prices ranging from one to five dollars for each person.[40]

Gracey tried to help readers understand the Armenians and the disruption of their lives caused by losing their homes and livelihoods. He described the style of underground housing favored by the refugees. These homes, typical of Armenian villagers in eastern Turkey and Russia, were designed to moderate both the heat of the summer and the cold of the winter. A visitor entered the underground homes by a low doorway in the courtyard of the home. The first room encountered was almost pitch dark, with a little bit of light coming through a hole in the roof through which the smoke from the cooking and heating fires escaped. These fires were made of dried dung, collected in the summer months and stored in the courtyard.[41] The floor was well trodden to make it hard. Because of extreme poverty, the dwellings were devoid of furniture, but coverlets found at the sides of the room furnished comfort for the families at night. As many as twenty-one people might sleep in one room. Often animals, mainly goats or chickens, shared the room with the family.

Gracey expressed his hope that an industrial work program among these refugees would profitably occupy their time. His plans for industrial work aimed to employ women to knit 20,000 pairs of socks, sew 5,000 men's suits, 5,000 dresses, and 5,000 coverlets for the children. Because he expected an additional 20,000 new refugees to arrive in the near future, he hoped to get the clothing manufactured before their arrival.[42]

Gracey also compared the current version of industrial work with earlier Board experiences following the Armenian massacres of 1895-1896. Just as industrial relief previously had saved the women mentally and morally, it now provided the same benefit in Erivan and Alexandropol (Gumri), giving the refugees hope and courage, and warming their hearts.[43]

In Marsovan, refugee girls rescued from deportation by local missionaries Francis Gage and Charlotte Willard now sewed for the American Anatolia Hospital of that city; they turned out from 1,000 to 1,300 units a week of new and mended garments and bedding. Distributed among the refugees in Marsovan were 500 Muslim *mohajirs* (settlers) from Turkey's eastern border who had fled west to Marsovan to escape Russian troops. They had left good homes only to arrive in Marsovan and find that the only available housing had been stripped of windows, doors, and any other creature comforts. The Turkish government gave the women a small stipend and tried to help them develop small businesses, but little could be done to assist them.

In addition to sewing, industrial relief in Marsovan included buying raw wool and cotton, then beating and spinning it into thread for weaving winter clothing and coarse cotton bags for flour. The missionaries lamented that this "better" class of Muslim women who knew only how to do the finer kind of weaving, like lace making, were reduced to weaving coarser products to sustain themselves.[44] The *Herald's* point in publishing this story may have been to illustrate to readers that ACASR lived up to its commitment to assist all refugees, no matter their ethnicity or creed. It may also have published this story to show the existence of refined Muslim women as well as the cruder types of Turks who had more often been portrayed in the *Herald*.

Graffam, the sole missionary in Sivas after her companion died of typhus, said she could put everyone in Sivas to work, if she could first get sufficient clothing for them so that they were covered. She had set up an industrial relief program in which carded and spun wool was knitted into sweaters that were then sold to the military for the troops.[45] She wrote that she was wonderfully sustained, but "long[ed] for someone to share the weight of her responsibilities."[46] All of the letters written by desperate refugee woman to husbands and fathers who were now dead came to her; the strain of reading these and the overwhelming need of the local refugees proved hard to bear.[47]

In Marash, Miss Cushman employed refugees who wove cloth to make garments for the refugees who had no clothes, food, or shelter. In Aleppo, industrial relief supplied shelter and some work for five thousand refugee women and children in five industrial sites.[48] Industrial relief in Constantinople provided a variety of jobs, including lace making, embroidery, knitting, cloth weaving, and sewing garments for the poor.[49]

The Board also described a letter it had received from Miss Stella N. Loughbridge, by then in Switzerland, who was able at last to write freely about her experiences in Talas and Caesarea before she left. She wrote in March 1917, stating that conditions in those cities did not differ much from what the Board already knew about the seizure of its mission school and hospital buildings. The Armenian students who remained in school there had been initially put in prison, but were subsequently sent to government orphanages. She mentioned about five or six thousand Armenians who had not been deported; some of these Armenians had become Muslims to save their lives, or were Protestants, Catholics, and soldiers who had somehow escaped the deportation of the Gregorian Armenians. Their lives were always precarious, however, and they were unable to refuse any of the demands of their Turkish neighbors for food, clothing, furniture, and even their daughter's hand in marriage. Eventually, they were required to become Muslims, and most did so to protect themselves. However, a Protestant pastor who had initially converted to Islam recanted a year later and returned to Protestantism, an action respected by the vali, according to Loughridge. He had not been in any way molested, she wrote, but was drafted into the Army.[50] The girls of the Board school at Talas were now serving as nurses in the Red Crescent Hospital at Zinjirdere, where they had absolute religious freedom, wrote Loughridge.[51]

On April 6, 1917, the United States declared war against Germany, but not on Turkey: on the other hand, Turkey unilaterally broke off diplomatic relations with the United States on April 21, 1917, allegedly under German pressure. Shortly before the month of April, Peet wrote that he was sure that the Turks did not want to break with the United States, but wondered if Turkey would be able to resist pressures to do so.[52]

The opening editorial of the May 1917 issue of the *Herald* expressed the Board's hope that the United States' entry into the war would not affect the Board's missionary work. It stated that America had entered the war not for national pride or ambition, or to gain territory or power, but for the welfare of the world: to affirm for all mankind, for weaker nations and oppressed peoples, the right to their own freedom.[53] In this commentary, the Board demonstrated it viewed America's entrance into the First World War as benevolent as its missionary enterprise in Turkey.

The Board remained concerned about the safety of its staff located in Turkey and the continuation of the relief work sponsored by ACASR, which vowed positively and emphatically that its relief work would continue. ACASR officials noted that all means of relief distribution remained open in Turkey and expressed confidence that if they were to be closed, others would be developed to take their place.[54]

So far, the *Herald* stated, no interruption of the Board's work in Turkey had occurred. Whatever happens, the missionaries will remain at their posts. But much of the *Herald's* reporting right after the break in diplomatic relations between Turkey and the United States appeared confused and uncertain, reflecting the Board's lack of information because of the inability to communicate with many members of its staff in Turkey. Nevertheless, the *Herald* felt comfortable in stating that the missionaries had encountered few difficulties with Turkish officials who had generally regarded them with respect; the Turks were not likely to risk the consequences of an attack upon them now. The Turks looked to the future, the Board stated, and therefore would be sure to safeguard the lives of American citizens living among them in Turkey.[55]

In spite of the Board's sanguine pronouncements, three of the Board's fifteen centers of work had been abandoned, and their staffs were either already in Constantinople or on their way there. In June 1917, the *Herald* informed its readers that they could not say with any certainty what the situation was inside Constantinople, let alone the rest of Turkey. Relief work was still progressing at Constantinople, Harpoot and Aleppo. Schools were still in operation at Brousa, Hadjin, and Adana. Some Turkish officials continued to exercise kindness and allowed the refugee work to proceed unhindered; others were said to be impatiently waiting to seize the Board's property. In the past, when Britain, France, and Russia declared war against Turkey, the Entente Powers' schools, hospitals, and property had been seized and their personnel interned; some Americans expected that they would experience the same fate. Nevertheless, the Board's staff continued their work unhampered, while trying to set up their relief activities so they could go forward without the Americans' presence. Several American women remained the sole missionaries at their stations, but they did not feel themselves in any danger, stated the *Herald*.[56]

To be sure, setbacks in delivering relief supplies occurred. Both relief ships, the *Caesar* and the *Des Moines*, had been unable to land in Syria as planned. If this problem could not be solved, stated the *Herald*, the vessels' contents would be sold and the funds used to further other relief activities. The Turks, it added, had done everything possible to facilitate the delivery of the relief supplies.[57] But the *Herald* failed to explain the reason for the failure of the ships to land and provide the relief needed for the suffering of Syria.

In general, asserted the *Herald*, Turkish officials seemed to present few problems in relief administration; Peet maintained that the use of relief funds gave the Board more standing with the Turks. "The Board's staff have been careful to use relief funds in a way that secured local cooperation and have worked cooperatively with the Turkish Red Crescent Society and a governmental committee, at the same time ensuring that its money was used for relief purposes only."[58] Peet's strategy to provide relief to the "less deserving Turks" in order to minimize opposition to helping the Armenians apparently had succeeded.

But new issues confronted the relief workers all the time. Early on, the missionaries recognized that large numbers of refugee children in the Caucasus lacked any means of support. The relief workers defined an orphan as any child who had lost his or her father, because the father of the family usually presented the only possibility of support for the child, regardless of the mother's presence. Relief workers estimated the number of orphans in this area as 175,000, out of a total refugee population of 250,000 as of March 1917. The numbers kept growing as stragglers from Harpoot, Erzerum, Moush, and Sasun managed to find their way through the Russian lines.[59] Remarkably well run orphanages in that area had been set up, according to relief worker Raynolds, but these served children without any parent at all, and those children were only one-tenth of the refugee population. The Russian government gave the refugee mothers a tiny amount of money, which was barely enough to keep them alive, but distribution of this stipend was often interrupted. The relief workers estimated that if they could give each child living with its mother a stipend of two dollars a month, it might be possible to keep the family together.

Raynolds described the situation well: the Armenians "are a race scattered and peeled, families already largely broken up, and it is desirable not to increase the process of disintegration."[60] Consequently, the missionaries endeavored to help the surviving Armenians maintain some sense of family life to meet their psychological as well as their physical needs. For Raynolds, supporting orphans had been part of his long service in Turkey. Some of the current orphans belonged to families whose parents themselves had been parentless and known to Raynolds during his twenty years in Van, particularly in the wake of the 1895 massacres when many had been cared for in Board orphanages. Many of those earlier orphans, he wrote, had grown up to be persons of influence who maintained their Christian faith. Orphanages were doubly important to him, not only as a humanitarian undertaking, but also as a means of evangelizing the children.[61]

To implement the Board's scheme of orphan support, the Committee organized a Home Orphan Department, with Mr. Yarrow,[62] Raynolds' colleague, in charge. The program began in Erivan where Raynolds spent most of his time locating, evaluating, and accepting orphans into the program. He employed three groups of investigators who made house-to-house canvases. The orphans remained in their own homes with their parent, almost always a mother,[63] but only one child in a family could be funded, even though several orphaned children were living in the home. The relief workers hoped to be able to support additional children when funds became available, but initially the number helped in Erivan was small.[64]

JULY - SEPTEMBER 1917

THE NEW YORK TIMES

ACASR continued to garner support from official circles. Mr. Elkus, former ambassador to Turkey, spoke at a luncheon meeting attended by many of New York City's most prominent men and described the enormous need for relief funds in Turkey. He expressed his conviction that, based on the sound reputation of ACASR throughout the whole of Turkey, he expected the Turkish government to continue to allow the missionary group to function without hindrance, even though government officials would have preferred the funds to be distributed through the Red Crescent Society. He added that the Turks grudgingly accepted ACASR's administration of the funds raised by Americans, but that ACASR had been invited to join the centralized plan for relief advocated by the American Red Cross. Elkus cautioned, however, that in addition to relief, a temporary measure, the Committee needed to begin to think about the reconstruction needed at the end of the war, when refugees would be returned to their former homes and would need funds to become self-supporting again. A cablegram from Peet, described as a forty-year resident of Constantinople, was read to the diners in which Peet estimated the total number of Armenian, Syrian, and Greek refugees to be one and one-half million. Peet furnished some figures on the cost of repatriation and rehabilitation, and added some comments about the role of Christian minorities in Turkey. Progressive elements, he wrote, deplored the extermination or significant diminution of the Christian races as they recognized the value of Christians in the future rebuilding of Turkey.[65]

From Tiflis, Willoughby-Smith also provided helpful information to ACASR via cablegram. He estimated the number of Armenian and Syrian refugees in the Caucasus to be 250,000; in eastern Turkey, 100,000. Of the quarter million refugees in the Caucasus, most were women and children and had no employment. Sadly, he wrote, the total continued to grow daily. Although ACASR expressed willingness to help the unfortunate mass of refugees, Willoughby-Smith estimated the minimum cost for each individual to be three dollars per month.[66]

Willoughby-Smith next outlined the staffing requirements to care for the sick, the old, and the infants, asking for one physician, two women for orphanage work, one well-trained man to lead the technical industrial work, and three or four general workers. He next set forth the sums needed:

repatriation	$1,000,000
orphaned children in homes[67]	$500,000
industrial relief	$500,000
farm animals	$150,000
orphanages	$100,000
medical relief	$100,000
seed	$100,000
Total:	$2,450,000

Willoughby-Smith also indicated that machines, looms, and engines for weaving wool would help to meet the needs for the coming winter, and would be of permanent value in establishing the industry.[68] These figures demonstrate the kind of long term funding that would be necessary to not only feed and clothe the refugees, but also to help them resume their lives.

In its September reporting, the *Times* reverted to an earlier model: graphic depiction of Turkish treatment towards Armenians. In large block letters, it headlined a story published on September 30, 1917, with the words "Armenians Killed with Axes by Turks." In that story, White, president of Anatolia College in Marsovan, who had recently returned to the United States, described the recent persecution of Armenians in that city. This included the separation of the men from their families, the massacres of the men, and the deportation of their families, including the continuous movement of women and children. As a result, the college official noted, no one knew the exact fate of countless refugees.[69]

This news story has some unique aspects that would have appealed to American Christians. When the men were taken away in groups to be killed, with trenches already prepared for their bodies, a group of Armenian boys from Anatolia College asked if they could sing. Given permission, they sang the famous Protestant hymn, *Nearer My God to Thee*, and were then promptly executed. White lauded the Armenian faculty members slaughtered during these events as "men of character, education, ability, and usefulness, several of them representing the fine type of graduates from American or European universities."[70]

THE MISSIONARY HERALD

By the time of the July issue, the *Herald* had a little more information to share with its readers. Turkish officials in Constantinople had informed the Swedish Legation that the Turks were not planning to occupy buildings of American institutions and that they intended in every way to act as gentlemen toward the United States government, reported the *Herald*. Even though many of the Board's missionaries had left Turkey, a considerable number still remained in that "disordered empire," waiting for a reply to their request for permission to leave Turkey.[71]

When allowed to leave, some of the missionaries settled in Berne, Switzerland, where earlier missionaries had already relocated. The Board planned to resume its activities at its abandoned stations with Swiss staff. To provide the services needed, ACASR would have to furnish $100,000 per month. Without these funds, stated the *Herald*, all of the Board's missionaries would have to be withdrawn from the Ottoman Empire. The Board hoped, of course, that "the good work of relief [would] go on uninterruptedly."[72]

The *Herald* hammered home its request for funds by using a large print advertisement at the bottom of a page announcing the need for the $100,000 right away. "Liberty Bonds! Red Cross Donations! Relief Funds! Y.M.C.A. Huts! Surely! But not by decreasing our abiding Foreign Missionary Work," read the advertisement.[73] The *Herald* sought to ensure that its patriotic readers did not forget to continue supporting the Board's missionary work.

As of June 1, 1917, the total collected by ACASR since its founding in 1914 amounted to $3,153,914.78. The funds were distributed through ten centers: Aleppo, Beirut, Sidon (in Syria), Cairo, Jerusalem, Constantinople, Baghdad, Tiflis, Tabriz, and Teheran. A map in the *Herald* with the heading, "Where Millions of Human Beings are Starving," showed some of the locations of the ten centers mentioned above.[74]

Information continued to pour into the Board as missionaries either left Turkey or worked in adjacent Russia, from which communication with Boston was possible. From Russia, Mrs. Maynard sent an article to the *Herald* that showed the kinds of unique roles the missionaries played in Turkey. Grisell MacLaren and Myrtle Shane, the only American missionaries present in Bitlis during the merciless slaughter of Armenians in 1915, worked in the military hospital there, headed by a Turkish physician, Mustafa Bey. The missionaries had remained in Bitlis to try to protect some local Armenian women and girls living inside their compound who had hidden when all of the other Armenian women had been killed. The missionaries devised a scheme to try to save these Armenians. They begged Mustafa Bey to inform the government that he needed the Armenian girls and women to work in his hospital. He agreed to do so, informing the authorities that absolutely no other women in Bitlis could do the required work in an acceptable manner. He then formally hired the women and girls in the hospital, where they toiled indefatigably, washing laundry, dressing wounds, cooking, sewing, carrying water, and otherwise serving the hospitalized soldiers.

Mustafa Bey continued to employ the Armenians, even after MacLaren and Shane were ordered to leave Bitlis by the American Consul at Mamuret ul Aziz. When the Turkish officials came to inspect the hospital, the women put on "funny bloomers" [the pants worn by Kurdish women], covered their faces and worked particularly energetically. The physician was so pleased with this arrangement that he continued to protect the women, dreaming up one excuse after the other, despite demands that the Armenians be turned over to governmental officials. When the authorities finally lost all patience and demanded that the Armenians be surrendered, Mustafa Bey pleaded illness and stated he would take care of the matter the next day. That night, however, Armenian volunteers in the Russian Army quietly slid down the snowy mountainsides into the steep-sided valley in which Bitlis is located and occupied the city. When the Armenian women and girls realized the town had been invaded, they immediately went to Mustafa Bey's house and informed the Armenian volunteers how he had protected them by employing them in the hospital. As a result, he escaped the fate of the rest of the Turks of Bitlis who were slaughtered indiscriminately by the conquering Armenians who now possessed the city.[75]

This stirring story appeared in print for several reasons. An entertaining story that would "grab" the readers' attention and remain in their minds, it also described the resourcefulness and power of MacLaren, Shane, and the Armenian women and girls. While the missionaries conceived of the ruse, the Armenians' willingness to take on new roles and to successfully enter into the deceptive plot saved their lives. They were not simply sheep, waiting to be slaughtered, but acted to affect their own fates. Most important of all, the story presents yet another tale of a good Turk, who at considerable risk to himself saved as many Armenians as possible. It adds to the store of knowledge about good Turks that the *Herald* had repeatedly published to help readers accept the principle that ACASR provided relief to all communities living in the Near East and not just the Christian minorities. The story would have reflected a fuller picture of the situation in Bitlis, if it had included the account of the Turkish massacre of the Armenians of that city in 1915.

As the year 1917 progressed, the *Herald* consistently supplied information to its readers about its relief programs, emphasizing the large number of refugees, the provision of aid to everyone, regardless of communal affiliation, and the frugality of the relief workers. Apparently, the Board felt it was necessary to reiterate these facts on a regular basis.[76]

The editorial department also described for its readers the impact on the Board's relief program of Turkey's breaking off diplomatic relations with the United States. The *Herald* assured its readers that Turkey would not block aid to the refugee populations the Board served in the Ottoman Empire.[76] Moreover, in the more remote areas of Turkey, where consular officials had been the leading administrators of relief, the Board had secured Swiss merchants and German missionaries to replace the Americans.

Nevertheless, the *Herald* expressed its concern that Turkey's break with America might cause American contributions to ACASR to slacken off. "[H]undreds of thousands of destitute people, women and girls and orphan children," cautioned the *Herald*, "have been kept alive so far, but they remain on the verge of starvation." Financial donations remained of vital importance.[78] Whatever the political and diplomatic situation, real people living within the Turkish Empire remained desperately in need of whatever aid could be provided to them. To show the enormity of the need, the *Herald* reported that in July, 1917, the American Red Cross Society had contributed $300,000 to ACASR, promising the same amount for each month of 1917.[79] This report demonstrated the support given to ACASR by an independent body, the Red Cross Society, and validated ACASR's policy of helping all refugees, regardless of ethnicity or religion.

The lengthy article on relief work in the Caucasus provided many more details than earlier accounts. The local Board employees, the Yarrows, Gracey, the Maynards, and Raynolds, agreed unanimously that industrial relief was the best way to help the refugees who had flocked to the Caucasus, but they recognized that such work called for large outlays of money for raw materials and close supervision, and that they could only meet the needs of some of the refugees. The concept of industrial relief was evolving because of the increased experience of the missionaries with it and the practical benefits to the refugees by providing the needed bedding and clothing. Mr. Yarrow, director of industrial relief in Erivan, saw that city as a good central location for organizing and administering work programs in the Caucasus.

The kind of work planned required three things: a maximum amount of hand labor; a modest supply of capital; and a finished product that could immediately be distributed or sold. Working with wool fit these criteria, because it had to be processed by hand, the finished product resulted in sorely needed socks or cloth, and their purchase in the Caucasus continued to be almost impossible.[80]

The process of washing and drying wool remained the same. The carding room, however, now employed about 200 refugee women sitting on small cushions to process it. Some opened the wool by hand; the rest carded it on crude hand machines through which it was pulled until it was ready for spinning. The prepared wool was then given to other women who took it home and spun it on wooden hand spindles, to which a rotary motion was given by rolling the spindle between hand and thigh. Once spun, it could be knitted into stockings. The work was organized so that women could alternate between carding, spinning, and knitting.[81]

Other refugee work involved the manufacture of suits. The Committee obtained cloth from Moscow and employed refugee tailors to cut the material in the Committee's workroom, from which the cut fabric was parceled out to 200 men and women for making into suits. The workers produced about 200-300 suits per day. These suits were then given to needy refugees who had recently arrived in the Caucasus and had therefore not received clothing when the earlier distribution had been made.[82]

The workers produced four sizes of suits for men, three for women, and two for boys and girls, and prepared material for infants. All of the outer clothing was sewn, while material for underwear was given out unfinished. Bundles were made up for each family, wrapped up in the underwear material and plainly marked and described. Each bundle included a pair of stockings and each woman also received a pair of shoes. Gracey was responsible for distributing the clothing and was either praised or cursed depending on his decisions.[83]

Another industrial activity involved the manufacture of blankets, since many refugees were sleeping on bare ground or floors with little or nothing to cover them. One hundred fifty women were employed in making good quality blankets, sewing covers for them, preparing the wool or cotton used, and sewing the blankets. To date, 5,000 blankets had been made. They would last the refugees for years. The blanket-making industry was suspended in the summer because of lessened need from the change in weather; those employed at making blankets were transferred to other work.[84]

In addition to wool, cotton was widely available in the Erivan region, resulting in establishing a cotton spinning industry at which 600 women were employed. The cotton was fluffed up first by men who used a long instrument that resembled a long, one-stringed fiddle bow. The cotton was caught on this string after which the men pounded the string with a heavy wooden mallet. After that it was spun into thread using crude spinning wheels made by the refugee carpenters. The women had to get down on the floor and literally keep their noses to the spinning wheel to produce the cotton thread, a very different process from spinning wool. The job was less enjoyable because the women could not chat while working as they did when spinning wool.[85]

Because it was so difficult to obtain cloth, weaving activity in the region of Erivan and Echmiadzin continued to increase, aided by portable looms built by refugee men employed for this purpose. Yarrow initiated this occupation by locating a sample loom at a technical training school; he took it to the carpenters, informing them he wanted a completed loom with a sample of cloth woven on it within three days. The carpenters rose to the challenge, produced the looms and the cloth, and began manufacturing the one hundred looms needed to give employment to several hundred men and women. Because the looms were portable, they could be taken by the refugees wherever they settled, thus giving them the opportunity to become self-sufficient in the future.[86]

This story displays the resourcefulness of the missionaries who investigated what kind of products was needed and how those products could be produced by the refugee population. This description also demonstrates the willingness of the refugees to do difficult work and shows that they wanted to be participants in their own rehabilitation. It therefore embodies what many believed to represent the traditional virtues of American society: resourcefulness, self-sufficiency, the work ethic, as well as other qualities that would appeal to a largely Protestant readership. It also showed the careful use to which contributions to ACASR were put, so that the donors could have confidence that their hard earned money was well spent.

The September 1917 issue also described in great detail the system used to serve orphans. The existence of so many widows with children to support led the committee to accept the idea of contributing a monthly amount to sustain the most needy of the fatherless children. Because of lack of funds, support had been reduced to two dollars a month given only to one needy child in a family in the cities of Erivan and Alexandropol. Only one hundred of the four hundred outlaying villages could be served. Ideally, stated Yarrow, financial relief ought to support several children from each family, and in many families, all of the children, but limited resources permitted financial assistance to be offered to only 3,000 children. The missionaries had asked for funds to help 10,000 children but recognized that the surrounding regions of Baku, Kars, and Erzerum also contained similar numbers.[87]

The missionaries had organized an efficient system for distributing orphan relief that ensured that funds were given out effectively and honestly. They established a centralized card index where information was kept on each child, including their address. To each mother whose child received assistance, the missionaries gave a card to be punched by the relief agent when the funds were distributed.

Although almost every family had a horrific story of how they had managed to survive, for Yarrow the most awful concerned a woman who returned her card, reporting that her infant child had died. When the missionary investigated further, he learned that the father of the child was one of the "fiendish" Kurds who had raped and murdered Christians after the Turks had launched their plan to exterminate the Armenians. The woman had struggled for several months to overcome her revulsion of the child who had resulted from the rape; eventually, unable to bear the constant reminder of her humiliation, she had choked the child to death.[88] Yarrow's failure to express any condemnation of the woman is pleasantly surprising. Despite his occupation and training, his response to this story of infanticide of the innocent child showed understanding and non-judgmental forbearance.

Yarrow's story also addressed the woman's honesty. She told the missionaries about her murder of the child and returned the card that would have allowed her to continue to collect the desperately needed funds, even though she might have deceived the relief worker at the home visit. The publication of this account in a missionary journal suggests the readers would also share in Yarrow's sense of humanity towards the woman. But by indicating the violent circumstances of the woman's insemination by a "fiendish" Kurd, the account also devalued the child's life compared to children conceived in a more traditional way.[89]

While aid workers in the Caucasus toiled under the auspices of a sympathetic Russian government, missionaries in Turkey, stated the *Herald*, also continued to work in that country without difficulty, for the predominating influence in the Turkish government was disposed to protect and even to aid American institutions and their representatives. This fact, maintained the *Herald*, strongly suggested that at the end of the war, America and the Americans would continue to be held in Turkey's favor. Although that hope turned out to be misplaced, it was a natural assumption at the time when the Turks displayed appreciation of the missionaries' role throughout Turkey.

OCTOBER - DECEMBER 1917

THE NEW YORK TIMES

In October, 1917, the *Times* published a letter received by ACASR from one of its workers, Harrison A. Maynard, describing the positive effects of industrial work, and requesting funds to expand the current operation. Maynard wrote that relief industries were currently employing 699-700 women, and asked for additional funds to support this work. If possible, he wrote, funds should be raised for this purpose, bearing in mind that widows and orphan girls especially benefit.[90]

Lack of funds was not the only problem facing ACASR. Despite the fact that 1,200,000 refugees were starving in Syria, a relief ship was unable to put into port at Beirut, according to a relief worker. He described the tragic disappointment of the people there, whose spirits had been kept up for weeks by the promised arrival by Christmas time of the American relief ship, the *Caesar*. Even though it meant life to thousands, the refusal of Germany and Austria-Hungary to grant the relief vessel safe passage to Beirut prevented it from being able to sail. The *Caesar*, laden with more than $250,000 worth of food and clothing contributed by Americans through ACASR ultimately had its cargo sold and the proceeds somehow sent to Beirut. Insufficient food supplies meant, however, less food for the refugees than expected. If the *Caesar* had been able to arrive, the people might have been encouraged to expect future relief ships. But its failure to dock led people to abandon all hope, reported the *Times*.[91]

As the climate changed to fall, President Wilson decided to use his bully pulpit, urging the American people to act. In the past, he wrote, he had encouraged people to give to ACASR on designated days. Recent reports from American diplomatic and consular officials, and other Americans returning from Western Asia, had assured him that thousands of lives had been saved from starvation thanks to the generosity of the American people. These same Americans, however, assured him that suffering and death from starvation and exposure would increase exponentially in the winter. According to the President, a total of 2,000,000 destitute survivors, including numerous women and dependent children who relied completely on relief assistance remained in desperate straits. Wilson called upon the country to contribute generously to these sufferers, and designated the American Red Cross or ACASR as agencies through which funds could be contributed.[92] Wilson's appeal points out the power of the relief agencies to obtain the support of the highest official in the United States.

The *Times* published two more stories on the Armenian issue that fall. Former Ambassadors Morgenthau and Straus spoke at "Armenian and Syrian Day" at Hero Land, a fair in New York. Morgenthau declared that the massacre of 800,000 Armenians and Syrians had been encouraged and aided by the Germans. Turkish authorities, he said, gloried in the fact that in thirty days they had accomplished what Abdul Hamid had not achieved in thirty-one years of his reign. They could have been stopped if they had not been encouraged by the Germans, he asserted. Straus adopted a similar theme when he spoke, arguing that Germany must also share the blame with Turkey for the annihilation of the Armenians.[93]

THE MISSIONARY HERALD

In November, 1917, the *Herald* informed its readers that the need for relief continued unabated. In Turkey and the surrounding areas, left undefined by the *Herald*, 2,140,000 people, Armenians, Syrians, and Greeks remained close to starving. One third of these were orphans. For the sum of five dollars per month, each of these individuals could be kept alive, but the monthly cost of doing so totaled $10,700,000, stated the *Herald*. Although the American Red Cross contributed $300,000 to ACASR each month for this cause, that donation provided only 1/35th of the amount needed. To save the refugees, the relief workers still needed the remaining 34/35ths. The funds coming into the Treasurer's office on a regular basis were insufficient to meet this need.

Having saved these remnants of subject races until now, said the *Herald*, it was unthinkable that Americans should let them die out by slow starvation.

> For their own sakes, for the sake of the lands yet to be rehabilitated, for the sake of the world and its need of these virile races, for the sake of the Christian name and what they have endured because they bore it, it is the plain duty of America, which has become in special sense the protector of these people, to tide them over this epoch of destitution.[94]

Moreover, added the *Herald*, most of these refugees were women and children, calling out to America for their very lives. Although Americans were hard-pressed with war taxes and higher prices, the *Herald* said, "we cannot drown that cry; we must not disregard it."[95]

In this editorial, the *Herald* expanded beyond the category of Armenians and Syrians to include Greeks, barely mentioned up to this point and then only sporadically. All these peoples had to be saved, argued the evangelical journal, not just for their own sake, but to help "rehabilitate" other lands, those who have not yet encountered Christianity.

Along with these exhortations, the *Herald* included some stirring accounts of persecution, rescue, and deliverance in its November and December issues. In November, the *Herald* included a report from Rev. Crawford, a Board missionary stationed in Trebizond, who wrote to the Board about the arrival of the Russians and the number of Armenians who came out of hiding as a result, some from as far away as Harpoot. Many of these Armenians had arrived in Trebizond by caique, sailboat, or rowboat from towns along the Black Sea coast, paying between twenty to thirty pounds sterling, up to sixty or eighty pounds each for a journey of two to six nights in an open boat, sometimes without food or water. Frequently the boats also carried Greeks from the coastal towns who reported that the Turkish authorities had become more and more oppressive. On July 7, 1917, reported the missionary, the Turkish army headquarters at Enderes issued an order that by July 25, 1917, no Greek man over the age of sixteen and under the age of fifty would be allowed in Ordu (a coastal town) but would be deported to the interior. Orders pertaining to families were to be issued later.[96]

At the same time, the *Herald* published a report from missionary Rev. Stapleton who had returned to Erzerum after withdrawing from that area in late 1916. He was pleased to inform the Board that the Russians were still in control of the city. He planned to help the Armenian refugees who had been repatriated to Erzerum and hoped to resume their earlier lives as much as possible. He urged the two new relief workers planning to join him to begin studying Russian as well as Armenian and Turkish.[97] His comments indicated that he believed this portion of Turkey would remain in Russian hands for some time to come, perhaps indefinitely.

Postcards continued to arrive at the Board's offices, this being the only means for the missionaries to communicate with the Boston headquarters. Those bearing August 1917 dates all came from different mission stations in Turkey and reported some news of local events. In Adana, the Board's hospital first had been seized for use to house the English, Hindu (Indian) and Russian prisoners of war captured by the Ottoman armies. Recently, it had again been converted into a hospital. Upon Turkish orders, the missionary doctor could no longer treat any patients for free. Since most of the patients were poor Muslims, the greatest hardships fell on them. The houses in the city left vacant when the Armenians were deported were now occupied by Muslims, many of whom were absolutely destitute. Armenians from all different parts of Turkey kept drifting into the city from the desert to which they had been deported. They lacked shelter, food, and clothing, and were trying to somehow survive.[98]

In December, the *Herald* published another letter from missionary Crawford about the deportation of the Greeks from Ordu. By this time, he wrote, families had also been deported, with no provision for food and shelter. As a result, many were dying daily by the roadside, unable to continue. In the market at Ordu, several Greek men who had not yet been deported were commiserating with each other, saying they were alive today, but who knew about the morrow. Upon hearing them, the Protestant pastor admonished them not to lose hope, because one never knows what God will bring about.

Within a few days, Greeks looking out at the Black Sea at dawn saw smoke on the horizon. As visibility improved, they saw a big Russian steamer that drew nearer and nearer. All Greeks able to get on small boats quickly went out to sea and boarded the Russian ship. The Protestant pastor and his wife, with the two little Armenian children they had rescued, decided to remain in Ordu because they were afraid there was no space for everyone who wanted to leave. When they left the docks and went back into town, they found their church, school, and home in flames. They returned to the docks, secured a boat to go on the Russian ship, and managed to board the vessel.

On August 25, 1917, at noon time, a young Greek man who had previously escaped from Ordu, came rushing into the Board's Mission House at Trebizond, shouting, "Come quickly to the landing. My pastor and his family and all the others have come." The Russian steamer had deposited all of the refugees on the dock at Trebizond, delivering a total of two thousand Greeks in all.[99]

These accounts are the kind of dramatic stories that the *Herald* liked to publish. It depicted the suffering of innocent people, the resulting depression and feelings that God had ignored their sufferings, followed by a rescue that demonstrated that faith in God was justified after all. The story also showed the kinds of situations faced by mission staff, and the emotional "ups and downs" that the missionaries contended with every day.

The December issue of the *Herald* also included a report from Dr. Ruth A. Parmelee, who had served in Harpoot since 1914 doing what she termed "emergency work." Although she had intended to be a "women's physician," the death of Dr. Atkinson in 1915 left the city without any medical services. Soon the influx of Armenian refugees, "[w]retched, ignorant creatures," consumed all of the missionaries' time. "[F]eeding and clothing them, teaching the children, and treating the sick who suffered from typhus and dysentery, and all the other ailments that come as a result of filth and poverty," used up all her time.[100] Eventually, the depleted ranks of their colleagues and Turkey's decision to break off diplomatic relations with the United States led the missionaries to abandon the Harpoot mission station.[101]

End Notes to The Year 1917

1. "Found Armenians Starving in Camps, *New York Times*, 1 January 1917, 9.

2. Meskene (also known as Meskéné, Meskeneh, Maskanih, and Meshseneh) is the site of an ancient city on the Euphrates east of Aleppo. It was on the deportation route leading to Der Zor in 1915.

3. Der Zor, also spelled Deyr es-Zor, Deir ez-Zor, Dayr az-Zawr and Deir al-Zur, is a town and province in the Syrian desert located about 285 kilometers southeast of Aleppo. In 1915, it witnessed grim scenes as many thousands of Armenians arrived at the end of forced death marches from Anatolia. Thousands died there and in surrounding areas. France occupied Deyr es-Zor in 1921 and made it the seat of a large garrison. In 1946 Deyr es-Zor became part of independent Syria. The Armenian Orthodox church in the town contains a memorial to the victims of the Armenian Genocide.

4. In this era of mass murder by governments, 60,000 might seem like a small number.

5. "Found Armenians Starving in Camps," *New York Times*, 1 January 1917, 9.

6. "Blocks Jewish Relief Plan," *New York Times*, 3 February 1917, 6.

7. "Cruiser Des Moines at Alexandria," *New York Times*, 4 February 1917, I, 4.

8. I have included Cleveland H. Dodge's full name to avoid confusion with D. Stuart Dodge.

9. "Predicts Turkey Won't Bar Relief," *New York Times*, 8 February 1917, 4.

10. "Calls Armenians Martyrs," *New York Times*, 26 February 1917, 9.

11. "Putting Sympathy into Action," *Missionary Herald*, CXIII (January 1917), 5-6.

12. Ibid., 6.

13. Bozanti (or Pozanti) is a town high in the Taurus Mountains. The rail line and highway that connect Tarsus and Cappadocia pass through it.

14. Sivas is about 170 kilometers northeast of Caesarea.

15. "Powerless to Escape," *Missionary Herald* CXIII (February 1917), 76.

16. Graffam died from heart failure while undergoing surgery in 1921. Missionary staff believed that her heart was weakened as a result of years of the stress and strain resulting from trying to save the Armenians she served. See Susan Billington Harper, "Mary Louise Graffam: witness to genocide," in *America and the Armenian Genocide of 1915*, ed. Jay Winter (Cambridge: Cambridge University Press, 2003), 214-239.

17. "To Sum Up," *Missionary Herald* CXIII (March 1917), 126.

18. "In the Interior," *Missionary Herald* CXIII (March 1917), 125.

19. "A New and Greater Difficulty," *Missionary Herald* CXIII (March 1917), 126.

20. Ibid.

21. "Turkey and the United States," *Missionary Herald* CXIII (March 1917), 106.

22. "Putting Sympathy to Work," *Missionary Herald* CXIII (January 1917), 5.

23. "Relief Work," *Missionary Herald* CXIII (January 1917), 26-27.

24. Ibid.

25. "Armenian and Syrian Aid," *New York Times*, 15 April 1917, III, 10.
26. "Ask $100,000 for Armenians," *New York Times*, 16 May 1917, 5.
27. "Armenian and Syrian Relief," *New York Times*, 20 May 1917, II, 3.
28. "Still Help Armenia as Deficit Grows," *New York Times*, 28 May 1917, 7.
29. "Curb Turkey, Says Colonel," *New York Times*, 30 May 1917, 3.
30. "Saving a Race," *Missionary Herald* CXIII (April 1917), 161.
31. Ibid.
32. Ibid., 160.
33. Ibid., 161.
34. Ibid.
35. Ibid., 160.
36. Ibid., 160-161.
37. The period for which they would be kept alive was not specified.
38. "Seeing It Through," *Missionary Herald* CXIII (April 1917), 161.
39. "Social Service in Turkey," *Missionary Herald* CXIII (April 1917), 176-178.
40. "Refugees in the Igdir District," *Missionary Herald* CXIII (May 1917), 243. Gracey did not explain what he meant by the "gallantry of the Russians."
41. Some of the Turks of rural Anatolia still use dried dung for fuel.
42. "Refugees in the Igdir District," *Missionary Herald* CXIII (May 1917), 243-244.
43. Ibid.
44. "Industrial Relief in Marsovan," *Missionary Herald* CXIII (June 1917), 288-289.
45. "Mary Graffam in Sivas," *Missionary Herald* CXIII (March 1917), 126-127; "From Sivas," *Missionary Herald* CXIII (April 1917), 188.
46. "From Sivas," *Missionary Herald* CXIII (April 1917), 188.
47. "From Crude Wool to Sweaters in Sivas," *Missionary Herald* CXIII (April 1917), 177.
48. "Cloth Weaving in Marash," *Missionary Herald* CXIII (April 1917), 177.
49. "Varied Work in Constantinople," *Missionary Herald* CXIII (April 1917), 177.
50. "Notes from Talas," *Missionary Herald* CXIII (June 1917), 291-292. Drafting this man into the Turkish Army probably amounted to a death sentence because of the use of Armenians as pack animals.
51. "Notes from Talas," *Missionary Herald* CXIII (June 1917), 292-293.
52. "Anxious Days in Constantinople," *Missionary Herald* CXIII (June 1917), 290-291
53. "The United States and the War," *Missionary Herald* CXIII (May 1917), 211.
54. "How about Relief Work in Turkey," *Missionary Herald* CXIII (May 1917), 212.
55. Ibid.
56. "A Crucial Hour in Turkey," *Missionary Herald* CXIII (June 1917), 263.
57. "How about Relief Work in Turkey," *Missionary Herald* CXIII (May 1917), 212.
58. "Anxious Days in Constantinople," *Missionary Herald* CXIII (June 1917), 290-291.
59. "175,000 Orphans," *Missionary Herald* CXIII (May 1917), 242-243.
60. "Refugees in the Igdir District," *Missionary Herald* CXIII (May 1917), 243-244.

61. "175,000 Orphans," *Missionary Herald* CXIII (May 1917), 242-243.

62. When a married couple served in Turkey, I have designated each member with "Mr." or "Mrs," when needed to avoid confusion.

63. This unusual program of home orphan care eliminated the need for expensive orphanages for children who still lived with a parent.

64. "Winter in the Caucasus," *Missionary Herald* CXIII (June 1917), 289-290.

65. "Elkus Urges Relief Work in Turkey," *New York Times*, 19 July 1917, 10.

66. These figures demonstrate the difficulty of establishing the number of refugees in the Caucasus, Turkey, and Syria. Relief workers repeatedly provided vastly different numbers of refugees. The number of Armenians who were exiled from their homes or killed is still subject to debate.

67. ACASR viewed children without fathers living with their mothers to be "orphaned" because the father was almost always the only means of support for the family.

68. "New Plea for Armenians," *New York Times*, 10 August 1917, 8.

69. "Armenians Killed with Axes by Turks," *New York Times*, 30 September 1917, I, 8.

70. Ibid.

71. "Later Word from Turkey," *Missionary Herald* CXIII (July 1917), 311-312.

72. Ibid.

73. Untitled, *Missionary Herald* CXIII (July 1917), 311.

74. "Where Millions of Human Beings are Starving!" *Missionary Herald* CXIII (July 1917), 310.

75. "The Days of Terror in Bitlis," *Missionary Herald* CXIII (August 1917), 372-373. The account indicates that Armenian volunteers massacred the Turkish troops they encountered in Bitlis, demonstrating that Armenian troops were more than willing to slaughter the Turkish troops they encountered without any evaluation of culpability. The story contains a factual error; it states that these events occurred in 1914, but from the facts provided, it is clear that they occurred in 1915 or 1916.

76. "Editorial Pointers," *Missionary Herald* CXIII (September 1917), 395.

77. Ibid.

78. "Turkey's Door Not Closed," *Missionary Herald* CXIII (September 1917), 395-396.

79. Ibid.

80. Systematizing Help in Erivan," *Missionary Herald* CXIII (September 1917), 418.

81. "Wool Department," *Missionary Herald* CXIII (September 1917), 418.

82. "Clothing Department," *Missionary Herald* CXIII (September 1917), 418-419.

83. Ibid.

84. "Bedding Department," *Missionary Herald* CXIII (September 1917), 419.

85. "Cotton Department," *Missionary Herald* CXIII (September 1917), 419-420.

86. "Weaving Department," *Missionary Herald* CXIII (September 1917), 420.

87. "Home Orphan Department," *Missionary Herald* CXIII (September 1917), 420-421.

88. Ibid.

89. Ibid.

90. "Armenian and Syrian Relief," *New York Times*, 7 October 1917, III, 4.

91. "1,200,000 Starving in Syria," *New York Times*, 22 October 1917, 9.

92 "Asks Aid for 2,000,000," *New York Times*, 29 October 1917, 20.

93. "Says Germans Aided Armenian Killings," *New York Times*, 11 December 1917, 13.

94. "What about the 34-35th's?" *Missionary Herald* CXIII (November 1917), 495.

95. Ibid.

96. "The Greeks to the Road," *Missionary Herald* CXIII (November 1917), 514.

97. "From Erzroom, Russia." *Missionary Herald* CXIII (November 1917), 514-515.

98. "Late News from Adana, *Missionary Herald* CXIII (December 1917), 571-572.

99. "A Black Sea Deliverance," *Missionary Herald* CXIII (December 1917), 570-571.

100. "Emergency Work for Three Years," *Missionary Herald* CXIII (December 1917), 573-575.

101. Ibid. In 1991, I visited the site. Not a single building remains.

Chapter 6

THE YEAR 1918

The political changes in Russia that led to the Treaty of Brest-Litvosk resulted in renewed Turkish attacks on Armenians and further threatened the lives of the freezing, starving refugees. The end of the war meant, however, that relief agencies could again work in Turkey and the Caucasus without impediment.

JANUARY - MARCH 1918

THE NEW YORK TIMES

Early in the year, the *Times* informed its readers that $4,445,000 had recently been sent to the Near East for relief purposes. When added to earlier contributions, a total of $6,854,893 had been contributed for the relief of "the suffering Syrians and Armenians."[1] The breakdown of the total funds paid out by this date was as follows: Constantinople had received almost two and one-half million dollars; Tiflis had been granted almost two million dollars; and Tabriz had been given slightly over one million dollars. Smaller amounts had been sent to other areas in the region, including Beirut, Jerusalem, Baghdad, Cairo, and Teheran.[1] The *Times* took pains to reiterate its standard statement that all administrative costs were paid by private parties, while relief distribution in the Near East was performed by missionary or consular employees who were independently paid and therefore required no salary from ACASR.[2]

While donations to ACASR were holding steady, the diplomatic arena had created additional problems for the hapless Armenians. For some time after the March 1917 revolution, Russian troops in western Armenia had been deserting their units and returning to Russia, thereby abandoning Armenians in Turkey who had somehow escaped the deportations or had returned to their homes to try to restart their lives. Because of the lack of any military restraint, fresh massacres had already broken out in the city of Samsun, a port on the Turkish coast of the Black Sea. The entire Armenian male population, including children, had been massacred, according to a report by an unnamed "official of one of the Central Powers." Thousands of those killed had been driven to Samsun by the Turks, who then slaughtered them at will.[3]

On March 4, the *Times*' readers awoke to read the startling news that the newly formed Bolshevik government of Russia had entered into the Treaty of Brest-Litovsk with Germany a day earlier. The treaty not only required the Russians to relinquish the territory they had conquered in Turkey during the war, but also the three districts (sanjaks) of Kars, Ardahan, and Batum, annexed by Russia in 1878, where large numbers of Armenians were still living.[4] The end of the Russian Army's presence in those areas meant that the Turks were now free to act with impunity. According to the *Times*, the Turks sought to stir up Georgians against Armenians and "appalling massacres" had taken place."[5]

The Armenian Correspondence Bureau at The Hague furnished additional information about the Turkish massacres. It noted that Turks returning to Trebizond after the Russian withdrawal had engaged in "fresh acts of savagery and rioting" in that city. For the Turks, stated the Bureau, the plan sought to make sure that not a single Armenian remained alive in the "reoccupied" territory.[6] In implementing this goal "[t]he Armenians were subjected to indescribable tortures. Sacks filled with children were thrown into the sea, old women and men were crucified or mutilated, and all young women and girls were handed over to the Turks."[7] Russian solders, separated from their units, likewise had been "shot, drowned, or burned to death." Although the article also indicated that Turkish sources related details of "alleged atrocities committed by bands of Armenians,"[8] the *Times*' bias in favor of Armenians shows up in its use of the word "alleged" when referring to Turkish claims against the Armenians. The newspaper failed to provide any details about the Turkish claims, yet provided extremely specific information about the Armenian Bureau's allegations

The *Times* followed this story with an editorial titled, "Armenia in the Last Ditch," in which the newspaper asserted that Armenian (and Georgian) troops, veterans of the Russian campaigns against Germany and Austria, had coalesced on the old Turkish-Russian border to try to defend their homes and to protect the hundreds of thousands of people who had fled across this border to escape the Turkish massacres. These troops, stated the *Times*, had inherited the war materiel abandoned by the Russian troops, outnumbered the Turkish troops, and possessed the determination needed to protect the republic of the Caucasus and the "remnants of the Armenian nation."[9] The

Armenian militia could not help but succeed against the Turks, gushed the *Times*, unless the Germans attacked from Odessa and sent her troops to overthrow the "last remnant of a Christian and cultured nation against which she has already tolerated outrages unprecedented in recent times."[10] The *Times'* editorial, however, illustrated how utterly ignorant the nation's premier newspaper was about the true state of conditions in western Armenia and the Caucasus.[11]

A news story published the next day may have provided some of the basis for the *Times'* report. ACASR relief worker William N. Chambers, now located in Switzerland, stated that he had received reports from fifteen places in Asiatic Turkey that corroborated the Armenian accounts about current large scale Turkish massacres. On the pretext that Armenian bands are actively killing Turks, the Turks are carrying out "general and bloody reprisals," he stated. It is very possible, he added, that similar atrocities will be inflicted on the Armenian residents of the Caucasus. Clearly, Chambers concluded, "[i]t is dollars to death, and America cannot afford to hesitate in this great humanitarian effort to save the remnant of the persecuted Christians in Turkey."[12]

Another ACASR representative in Persia sent to ACASR's headquarters a description of the conditions facing the refugees in that land: "Men and women, once in good circumstances, self-respecting and respected by others, now hungry, helpless, and friendless, crawl away out of sight, die unseen, and lie unburied. This is not fiction; I have seen them." Even if the war should end soon, he wrote, ACASR will have to provide continuing relief through the winter of 1918 and 1919, and to a lesser degree for some years to come.[13]

The Board's staff continued to view the new threats to Armenians as part of Germany's and Turkey's geopolitical aims. Dr. F. W. Macallum,[14] a twenty-five year resident of Constantinople as a Board missionary, and mostly recently part of the ACASR team working in the Caucasus, furnished such an analysis when he spoke to the Harlem Branch of the Young Men's Christian Association (YMCA) in late March, 1918. His talk, called "The Armenians in the Caucasus and Their Present Peril," presented a full-blown evaluation of the current aims of both Germany and Turkey. Thwarted by the Soviet's capture of Odessa, and Turkey's control of Baku, the Germans, stated Macallum, had devised a new project by which to reach India: the Berlin-Batoum-Baku-Bombay line. Enver Pasha, one of the ruling triumvirate of Turkey, was "dreaming of occupying the throne" of a Pan-

Turkic empire, stretching from Gibraltar to the Pacific Ocean, including the lands of North Africa, Turkey, the Arabian peninsula, the Caucasus, Russia, central Asia, Afghanistan, and India, according to Macallum. The only obstacle to the fulfillment of this plan was a

> ...band of perhaps 25,000 or 30,000 Armenians and Georgians in the Caucasus, who are menaced every moment by Tartars secretly waiting for the German and Turkish advance so that they can surround the helpless Armenians and Georgians and wipe out those that have not already succumbed to German cruelty.[15]

Macallum, who saw Germany as the armorer of the Muslim Tatars, claimed that Russian soldiers who abandoned the front to return to their homes had sold their rifles and other arms to the Tartars. The latter had purchased the weapons with gold obtained from the Germans. But for Macallum, Germany's, culpability extended far beyond these recent actions. "The whole thing could have been stopped by one word from the Kaiser," he said.[16]

THE MISSIONARY HERALD

A crucial issue faced by the United States in 1918 concerned whether the United States should declare war on Turkey and Bulgaria. The Board's answer in the January issue of the *Herald* was loud and clear: "[W]e say, unqualifiedly, 'No.' It would be a tactical blunder, an outrage against humanity, and a moral crime."[17] The Board claimed that Turkey did not want to wage war against the United States and had taken great pains to avoid any action that would goad the United States into such a conflict. It was Germany, opined the *Herald*, that "schemed" to convince Turkey that the Turks must engage in war against the United States.

The *Herald* then asked a second rhetorical question: "Are we tactically to improve the position of the United States by effecting what Germany desires, and by alienating from us two of her unhappy allies that 'incline to our side?' Such a course would be a piece of political folly."[18]

This question lay at the heart of the Board's work in Turkey. If the United States declared war against the Ottoman Empire, the Board's operations might be seriously compromised. A declaration of war, stated the *Herald*, would most likely lead to further seizure of mission property, internment or expulsion of the Board's staff, the end of ACASR's relief work, and "beyond doubt" the starvation of the remaining Armenians who had somehow still survived. In addition, the Board argued:[19]

> It might easily mean, also, the wiping out of other subject races as the German overlords cleared the land of every obstacle to their domination. The way would be open for the last and worst era of atrocities that the *Ottoman Empire* has yet staged. [The emphas is mine.][20]

If the United States had entered the war solely to rid the world of an "irreconcilable foe of the world's progress," stated the *Herald,* it would be a "moral crime" to force another nation to become a belligerent, when that country desired to stay out of the fray. Indeed, the Board further stated: the United States had engaged in warfare only to defend human rights from "the attack of an arch-enemy;" it must therefore refuse to extend that war any further than necessary.[21]

The deceptive sophistry shown by this editorial demonstrated how far the Board was willing to go to rehabilitate Turkey and to convince its readers that Germany was the true evil doer. Despite Turkey's slaughter of Armenians, the Board's own constituency, the Board now found it expedient to minimize Turkey's misdeeds and to label Germany the miscreant. Knowing that one of the slogans used for fund raising purposes was "Remember the Starving Armenians," the *Herald* claimed that war between the United States and Turkey would cause "the starving to death" of those Armenians who had managed to survive thus far. Moreover, those who supported war with Turkey would be allowing Germany to dominate that country, which would produce even greater atrocities by the Turks.[22]

The Board's concerns about its staff, property, and relief activities constituted legitimate issues; declaring war against Turkey would probably have made it more difficult for American relief activities of the kind conducted by ACASR to continue. In fact, such a declaration might have made it extremely difficult to get the necessary documentation not only from the Turks, but also from the American authorities to import the necessary relief supplies. The ACASR's relief efforts often spelled the difference between life and death for the recipients and any hindrance to the delivery of that aid had to be very carefully weighed. But, after spending close to eighty years of mission work in Turkey and witnessing first hand the events of 1915 and 1916, to pretend that *Germany* was the main force behind the Armenian Genocide was dissembling of the highest order. The missionaries in the field knew full well that the Turks had instigated the massacres; they had seen their Armenian congregants killed or led off under threat of death; they had heard reports from responsible persons about the conditions of the deportees in the camps, on the deportation trail, and in Der Zor itself. Knowing about the role of the Turks in these events, the *Herald* nevertheless blamed Germany for the Genocide.

During the war years, and earlier, the *Herald* had informed its readers about Turkish atrocities, possibly as a means of motivating contributions to relief funds for its Armenian constituency. In its publications it had on occasion used such incendiary terms as "fiendish," to describe the Turks. Having created such a negative image of Turks for one purpose, the Board now needed to formulate another perception. One of the easiest ways of doing that was to transform the once "evil Turk" into a beneficent but unwilling dupe of the Kaiser. The motive for making such a switch is clear.

This is not to say that others did not also find Germany responsible. Many news stories and letters to the editor of the *Times* found Germany culpable, at least partially, for the Armenian Genocide. But in the Board's case, their employees were on the ground and knew what had really happened (and was continuing to occur). Few of the Board's Turkish staff would have endorsed the idea that Germany was behind the Turk's genocidal actions.

One possible explanation for the change in the Board's thinking may have been optimism about the outcome of the war. The January issue of the *Herald* included an editorial about the entry of General Sir Edmund Allenby and his British troops into the city of Jerusalem. The conquest of nearby Palestine may have suggested to the Board that the Entente Powers would win the war, or at least take over part of the Near East. A defeated Turkey might be very willing to allow ACASR free rein in its territories, especially if the Turkish authorities were somehow found not culpable for the murder and deportation of Armenians; assigning Germany absolute guilt proved the easiest way of absolving the Turks of their responsibility for the Genocide.

In addition, the Board's long time goal was to convert Turks, the very group whom it had recently "demonized." The demographic shift in Turkey's population, as the ratio of Christians to Muslims changed because of the destruction of the Christian minorities, may have suggested to the Board that it now needed to change its orientation.[23] The missionaries had previously shifted their attention from Turks to Armenians because of the death sentence imposed upon Turks who abandoned the Muslim faith. Perhaps the mission board now felt that without a missionary identification with Armenians, Turks might be more open to the Christian message. They may have also hoped that the modernizing changes wrought by the First World War might have encouraged government officials to permit Muslims to convert to Christianity without penalty. The vicissitudes of war might also have opened Turkish hearts to the Gospel, especially when they learned of the many Board missionaries who died ministering to the needs of both Turks and Armenians. Yet, unless the Board was able to switch its supporters from viewing Turks with opprobrium and make them look like the unwilling partner of Germany, it might be impossible to raise the funds needed to succeed in its evangelistic plans for Turkey.

Despite this initial foray into the politics of the Genocide, the *Herald* continued to provide more conventional reporting by frequently publishing news of relief activities and their funding, but not in every issue, possibly to avoid boring their readers or inducing what is currently called "compassion fatigue."[24] One way to keep funds coming was to describe the kind of positive activities undertaken by ACASR, and the more exciting the better. One such article was the story about ACASR's workers who had entered Russian territory in Turkey to do relief work.

The Russian occupation (for a time) of a significant part of the eastern provinces of Turkey meant that the missionary staff in Erzerum could now communicate with the Board. Under the heading "Activities in Russia," the *Herald* published the contents of a letter Rev. Stapleton had written in the summer of 1917 to describe the work he was doing to foster self-sufficiency in the nearby villages. Largely peopled by Armenians who had been repatriated to their former homes under the peace and security provided by the Russian presence, these hamlets, a survey showed, lacked oxen or plows, resulting in fallow fields and a lack of dung to make the fuel needed for the winter. Stapleton had advised ACASR staff that the villagers needed 300,000 rubles during the summer months of 1917 to purchase the oxen necessary for farming, but the relief committee in the Caucasus voted to furnish his area with only 15,000 rubles a month. "What the people will do this coming winter is a big question," he noted. In the city of Erzerum itself, ninety women worked five days a week sewing garments, including stockings and bed clothing, to be used in the winter. The garments were parceled out to the poor, including some of the seamstresses themselves, a large number of whom were widows. The seamstresses earned one ruble a day for six hours of work, and most of them received their bread from a relief committee that supplied the poor.

Protestant church services were held for Armenians, few of whom came, wrote Stapleton, but Russian Baptists conducted services for the troops whose "earnestness ... [was] indeed an inspiration. How they do enjoy the singing, and they will stay for an hour after their own service, while I play for them their favorite songs...."[25] The lack of enthusiasm shown by the Armenians for Protestant church services is surprising because Armenians represented the primary beneficiaries of relief funds. Their apathetic response to such services could have been construed to be indifference towards their benefactors.

The March issue included an account of the difficulties experienced by ACASR workers who went to the Caucasus, leaving from San Francisco on July 18, 1917. After arriving in Vladivostok, they were detained there for several weeks until they received authority to proceed to the Caucasus. During their detention, the missionaries spent their time studying Russian, teaching English, and doing YMCA work. Once Consul Willoughby-Smith of Tiflis obtained permission for them to resume their travel, the relief workers booked reservations on the Trans-Siberian railroad, leaving Vladivostok on November 15, 1917. After traveling on the railroad to Tashkent, they crossed the Caspian Sea to Baku by ship, thereby avoiding the turmoil and crowded roads of European Russia; from Baku they traveled the 260 miles to Tiflis, and from there went to Erivan. Included among the eight relief workers were five new recruits.[26]

The ACASR workers already on site had purchased a building for an orphanage in Erivan that would also give the workers a center for their permanent relief activities, according to a letter from Mr. Yarrow. (Yarrow took pains to point out that the decision to purchase the building was a unanimous decision by Yarrow, Raynolds, and Gracey.) In addition to the orphanage, the workers continued to operate what was called the Home Orphan Department. This program had been in place for some time and had been described fully in earlier issues of the *Herald*. (The *Herald* staff apparently found it important for the readers to read again about the arrangements for supporting fatherless orphans living with their mothers, or felt that the turnover in readers was such that current readers might not be familiar with this program.) Feeding just one child per family, the missionaries estimated they were caring for 5,000 orphans in over 250 villages in the province of Erivan alone; there were villages that they had not yet entered. Yarrow hoped to increase the number of orphans served to 10,000, so that all of the children in a fatherless family could eat. Although the evangelists did not like to give aid without corresponding work, they recognized that orphans and widows could not work sufficiently to be able to feed themselves. Yarrow estimated that similar numbers of orphans in the provinces of Kars, Erzerum, Trebizond, Erzingan, Bayazid, and Van required help.[27]

But according to a later letter from Yarrow dated September 28, 1917, and received in Boston in late January, 1918, the news from the Caucasus was not quite so positive. Although the missionaries had opened new branches of industrial relief in the Armenian cities of Echmiadzin, Garmaloo, and Erivan, Yarrow reported that his visits to some of the surrounding villages made him

> much depressed at the general situation. For over two years these wretched people have been living from hand to mouth, with conditions getting gradually worse... [T]housands and thousands are weakening and will eventual die, from long-continued lack of sufficient nourishment.[28]

Yarrow was, however, encouraged by the presence of additional recruits for the work: two Friends (Quakers), Mr. Heald, who handled the Alexandropol refugee work, and Mr. Walsh, lured away from Polish relief work, both English. Walsh, a trained mechanic, was particularly welcomed because he would be able to help with future reconstruction work. Employing these two men proved a bargain; the only expenses were their room and board; they came with their own income, presumably from the Friends.[29]

Plans for improving medical care for the refugees also brightened Yarrow's outlook. The missionaries had organized a medical clinic in Erivan, run by Garabed, a male nurse from Dr. Ussher's hospital at Van, who was aided at the clinic by a woman nurse, Vartanush, also from the Van hospital. Both were Armenians.[30] The ACASR workers also expected to locate a pharmacist soon. In addition, they hoped to hire a "fine-spirited local Armenian doctor" to run the clinic for as much time as he had to offer. Yarrow planned to set up a similar endeavor in Alexandropol.[31]

Dr. Raynolds supplied news in the next issue about Garabed's work. During the first four months of 1917, Garabed saw 637 patients, gave medicine to 567 of them, and assisted as well 274 new-born babies, giving flannel for first wraps to 218 of the infants. He also furnished small comforters to 126 mothers, and large comforters to fifty-nine others. The

Armenian nurse also donated small amounts of money, averaging ten roubles each, to 3,437 sick and poor.[32]

Raynolds, in charge of individual cases of need in Erivan, where about one hundred old, infirm, and helpless individuals received a regular monthly allowance, also provided temporary assistance to others who had fallen sick and were unable to work. His work included supplying sterilized milk to 100 babies and twenty-five other patients. Recently, Raynolds welcomed the arrival of Dr. Kennedy, a physician, sent to Erivan by the Lord Mayor's Committee of London who was seeing patients in his office or in their homes and who hoped to establish a small hospital for severe cases.[33]

Mr. and Mrs. Maynard also reported to the Board by letter written in Erivan on October 11, 1917. Now secretary and treasurer of the local ACASR, Mr. Maynard supervised the distribution of all supplies for industrial work, whether raw materials or finished products. This work, which employed about five thousand refugees, saved both body and soul of the refugees, he wrote. The refugees had not been beggars before, he stated, and now they begged only for work. He also described for the readers the forms of industrial relief offered in Erivan, much as Yarrow had done earlier, expressing special pride in that everyone employed in the industrial work process, the managers, foremen, teachers, and all others except one were refugees. That exception was a Russian Armenian, chosen for his language abilities. Maynard wrote of the stress experienced when he had to refuse to employ desperate refugees who begged for work:

When a man pleads for work with tears in his voice, if not in his eyes, it makes one sick to refuse him. Most of them, I suppose, have not only their families dependent upon them, but also women and children of their brothers' families, for more men than women seem to have been killed. They have a look of despair. Many show signs of insufficient nutrition. It will be worse in the winter.[34]

He also wrote that he wished the contributors to ACASR could see the good uses to which their donations were put.[35]

Mrs. Maynard also wrote to the Board, describing a refugee conference held in Erivan at which the Armenian guerilla fighter Antranig was lionized. He was a simple man, she wrote, a carpenter, but he had the knack of organizing and leading men. Antranig, she wrote, saved the remaining Armenians in Bitlis who had somehow survived the earlier massacres there.[36] An Armenian physician, Dr. Bonapartian of Harpoot, also spoke at the meeting. While serving as a military doctor in the Turkish Army near Erzerum, he learned about the widespread massacres of Armenians. Fearing he would also be killed, Dr. Bonapartian escaped and went over to the welcoming Russian lines. Other business at the conference included sending telegrams of thanks to President Wilson, Barton, Willoughby-Smith, the United States Ambassador at Petrograd, Lord Bryce, and others. The event ended happily with the Americans entertaining the Armenians, and with toasts on all sides. Mrs. Maynard carefully pointed out that the missionaries toasted in lemonade.[37]

Although the Board seemed anxious to rehabilitate the image of Muslims among its supporters, the *Herald* was not above criticizing Muslim activities to help the needy. The Muslims, wrote the *Herald*, called their society for medical and relief work the "Red Crescent," a blatant copy of the idea of the Red Cross. Much of the work resembled that of the Red Cross, wrote the *Herald*; both societies established and maintained field hospitals with ambulances, doctors and nurses, and both provided food and clothing for those made destitute by the war. But, stated the *Herald*, a fundamental difference existed between the cross and the crescent. In contrast to the Red Crescent, which suggests ambition and power, "the Red Cross represents the idea of sacrifice and service to the uttermost. It tells its purpose and its motive in its very name." Nevertheless, stated the *Herald*, "...we welcome the Red Crescent Society and its work for the suffering. Its inspiration, after all, comes not from the Crescent, but from the Cross."[38] The *Herald* thus disparaged Turkish attempts at service, not because of something that the Red Crescent Society had done or failed to do, but because it was a Muslim organization.

The Board not only saw the Red Crescent Society as inspired by the Christian cross, it also viewed the conquest of Palestine by General Allenby as symbolic of the triumph of Christianity. "The capture of Jerusalem by the British forces is an event that thrills the Christian world," the Board wrote. Reminding its readers that the Board had sent its first missionaries, Pliny Fisk and Levi Parsons, to the Holy Land in 1819, almost one hundred years earlier, the *Herald* judged General Allenby's conquest of the Holy Land a "staggering blow" to both Turkish prestige and the whole Islamic world. Although the British Army's entrance into the city did not outwardly resemble Christ's arrival on a a donkey, admitted the *Herald*, the two events were linked: "Blessed is he who cometh in the name of the Lord," exulted the *Herald*.[39]

All of the *Herald's* readers would have been familiar with the story of Christ's entrance into Jerusalem from annual "Palm Sunday" enactments in their own churches, if not from their own Bible reading. Linking General Allenby's entrance into Jerusalem, however, with that of Christ's demonstrates the tendency of belligerent nations to equate their doings with God's will, while indirectly (and sometimes explicitly) implying that their opponents' actions were not.

As a mission board whose aim was to bring about the Kingdom of God on earth, the Board devoted a full page in the *Herald's* January issue about the need for additional missionaries. Estimating that 175 missionaries and relief workers were needed in Turkey, the Board wanted to move forward in selecting and training recruits, so that workers could leave the United States as soon as the war ended.[40] Through this advertisement, the Board made it plain that it expected the Allies to win the war within the next few months.

Henry H. Riggs, a long time Board worker at Harpoot, responded to these plans with a lengthy essay published in the February 1918 issue of the *Herald*, titled "Turkey Calls to the American Board." In that article, H. H. Riggs took issue with the Board about the number of recruits needed. One hundred seventy-five was "pitifully inadequate," he maintained. Because of the Turks' genocidal murder of both Protestant and Gregorian clergy, the Gregorians as well as the Protestants were looking to the missionaries for spiritual guidance, stated H. H. Riggs. The Muslim rulers of Turkey had suffered setbacks: military losses, the repudiation of the Caliph, the defection of the Arabs, and the fall of Jerusalem. These events, Riggs predicted, would lead to religious liberty in Turkey by the end of the war. Indeed, he added, the Board, which had spent the last century planning to covert Muslims and had failed, even though it had spent one-third of its resources on Armenians, would now have opportunities to introduce the Word of God to the other four-fifths of Turkey. Moreover, wrote H. H. Riggs, the Turks now realize "that the extermination of the Armenians was a crime for which they must answer at the bar of God and man."[41]

Riggs also spoke enthusiastically about Kurds, who he believed naturally felt closer to the missionaries because of their own Christian ancestors. On the whole, Riggs claimed, they had sided with Armenians, doing much to rescue and assist the Armenians. By the end of the war, he prophesied, they will no doubt ask the Board to send evangelists to them to help establish mission schools and centers.[42]

Riggs' essay represents the kind of panglossian longing the Board's staff frequently fell victim to over the course of their long ministry in Turkey. Success on the mission field of Turkey was always "right around the corner," if only sufficient personnel could be obtained to do the job. Riggs' article may therefore have been published to enable the Board to go to its supporters, citing the "rebellion in the ranks" of experienced mission staff demanding significantly increased support for the Board's programs in Turkey. The article does, however, acknowledge that the Turks were responsible for the extermination of Armenians, a change in position from those who saw Germany as the instigator and beneficiary of the genocide. Whatever the merits of the article, it kept before the *Herald's* readers the Board's primary goal of converting Muslims and suggests that the Board had been interested in the Armenians only as a stepping-stone to Muslims.

Regardless of what would happen in the future, the more immediate concern was relief work. In Constantinople few problems occurred. The Board's staff received funds without difficulty and distributed them easily. Turkish officials were cordial and allowed the Americans such privileges as being out on the street after curfew. Some of the Board's academic institutions operated without hindrance.[43]

But if Constantinople showed relative calm at this point, Moscow was in a state of upheaval. Although the Board staff actively conducted YMCA work in the Russian city, an area only tangentially related to the Board's work in Turkey and the Caucasus, the *Herald* reported changes sweeping through the Russian Church. Radical reforms, resulting from the Russian Revolution, now mandated that the Russian Church's priesthood be elected; both clergy and laity had the power to choose the bishops and other higher clergy, wrote the *Herald*. "The religious tyranny in which 180,000,000 have been held fast is broken," crowed the Board in its January issue. But the new era did not open Russia's doors to Protestants only, the *Herald* warned; the Vatican, particularly the Jesuits, was also seeking converts in Russia.[44]

The March issue of the *Herald* included news about additional ACASR workers who were being sent to Tiflis via Vladivostok to supplement the Yarrows, the Maynards, Raynolds, and Gracey. Setting out on a twelve-day railroad journey from Vladivostok, the Board's staff clashed with soldiers who threatened to throw them off the train but never carried out their threats. Such was the propensity for violence in Russia that government officials had posted a notice in all seriousness in the railroad cars that said, "Please do not shoot in the cars, or kill the engineers or guards. All the world will hear of it. Don't throw passengers out of the window while the train is in motion." The new relief workers reached Moscow safely, only three days after revolutionary fighting erupted in that city.[45]

The missionaries' presence in Russia caused them to take a fresh look at the Russian Church. Veteran Board missionary Fred Field Goodsell, then doing YMCA work in Moscow, wrote an essay published two months later in the *Herald* that signaled more favorable views of the Orthodox Church. Extolling its mystical services resplendent with glorious liturgies and beautiful icons, Goodsell argued that the Russian Church could not be ignored; in addition, it had had the most experience of any Church in dealing with Islam. He hoped the revolutionaries' proclamation of new religious freedoms meant opportunities for the development of other religious groups. What will be the "dominant spiritual influence in Russia?" Goodsell asked. "Will it be German *kultur*, with its Christlessness, or the ideals of humanity and brotherhood and justice … as championed by the noblest statesmen of the Entente Powers, including Russia?"[46] Unsure of what the Board's future role in Turkey would be, the tantalizing prospect of dispatching Board missionaries to Russia suggested by Goodsell's essay must have intrigued many readers of the *Herald*.

APRIL - JUNE 1918

THE NEW YORK TIMES

As starvation continued to stalk the refugees in the Caucasus, massacres broke out anew. The *Times* reported the slaughter of Armenians and Greeks at Trebizond, calling the city that "favorite butcher shop of Armenians and Greeks." "Turkey for the Turks," the paper stated sarcastically.[47]

The renewal of the Turkish offensive in the Caucasus, its effects on the civilian population, and the culpability of Germany served as the subjects of several articles in the *Times* in April.

In a story headed with large capital letters reading "Asks Berlin To Stop Killings By Turks," the Russian People's Commissariat for Foreign Affairs reportedly complained to Berlin that the slaughter of Armenians was continuing at a rapid pace.

> The offensive of the Turkish troops and detachments on the Caucasian front has been followed by the murder of the whole

Armenian population. The peaceful population of women and children has been killed without mercy and their property has been plundered and burned.[48]

The demobilization of the Russian troops facilitated the renewed slaughter of Armenians, as conditions deteriorated to their nadir, reported the *Times*.[49] Now even American missionaries were threatened by the Turkish advance.[50]

The Russians insisted that the Treaty of Brest-Litovsk had mandated that the people of Ardahan, Kars, and Batum *alone* would determine their own destiny. The Turks ignored these treaty provisions, stated the *Times*, and continued their old policies of annihilating Armenians. This horrific evil, continued the newspaper, lay squarely at the hands of the German government, whose treaty with Russia had helped Turkey to obtain these regions.[51]

The Russians also forwarded a desperate plea to the President of the German Reichstag and the German Ministry of Foreign Affairs from the Armenian National Council, described as the supreme body for the expression of the will of the Armenian people. Echoing the claims of the Russian People's Commissariat for Foreign Affairs, the Armenian organization urged the Germans to stop their ally from invading the undefended country between Russia and Turkey and killing every Turkish Armenian and Russian found there: "It rests with Germany to prevent the habitual excesses of the Turkish troops, increased by revengefulness and anger."[52]

By late May, the *Times* reported that the Turks had extended their new offensive all along the Caucasian front. Under the headline "Blames Germany for Turk Massacres," the *Times* noted that "[a]nother Armenian massacre has been begun." "Negotiations between the Caucasian Diet and the Turks had broken down because of the exorbitant demands of the Ottoman government," stated the Russian Commissioner for Foreign Affairs who sent the following telegram to the German Foreign Office:[53]

> In the Turkish advance on the Caucasus the peaceful population, including women and children, is being cut down ruthlessly by the thousands. The treaty we were forced to sign at Brest-Litovsk provided that the populations at Ardahan, Kars, and Batum should have full freedom and the right to control their destiny in their own way. The events in these regions show that the policy of extermination which has been followed for the last ten years is still being pursued.[54]

Conditions in the Caucasus remained bleak. Under the heading "Slay 10,000 Armenians," the *Times* charged that ten thousand Armenians had been killed within a fortnight.[55] Approximately two weeks later, under the headline "New Slaughter of Armenians," the newspaper described a conference of the Labor Party in Britain at which Mikael Varandian, an Armenian journalist from Tiflis, spoke. After recounting the Turkish atrocities occurring earlier in the war, Varandian informed the conference that the Turks had sent Socialists "invented for the purpose" to Scandinavia to declare that Armenians had brought retribution upon themselves by first killing Turks. Now that the Georgian Army had ceased fighting after the capture of Batoum, the Armenians represented the sole force resisting the Turks.[56] While these *Times*' stories did not contain solicitations for donations for ACASR, the newest outbreak of warfare, together with the renewed attacks on Armenian civilians, pointed to the ongoing need for relief.

In the United States, ACASR, now renamed the American Committee for Relief in the Near East (ACRNE), continued its advocacy for Armenian refugees. On June 28, 1918, it sponsored a luncheon held in Manhattan "for prominent editors, authors, and writers." A split in thinking, however, arose between Cleveland H. Dodge and Henry Morgenthau. The news story, labeled "Divergent Views in Near East Situation," with the sub-heading "Cleveland H. Dodge Against War with Turkey, Morgenthau for Intervention," asserted that Dodge opposed a declaration of war against Turkey because "as long as we hold a threat over the Turks, they will behave themselves, but the minute war is declared there will be great trouble." Indeed, he added, they will "gobble up everything we have in the Empire," undoubtedly including the mission properties. Morgenthau, on the other hand, rejected the idea that no country should intervene in the affairs of another, but instead wanted all Americans to understand the gravity of the Armenians' situation so they would give generously to provide the needed funds. At the literary meeting, ACASR announced a campaign to raise $30,000,000 for relief work during the week of November 23 to November 30.[57] This quarter of the year ended without any resolution of the Armenians' situation.

THE MISSIONARY HERALD

The *Herald* looked forward, hoping for an end to the war that had now lasted almost four years. What changes would the end of the war bring in Turkey, asked the *Herald*. Quoting Sir William Ramsay, "an eminent student of Asia Minor and of modern Turkey," the magazine presented American missionaries as examples of economic management, moral vigor, and the highest standards of conduct. Thus, said the *Herald*, the Board's missionaries would be perfectly positioned and eminently qualified to help create a modern Turkey. As the Board was now actively recruiting 175 new men and women for service in Turkey, Ramsay's endorsement could not have come at a better time.[58]

Composed in November, 1917, but published in April, 1918, a letter from Crawford of Trebizond recorded the kinds of plans the missionaries had for Turkey before the signing of the Treaty of Brest-Litovsk. Crawford intended to open an American orphanage and to do other relief work in Trebizond for Armenians who had been saved during the winter of 1915-1916. Having located some abandoned Armenian homes, the missionary was organizing repairs the day after the Russians had taken the city. That same day, a delegation from wealthy Russian Armenians

> ...assumed all this work. ... [T]he great, bighearted Russians themselves formed the "Union of Cities," and a similar society the "Union of Provinces," and these have cared for the sick, clothed the naked, and provided food, soup kitchens, etc., for the poor and hungry, of all sorts and classes and nationalities.[59]

All such plans ended, of course, when the Russians abandoned their Turkish front.

The *Herald* often published stories about individual male evangelists that portrayed a kind of "missionary adventurer," a type of "muscular Christian" who was able to handle himself in a variety of situations. A typical account concerned missionary train travel in the Caucasus in 1918. On occasion, Mr. Maynard had to make a trip to Tiflis to consult with Willoughby-Smith about issues involving Russian transport. With a system of regular conveyance, ACASR could supply flour and sugar to twelve thousand refugees. Forced to travel in third class, Mr. Maynard accompanied by his colleague Mr. Yarrow found themselves sharing a train car with exceptionally filthy soldiers who were infested with "live things which it is not polite to mention." The soldiers assumed that the evangelists were spies and conducted a little trial of them on the train. After the soldiers had found the two men "not guilty" of these charges, a German-speaking soldier approached them and spoke to them in German. The missionaries wisely answered: "we do not understand 'Russian'."[60]

Despite the relatively short distance, the train pulled off the tracks and waited at numerous junctions and sidings along the way. After accusations by a soldier that the missionaries had stolen twenty-five rubles from him, the ride got even more uncomfortable. Finally, a kind-hearted nurse took them on to the military hospital train and they were able to sleep in a clean and comfortable bed.[61] The story provides a detailed picture of the difficulties involved in obtaining food for the refugees, as well as the acumen of the relief workers. The savvy missionaries were made of stern stuff.

Rev. Stapleton of Erzerum had written earlier of his concern about the spiritual welfare of Armenians. Although his program of industrial relief went well, he was disappointed that only ten congregants took Holy Communion: "[A]t this time of such suffering [it is sad] that so few avail themselves of this one means of grace." Stapleton looked forward to opening day schools in the city that would early on inculcate in the children a closer relation with God. Stapleton was also learning Russian, he wrote, and busy in many different ways, but lonely for lack of letters. Commenting on Stapleton's letter, the Board wondered whether he was still in Erzerum after the Turks had recaptured the city.[62]

In that section of the magazine called "The Portfolio," the *Herald* reprinted an article written by religion writer William T. Ellis. Originally published in the *Saturday Evening Post*, the essay, which described the work done by ACASR, began by asking the reader to visualize a

> ...monkey-faced babe. When little children are starving, their skin grows taut and their eyes pop out until they look like wee apes. This particular child [was] trying to draw food from empty breasts that hang limp against the bony body of a woman who looks to be seventy years old. By all reason and expectation, the miserable morsel of humanity should have perished within a month of birth, for the mother has scarcely clothes or food for herself, or yet nourishment for her child.
>
> [A] great and beautiful and heart-breaking hope sustains her, and myriads of others–that the Americans will come with relief.... In the far, waste places of earth, where famine stalks, the name that is synonymous with rescue and life is America."[63]

Having captured the reader's interest through this imagery, the rest of the story described the ACRNE's funding, highlighting that all contributions went to relief work and nothing to administrative costs. "Yankee ingenuity," wrote Ellis, developed the concept of industrial relief in all its permutations. The article also tied successful relief administration to the outcome of the war, for refugees could be resettled in their homes once "we have put the firm of William, Mohammed & Co. Out of business,'" stated Ellis. Ellis also praised the missionaries for their ability to withstand the emotional strain of helping the refugees who struggled to survive amidst such widespread misery.

> Only those who have had to listen to the cry of the starving for food when there is no food, to the frantic pleas of a mother that their little children be accepted as a gift, and to the despair of men who are helpless to care for their families, can know what a toll is extracted from the spirit.[64]

In the same issue of the *Herald*, the Board presented its assessment of the changes occurring in the Muslim world. Islam, boasted the *Herald*, no longer remained a united religious body, but was rapidly breaking away from its traditional conservatism. Having lost Mecca and Medina, the holy places of Islam, the "discouraged and disheartened Moslems of Turkey have the right to expect from the American Board and its missionaries, that they now prepare to teach them the content, claims, and promises of our blessed Christianity." And, concluded the *Herald*, the missionaries in the field have recognized this and were preparing themselves to address this historic opportunity.[65] At long last the missionaries believed they had the possibility of fulfilling the Board's original purpose – conversion of the Muslims.

As had already been reported by the *Times*, the political situation in eastern Turkey and the Caucasus had begun to unravel, with ominous portent for Armenians and the Board's ministry to them. The "surrender of Russia [in the Treaty of Brest-Litovsk] added heavily to the burdens and anxieties of American Board missionaries in Turkey and the Russian Caucasus," stated the *Herald*.[66] By treaty, the *Herald* continued, the Turks had now regained the territory seized by the Russians during 1875 and again in 1916. The Ottomans had recovered the Turkish cities of Trebizond, Erzingan, Erzerum, and Van without a struggle and had now subjected them to "the cruel devices of the Turk, reinforced by German pressure."[67] Warned the *Herald*:

Turkey may even march unresisted [sic] across what used to be the border into the [Russian] district of Echmiadzin and Erivan, with its large Armenian population, increased by the refugees who dragged themselves thus far and thought they had reached safety. With no government to protect them and no arms to defend, unless, indeed, they may be able to arm themselves for self-defense, these wretched people are again exposed to the cruel devices of the Turk, reinforced by German pressure which has been for some time exerted upon the Tartars, to encourage an attack upon these Armenians and the Georgians, their fellow-Christians in that region.[68]

Turkey had also demanded and had received the town of Batoum on the Black Sea coast, stated the *Herald*. The Turks were such "keen schemers themselves," continued the *Herald*, they must have recognized Germany's motives in forcing Russia to yield to Turkey, and that Germany had intended to seize the port of Batoum to establish a permanent German force in the region. As a result of German ambitions on the Black Sea that would have made Turkey a vassal of Germany, the *Herald* opined, Turkey had become disillusioned with Germany.[69]

But, because the changes brought about by the Bolshevik Revolution allowed Turkey to regain her territory, the Turks had grown arrogant and become a menace to Russian Armenia. Now Turkey could also threaten mission interests and perhaps the lives of the American missionaries themselves. The situation, stated the *Herald*, was grave. Worst of all, the fighting had hampered relief efforts.[70]

Communication between the Board and its staff in the Caucasus remained difficult at best. The State Department indicated that it had received no direct communication from Willoughby-Smith since the latter part of February, 1918, nor had the British government heard anything from its staff in Tiflis. Both the missionaries and the Consul had sent dispatches by courier to Tehran, Persia, which had been subsequently forwarded by cable to the State Department. In May, the *Herald* reported that conditions in the Caucasus were continuing to deteriorate, with the Turks attacking to the north and seizing territory which the government in Tiflis had decided to defend. The government, made up of Armenians and Georgians, was united against what the *Herald* called a common enemy made up of "Turks, Tartars, and Teutons."[71] In view of this confusing state, ACRNE felt unable to send the $400,000 desperately needed for relief purposes in the Caucasus. While the

Board had little fear that its missionaries would be harmed, the people whom they served, the Armenians, were terrified.[72] The role of Turkey in these events had led the Board to shift its position, now portraying Germany as "reinforcing" Turkey's nefarious activities, rather than as their instigator.

On a different note, Board missionary Isaac Camp, a British citizen, on his return trip to Sivas had been detained in Egypt and joined General Staff Intelligence of the British Egyptian Expeditionary Force. In that capacity, he had been temporarily appointed acting Governor of Bethlehem, until the British named a permanent governor. At Christmas, his responsibilities led him to attend midnight High Mass in the Church of the Nativity and altered his view of other clergy serving in the Near East. He wrote glowingly of the service of the Catholic priests and nuns in the Holy Land, looking upon them "with a great deal more catholicity of judgment than a few years ago," because "many of them have stood by their guns as nobly as our own people have in Asia Minor; and they have been persecuted by the Turk and their work and buildings despoiled in an almost unbelievable fashion."[73] The *Herald's* decision to include this laudatory article about the behavior of the Catholic clergy of Bethlehem demonstrates the *Herald's* propensity for presenting conflicting views about the same issue. Whereas the Board typically decried the influence of the Vatican, here it speaks well of Catholic clergy through the report of one of its staff.

In June 1918, the *Herald* brought its readers up to date about the activities of long time missionary, Dr. Raynolds. Raynolds' letter from Erivan of November 20, 1917 had not been received by the Board at its headquarters in Boston until April 1918. In his missive, Raynolds described a young Armenian man who had gone to seminary in Harpoot, escaped the massacres there with the help of the local Kurds, worked for the missionaries for a time in Van, and ended up in Tiflis where he was ordained at a service where 200 to 300 people were present. Once again, the *Herald* presented a brief biographical sketch that helped humanize the Armenians to whom so much of the relief funds were directed.[74]

The Board continued to look for new staff for the Near East. The *Herald* pointed out that no new missionaries had been sent to Turkey for the last four years. During that time, some twenty missionaries in this field had died or retired, and probably two-thirds of the native Christian leaders "have miserably perished." Those who remain were "greatly incapacitated in strength and vitality." New blood was necessary, said the *Herald*, so the Board could keep to its standard of efficiency practiced at the beginning of the war. Indeed, the magazine concluded by again reminding its readers of the Board's ultimate mission to convert the Muslim population. "The discouraged and disheartened Moslems of Turkey have the right to expect from the American Board and its missionaries that they ... teach them the content, claims and promises of our blessed Christianity."

JULY - SEPTEMBER 1918

THE NEW YORK TIMES

Readers sympathetic to the plight of the Armenians must have been pleased to read in the *Times* an announcement that an additional appropriation of $900,000 had been made by the American Red Cross War Council to ACRNE. During the previous year, the American Red Cross had contributed $3,000,000 to the relief agency.[75]

But the situation in the Caucasus remained perilous. After the withdrawal of the Russian forces, Armenia, Georgia, and Azerbaijan had formed the Transcaucasian Republic; after Georgia and Azerbaijan withdrew and made separate peace with the Turks, the Armenians were now forced to "go it alone." Thus, the National Armenian Council had also been coerced to sign a peace treaty with Turkey, conceding that the districts of Erivan and Echmiadzin as far as the River Karsagh on the east constituted an independent Armenian Republic. The Armenian Council signed the agreement, as the only way to save a large section of the Armenian population from extermination.[76] The Armenians from Kars and Alexandropol, who had survived thus far, had to again flee the advancing Turkish Army.[77] In the United States, ACRNE continued to solicit funds; the newspaper reported that since the beginning of the war, the Committee had raised $13,000,000.[78]

THE MISSIONARY HERALD

While the *Herald* described these political and missionary issues, it also expressed its concern for the Board's missionaries. Lack of communication with the outside world and the sense of isolation continued to be highly stressful for the missionaries in the Caucasus. For months on end, they were cut off entirely from the outside world. The news they received often proved erroneous. One such news account stated that British had forced the Straits and had taken Constantinople. The missionaries had also heard that Germany had driven the Allies back in France.[79]

The reports provided by the *Herald* were not contemporaneous, of course, but they nevertheless provided readers with heroic tales about the missionaries serving in the Near East. In the Caucasus, the Russian government had terminated its grants to families and orphanages. This meant that ACRNE remained the only source of sustenance for the starving refugees. To the lack of food was added the misery of a severely cold climate. Yet the missionaries continued to work energetically to save as many refugees as possible.

With the additional staff that had arrived from the United States, ACRNE had been able to extend the program of industrial relief so that 8,000 women were employed at approximately thirty rubles a month, with some 240,000 rubles in circulation. About two thousand men were employed as carpenters, building spinning wheels and looms and fitting out the new buildings at the orphanages for school rooms and hospital uses. The men earned about one hundred fifty rubles a month, bringing about 540,000 rubles into circulation. Through these employment programs about ten thousand families managed to survive.

One of the services provided by the missionaries was a soup kitchen. It produced soup primarily for the women who came from distances to get wool or cotton to spin. During the severe cold weather, they suffered greatly; they had thin clothing and no food, yet some came on foot over the mountains as far as twenty miles in those conditions. The women could eat the warm soup in a heated room before they had to venture out in the cold again. The doctor would also refer people more hungry than sick, and they would benefit from the soup kitchen as well. When refugees flooded in after the fall of Erzerum, the missionaries borrowed a wagon soup kitchen from the military authorities and took the soup to the refugees.[80]

As mentioned in an earlier issue of the *Herald*, Dr. Raynolds had instituted a medical department by locating an Armenian nurse, pharmacist, and doctor; by creating a hospital out of a trashed house with broken windows; and by providing bedding consisting of mattresses, pillows, and comforters, as well as sheets, towels, and clothing made by the refugees themselves. The needs of the medical department furnished extra employment for weavers, seamstresses, and carpenters, as well as kitchen and laundry staff.[81]

When the Armenian refugees arrived by the thousands from Erzerum, many had frozen hands and feet and required immediate medical care. Although they needed food, the bakers were able to bake only the coarsest kind of corn or rye bread, and it was almost black. Often there was no bread at all. Towards spring, potatoes and grain were sometimes available. Even the missionaries lacked sufficient fuel to keep warm. Raynolds wrote: "I never want to see another place so destitute of everything as Alexandropol was last winter."[82]

In December, ACRNE worker Rev. Theodore Elmer arrived in Erivan, with instructions to go to Echmiadzin, the seat of the Armenian Church, rent a house, live there alone, supervise the on-going work in that city, and begin new relief operations in Ashdarag, a town lying thirty-eight miles to the north of Echmiadzin. Elmer found it extremely difficult to find a house to rent because the town was crowded not only with refugees, but also with the soldiers and officers of the Armenian army, which was preparing to leave for Erzerum to help defend it.[83]

Because cotton spinning had long been an industrial relief program in Echmiadzin, Elmer took it over and increased the number of workers; by the time he left Echmiadzin, forty looms were in operation, and the cloth made was used for making underwear for the orphans. Seven hundred women were employed in spinning the cotton yarn for these looms. Almost every person who worked supported an entire family of refugees. Most of the refugees in Echmiadzin lived in terribly crowded, unsanitary conditions in an old khan and stable belonging to the monastery. In the stable Elmer had found 150 dead horses that the Russians had allowed to starve to death. He got the carcasses moved out.[84]

Elmer also addressed the refugees' spiritual needs by hiring an Armenian priest to visit the sick and perform the last rites over the dead. Every day, refugees died from small pox, typhus, and dysentery. Employing a Gregorian priest showed a significant accommodation by this relief worker who worked for the Board, an organization that had long seen the Gregorian Church as decadent, priest-ridden, and lacking in spirituality.[85]

Elmer's work was so well received by the Holy See at Echmiadzin that the monastery's administrators asked him to take over their non-functional wool shop. The Catholicos, the head of the Church, gave him two large rooms in the refectory of the old monastery close beside the cathedral. The biggest problem, wrote Elmer, was finding trustworthy men to oversee the work.

(Elmer did not indicate what he meant by "trustworthy.") Elmer reorganized the work and employed fifteen hundred women to prepare and spin the wool into yarn, which was then woven into clothing for the orphans. "No cloth could be bought in Echmiadzin for any price," said Elmer.[86]

Elmer had also started a similar industry in Ashdarag. Refugee men were employed to build roads and improve the grounds of an ancient church. He also initiated the construction of an irrigation canal from Erivan, with its excess of water, to Echmiadzin, which had little. The local residents and priests were supportive of this enterprise. Immodestly, Elmer reported he was rapidly becoming the most influential man in this Mecca of the Armenians.[87]

The relief work, however, came to a sudden stop. Fearing Turkish attack, Willoughby-Smith issued an order in March, 1918, requiring that all relief workers leave the Caucasus immediately. The missionaries were heartsick. For more than three years the refugees had been saved from death by the enormous energy expended by the relief workers; to have to leave them now was devastating. The refugees were also traumatized by the exit of the missionaries, some giving way to utter despair. Many of the workers employed by the missionaries were educated men and women from the Board's own mission schools. The missionaries tried to console themselves with the thought that the overseers of the industrial relief were sufficiently skilled to be able to continue the work without the presence of the missionaries. Sufficient funds had been left to carry on the work for three weeks to a month, and the missionaries hoped to be able to provide on-going funds. Yet no one could deny that it was extremely difficult to leave.[88]

The journey out of the Caucasus was perilous. On March 19, the relief workers began their journey from the Caucasus, traveling first by a train with missing windows to Tiflis, and from there to Baku. The Tartars were willing to let them pass through their territory as long as the workers did not try to bring any Armenians with them. Stranded in Baku for two weeks, the missionaries witnessed a battle lasting three days in which the Armenians and Russians fought the Tartars. Blood and human brains were splattered all over the pavements and dead bodies littered the streets. Finally, the relief workers managed to hire a private steamer to cross the Caspian Sea and reach Astrakhan. From there, they traveled up the Volga River and on to Vladivostok, hoping to return to the Caucasus sometime soon.[89]

On May 27, 1918, the State Department received a cable from the American Consul at Vladivostok, informing the Department of the welfare and the current location of the missionaries who had been sent out of the Caucasus by the State Department. Some of the withdrawn missionaries had remained in Russia to do YMCA work along the route of the Trans-Siberian Railroad, or in the port city of Vladivostok. Elmer found employment doing relief work in Persia. Other members of the Caucasus team – Raynolds, the Whites, Miss Orvis, Mr. Partridge, and the Yarrows – headed for Peking (Beijing). Stapleton, formerly of Erzerum, temporarily relocated to Japan.[90]

The Crawfords also contacted the Board, informing it in a letter dated February 14, 1918, that they intended to remain in Trebizond, despite the Russian pullout. They hoped that they could be of use to the terrified Christian population, which had seized any kind of transport available, even crowded, unseaworthy, open boats in the middle of winter, to try to escape from Turkey.[91]

The inability to communicate with its staff remained one of the Board's chief complaints. Because Turkey was allied with Germany against whom the United States had declared war, permission to correspond with staff members in Turkey had to be granted by the War Trade Board in Washington, D.C. Permission was difficult to obtain. For example, the Board was permitted to send one letter per month to Mr. Fowle, who resided in Constantinople. That letter had to be reviewed by the War Trade Board's censors and the State Department. Fortunately, Mr. Chambers was located in Switzerland and could receive brief notes cleared by the Ottoman censor from the mission staff in Turkey, and could then forward the letters to the Board.[92]

Whatever the Board's fears about the Armenian remnant in the Caucasus, it rejoiced that conditions inside Turkey itself had improved, that Turkish officials had become increasingly friendly and more inclined to cooperate with relief workers, and that relief funds now reached the twenty relief centers inside Turkey with greater speed and efficiency.[93]

The *Herald's* portrayal of Turkey as it regained its territory lost to the Russians in 1916 and 1878, and threatened to seize Russian Armenia, illustrates the mixed opinions the Board held about Turkey. In fact, the *Herald's* statements frequently contradicted each other, or at the very least must have puzzled its readers. If the Turks were so cooperative inside Turkey, why should there be such grave fear about the Turkish advance into the Caucasus? Would the Turkish Army in the Caucasus directed from Constantinople be so different from the Turkish officials in Constantinople itself? The *Herald* left these questions unanswered.

OCTOBER - DECEMBER 1918

THE NEW YORK TIMES

The *Times* provided little reporting about the situation facing the Christian minorities in the Near East during the last three months of 1918. In October, the paper reported that a new survey of current needs had been undertaken by ACRNE. The newly named committee launched a week long nation-wide campaign to raise additional funds of $30,000,000 for its efforts in western Asia. ACRNE determined the number of needy to be 2,000,000, with about 935,000 within reach of the distributing forces of the American committee.[94]

The *Times* kept its readers abreast of new massacres and reported the escape of Armenians, Assyrians, and Russians who had broken through the Turkish front in Mesopotamia and thereby escaped from their camps in the desert. The story, headlined "Persian Armenia Ravaged by Turks," also mentioned that British cavalry had beaten back Turkish troops in pursuit of ten thousand refugees who were in Kurdistan or wandering in the hills nearby. Nevertheless, the Turks had massacred some three hundred old men in Urumiah, while 600 Christian women had been distributed among the Turkish troops and the Muslim population of that city.[95] This story was placed on page six of the newspaper. Although similar stories had been front page news in the past, the pending conclusion of the war may have eclipsed the routine tales of massacres in the Near East.

The war ended on November 11, 1918. But if the Armenians thought their troubles were over, they were mistaken. Two days after the Armistice, the *Times* reported that fresh murders of 15,000 Armenians had occurred in a town fifty miles southwest of Bitlis.[96] Later that month, Turkish troops commanded by Nourri Pasha, brother of Enver Pasha, former Minister of War, slaughtered Armenians in the district of Azerbaijan[97] on the border of the Caucasus. Nourri Pasha claimed that he was beyond the jurisdiction of the Constantinople government, which had been defeated in the war, and that he had been requested by the Muslims of Azerbaijan to suppress the revolt of the Armenians. For the Armenians, nothing had changed.

Because Americans at home needed to understand the current situation of the refugees in the Near East, ACRNE announced that the U.S. government had informally incorporated a committee of seven men "to go to the Near East and to prepare for the relief work that the U.S. is to do in that part of the world." The seven men chosen included Barton, Edward C. Moore, Peet,

Harold A. Hatch of New York, Justice Victor Dowling, Rabbi Stephen S. Wise, and John H. T. Main. The men were to proceed on December 31, 1918 in a government relief ship from New York to London and Paris, where they would solicit funds for the relief efforts from the Allied governments. Simultaneously, ACRNE would launch its campaign to raise $30,000,000 for refugees in the Near East.[98]

Despite Turkey's defeat in the war, reported the *Times*, the Turks were pursuing "a brutal attitude toward the Christian populations of the empire and were inciting the Ottoman people to fanatical outrages against the non-Moslems."[99] The Turks, for instance, the *Times* reported, had massacred 10,000 Armenians while evacuating the towns of Baku,[100] Olti, and Ardahan. In some towns, the entire Armenian population was slaughtered. The Young Turk government, the governing body of Turkey during the war and earlier, had reorganized and now opposed the newly established pro-Allied government. The new government, reported the *Times*, was "too weak to enforce respect and obedience." The hapless government was unable to stop violence within its own territory, showing, said the newspaper, that anarchy reigned in Turkey.[101]

President Wilson joined the effort to save the refugees of the Near East by appealing to the public to increase its generosity, so that the more than 4,000,000 Armenian, Syrian, Greek, and other exiles and refugees could be saved. Pointing out that the period for rehabilitation was now at hand, he urged the public to give more generously than it had in the past. The refugees are in "a starving, shelterless condition," the President said, adding that the vast majority of the refugees were women and children, including 400,000 orphans. At the bottom of this article was a short statement from Dutton,[102] in which he declared that the Turkish atrocities had been confirmed. He added that starvation had become so common that "heroic men and women who have strained every bit of energy to save lives now have the unthinkable task of picking out those who shall perish."[103]

To further display governmental approval of ACRNE's work, the *Times* reported that Washington had lent a ship to the committee that would sail about January 15 to transport physicians, nurses, agricultural workers, farm implements, and other supplies to the Near East. The committee continued to describe the refugee conditions in attention-getting ways: Charles P. Gates, President of Robert College, a missionary institution in Constantinople, deemed the situation "desperate." He noted that two million "deported

Armenians, assembled at various towns in hopes of returning to their homes, were starving, and ... only 40,000 of these might survive." The monthly death toll was 20,000.[104]

On December 30, 1918, the *Times* ran two stories: one described a message from the Secretary of the Navy in which he declared himself as deeply supportive of the mission of the relief committee. He encouraged all Americans to make contributions to the cause.[105] James Cardinal Gibbons called the refugee situation the "greatest tragedy of the war" and issued an appeal to all Christians to contribute to this effort even if they had already had done so.[106] These final news stories show the kind of energy expended by the newspaper to keep the issue of the refugees before the American public to encourage them to give generously to the campaign to be kicked off in January. Thirty million dollars were needed to save the more than four million Armenians, Syrians, Greeks and others who had somehow managed to survive, despite the Turkish plan to destroy them. The fate of the refugees now largely rested in American hands.

THE MISSIONARY HERALD

As it did so often, the *Herald* used a story about the death of a young Armenian at the hand of the Turks to describe the kind of situation facing the Armenian refugees. The *Herald* reported that Mr. Partridge, formerly principal of the college at Sivas, had been among the relief workers ordered out of the Caucasus. He had ended up temporarily in Shansi, China, and had preached a sermon translated by a young man, Mr. Kung, whom he had met at Oberlin College years earlier. At that time, Kung had introduced Partridge to his roommate, a young Armenian man who subsequently completed his education and returned to Sivas to teach in Partridge's school. In 1915, the Armenian man was arrested, imprisoned, and urged by prominent Turks to recant to save himself. He refused and was murdered, "one of the numberless Christian martyrs of the Armenian race," wrote the *Herald*.[107]

ACRNE, reported the *Herald*, represented the only organized agency caring for the stricken non-Muslims in Turkey, the Caucasus, and Persia. So far it had raised and dispersed $12,000,000. Thirty million dollars now had to be pledged, stated the *Herald*, with a special effort made in the next month, November, 1918. Barton and Vickery, the executive secretary of the Board, had traveled for a month throughout the U.S. to raise this money. They met with local state committees in many cities throughout the West Coast, in the

Midwest, and on the East Coast. In most places they were hosted by the Chambers of Commerce, Boards of Trade, and other civic organizations. They found among all classes of people and in every faith, including Judaism, Roman Catholicism, Mormonism, and Protestantism of every variety, the firm determination to "defeat, if possible, the concerted endeavor to destroy the non-Moslem populations of Turkey."[108]

The October issue of the *Herald* included a five-page description of Partridge's escape from the Caucasus together with the other ACRNE workers. The article added new information on the heroic adventures of the relief workers, telling that not only the Turks, but also the Germans and the Tartars were advancing on Tiflis. The missionaries accepted Consul Willoughby-Smith's direction, Partridge wrote, because they would most likely have been interned within a few days and prevented from performing further relief work. The rest of the lengthy article dealt with the experiences of Partridge and his colleagues on the way to Vladivostok, a trip that took seventy-five nights. Only one time in all those nights did Partridge sleep in a bed with a complete outfit of bedding.[109]

The *Herald's* November opening editorial, "The Red Triangle," described the work of the YMCA, whose workers displayed "devotion, loyalty, unstinted service, and the Spirit of Christ at work among the men in khaki." Under this magic symbol, "the most widely known and potent religious symbol in the world," second only to the Cross, wrote the *Herald*, no less than seventeen of the Board's missionaries have worn its uniform, have delivered its message, and have revealed its spirit.[110] This relationship between the Board's missionaries and the YMCA demonstrates the interplay between the Protestant missionary organization of the Board and other Christian organizations involved in service at that time.

The Board also reported in November on its occupied missionary stations, especially about Miss Graffam in Sivas, who had spent the war years alone after her colleague died from typhus. Writing in July 1918, the missionary described how all of the buildings in the mission compound had become orphanages, a scene that would become commonplace all over Asia Minor. In Sivas, four campus buildings had been converted to orphanages, and the Turkish governor had asked her to "take an interest" in organizing another new orphanage in the local Gregorian monastery. The monks apparently had been killed or exiled.[111]

As its "wrap-up" of the year, the Board discussed its plan for the coming year. As soon as the war ends, wrote Barton, new and returning missionaries would enter the field in Turkey, and those who had stayed at their posts would immediately be relieved, so that they might recover from their wartime experiences. Large numbers of missionaries would be needed to help the repatriated refugees to resume their lives in Turkey. Barton wrote:

> The non-Moslems for four years have been hunted and driven like beasts across desert and through mountains, starved, crushed, broken; tens of thousands of them have fallen, and their bones in their glaring whiteness cry out against their murderers. Millions yet survive, and wait in patience the dawn of the day of emancipation, when they need no longer cringe under the blows of a soulless taskmaster, and when they can return to their shattered homes, from which neither they nor their children shall be compelled again in terror to flee. Amidst all these scenes of horror your missionaries have remained.[112]

The Board believed that the refugees would at last be left in peace to restart their broken lives.

Although the *Herald* lamented the cost in human life and treasure, it rejoiced exuberantly at the war's end, saying: "[t]he tyranny of unbridled might is broken. The world is free as it was not before. ... The victory has been won. Praise God!"[113] The peoples of the Ottoman Empire, it added, "face the future, destitute and heartbroken indeed, but with the stir of a new hope." Unlike the armies that had ravaged the Armenians, a new army of "relief and reconstruction" would now redeem the country, wrote the *Herald*. ACRNE's commission to the Near East would take with them one hundred or more persons to begin the work of reconstruction and redemption for the refugees who were still suffering, and so that the more than fifty Board missionaries who had endured the terrible war years could return home.[1154]

The Board opined about the future role of Turkey. While that question would be settled by the Allies, it said, the common consent of public opinion indicated that Turkey had to get out of Europe, relinquish control of the Dardanelles, the Bosporus, or Constantinople, and no longer rule over dependent races. All of these safeguards would prevent the new Turkey from ever abusing its Christian minorities again, stated the *Herald*.[115] How wrong the *Herald* was.[116]

End Notes to The Year 1918

1. "Armenian and Syrian Relief," *New York Times*, 6 January 1918, II, 3.
2. Ibid.
3. Ibid.
4. "Thousands of Armenians Massacred at Samsun," *New York Times*, 4 March 1918, 1. Because this information came from an "official of one of the Central Powers," it had more credibility than if it had been provided by Armenian sources only.
5. "Peace Signed, German Advance Begins," *New York Times*, 4 March 1918, 1.
6. "Thousands of Armenians Massacred at Samsun," *New York Times*, 4 March 1918, 1.
7. "Massacre in Trebizond," *New York Times*, 18 March 1918, 2.
8. Ibid.
9. Ibid.
10. The "republic of the Caucasus" formed a political unit in the Caucasus after the Bolshevik Revolution. The republic of the Caucasus was made up of Azerbaijan, Georgia, and Armenia and claimed that Soviet Russia had no jurisdiction in these areas. See Richard G. Hovannisian, "Armenia's Road to Independence," in *The Armenian People From Ancient to Modern Times, vol II, Foreign Dominion to Statehood: the Fifteenth Century to the Twentieth Century*, (New York: St. Martin's Press,1997), 393-394.
11. "Armenia in the Last Ditch," *New York Times*, 21 March 1918, 12.
12. Richard G. Hovannisian, "Armenian's Road to Independence," *The Armenian People From Ancient to Modern Times, vol. II*, 290. Hovannisian asserts that the Armenian and Georgian troops made up no more than several thousand men who tried to defend a border previously secured by as many as 500,000 Russian troops.
13. "Armenians to Fight," *New York Times*, 22 March 1918, II, 3.
14. "Call for Clothing for War Sufferers," *New York Times*, 24 March 1918, II, 3.
15. The *Times* misspelled his name as "McCullum."
16. "Kaiser and Turks Plan Drive to India," *New York Times*, 18 March 1918, 2. The band of Armenians and Georgians mentioned by Dr. Macallum appears to be the militia described by the *Times* in its editorial of March 21, 1918.
17. *New York Times*, 18 March 1918, 2.
18. "Leave Turkey and Bulgaria Out," *Missionary Herald* CXIV (January 1918), 3-4.
19. Ibid., 3. The idea that Turkey inclined to the side of the U.S. seems particularly far-fetched.
20. Ibid.
21. Ibid.
22. Ibid., 3-4.
23. Ibid.
24. The actual number of Armenians who died during the First World War is contested by Turkish and Armenian scholars. One scholar who has studied this extensively is Taner

Akcam, a Turkish historian. He offers 800,000 as the number of Armenians killed at Turkish hands. Armenian scholars sometimes offer the number of 1,000,000. One of the problems is how to define massacre. Do you count only those persons directly killed by Turks or include those who escaped from Turkey to save their lives only to die of starvation in the Caucasus? Are those who were weakened by their travails and subsequently died from typhus included in the number of Genocide victims?

25. "Keeping Races Alive," *Missionary Herald* CXIV (March 1918), 106.

26. "Activities in Russia," *Missionary Herald* CXIV (January 1918), 23-25.

27. "In the Caucasus," *Missionary Herald* CXIV (March 1918), 130.

28. "The Orphanage," *Missionary Herald* CXIV (January 1918), 27.

29. "In the Caucasus," *Missionary Herald* CXIV (March 1918), 130.

30. "Relief Work in Erivan," *Missionary Herald* CXIV (January 1918), 26-27.

31. The missionaries provided only first names for Garabed and Vartanush, despite their standard practice of using a title and surnames for fellow evangelists.

32. "Relief Work in Erivan," *Missionary Herald* CXIV (January 1918), 26-27.

33. "A Doctor Goes to the Erivan Relief Force," *Missionary Herald* CXIV (February 1918), 74.

34. Ibid., 74-75.

35. "In the Caucasus," *Missionary Herald* CXIV (March 1918), 130-131.

36. Ibid.

37. This story of the Armenian troops who captured Bitlis was included in Chapter 1917.

38. "Toasts in Lemonade," *Missionary Herald* CXIV (January 1918), 26.

39. "Red Cross and Red Crescent," *Missionary Herald* CXIV (February 1918), 59.

40. "He Hath Redeemed Jerusalem," *Missionary Herald* CXIV (January 1918), 4.

41. "Our Greatest Missionary Call," *Missionary Herald* CXIV (January 1918), 53.

42. "Turkey Calls to the American Board," *Missionary Herald* CXIV (February 1918), 64-67.

43. Ibid., 67.

44. "Items from Constantinople," *Missionary Herald* CXIV (March 1918), 129.

45. "Religious Crisis in Russia," *Missionary Herald* CXIV (January 1918), 7-8.

46. "Thanksgiving Day in Moscow," *Missionary Herald* CXIV (March 1918), 129-130.

47. "The Religious Consciousness," *Missionary Herald* CXIV (March 1918), 114-115.

48. "Taalim El Alman," *New York Times*, 1 April 1918, 10.

49. "Asks Berlin to Stop Killings by Turks," *New York Times*, 14 April 1918, I, 3.

50. "Aid for Armenia and Syria," *New York Times*, 22 April 1918, 10.

51. "Turks Killing Americans?" *New York Times*, 29 April 1918, 3.

52. *New York Times*, 14 April 1918, I, 3.

53. "Murder of Mar Shimun," *New York Times*, 15 April 1918, 4.

54. This office was called the "Russian People's Commissariat for Foreign Affairs" in the *Times* story of 14 April 1918. It appears to be the same agency.

55. "Blames Germany for Turk Massacres," *New York Times*, 21 May 1918, 2.

56. "Slay 10,000 Armenians," *New York Times*, 8 June 1918, 5.
57. "New Slaughter of the Armenians," *New York Times*, 22 June 1918, 3.
58. "Divergent Views on Near East Situation," *New York Times*, 29 June 1918, 9.
59. "The Missionary May Save Turkey," *Missionary Herald* CXIV (April 1918), 164.
60. "The Big-Hearted Russians," *Missionary Herald* CXIV (April 1918), 180-181.
61. "Suspected as Spies," *Missionary Herald* CXIV (April 181), 181-182.
62. Ibid.
63. "As It Was in Erzroom," *Missionary Herald* CXIV (April 1918), 179-180.
64. "Help from America," *Missionary Herald* CXIV (June 1918), 238-239.
65. Ibid.
66. "The Moslem Claim," *Missionary Herald* CXIV (June 1918), 250-251.
67. "Russia Increases Turkey's Menace," *Missionary Herald* CXIV (April 1918), 160-161.
68. Ibid.
69. Ibid.
70. Ibid.
71. Ibid.
72. "Turkey's Menace in the Transcaucasus," *Missionary Herald* CXIV (May 1918), 201.
73. Ibid. The Board also mistakenly reported in this article that the Bolsheviks had given the Transcaucasus to Turkey, including Erivan and the railroad line to the Caspian Sea. This account published in May also contradicts the article in the April 1918 issue about the possible threat to the missionaries.
74. "Governor of Bethlehem on Christmas Day," *Missionary Herald* CXIV (May 1918), 232.
75. "A Pastor Ordained at Erivan," *Missionary Herald* CXIV (June 1918), 276.
76. "$900,000 More to Armenia," *New York Times*, 10 August 1918, 7.
77. "More British in Russia," *New York Times*, 17 August 1918, 1.
78. Ibid.
79. "Conference Hears of America's Relief," *New York Times*, 20 September 1918, 14.
80. "In the Caucasus," *Missionary Herald* CXIV (August 1918), 369.
81. Ibid., 372.
82. Ibid.
83. Ibid.
84. This refers to the Armenians who tried to block the Turkish advance after the Russians withdrew from the war.
85. "Like Dante's Hell," *Missionary Herald* CXIV (August 1918), 373-375.
86. Ibid.
87. Ibid.
88. "An Irrigation Canal," *Missionary Herald* CXIV (August 1918):. 374.
89. "Ordered to Leave the Country," *Missionary Herald* CXIV (August 1918), 374-375.

90. Ibid.

91. "A Turkey Bulletin," *Missionary Herald* CXIV (July 1918), 322-325.

92. "The Story of Trebizond," *Missionary Herald* CXIV (July 1918), 323-324.

93. "A Turkey Bulletin," *Missionary Herald* CXIV (July 1918), 322.

94. Ibid., 322-324.

95. "For Relief in the Near East," *New York Times*, 6 October 1918, II, 2.

96. "Persian Armenia Ravaged by Turks," *New York Times*, 6 October 1918, 6.

97. "Turks Are Still Slaying," *New York Times*, 13 November 1918, 10.

98. *New York Times*, 25 November 1918, 3.

99. "Plan Armenian Relief," *New York Times*, 21 December 1918, 22.

100. "10,000 Armenians Fell in Turkish Massacre," *New York Times*, 8 December 1918, 6.

101. Baku does not seem to belong with the other two cities, Oltu and Ardahan, which are located in northeastern Turkey. It is possible that the paper meant "Batum" (Batoum) instead.

102. "10,000 Armenians Fell in Turkish Massacre," *New York Times*, 8 December 1918, 6.

103. Professor Samuel Train Dutton was Secretary of the relief organization ACRNE.

104. "Wilson Aids Relief Fund," *New York Times*, 12 December 1918, 9.

105. "To send Relief Ship," *New York Times*, 26 December 1918, 2.

106. "For Near East Relief," *New York Times*, 30 December 1918, 9

107. "Gibbons Issues Appeal," *New York Times*, 30 December 1918, 3.

108. "Armenia and Shame!" *Missionary Herald* CXIV (October 1918), 435-436.

109. Idem., 436.

110. "Eight Thousand Miles Across Asia," *Missionary Herald* CXIV (October 1918), 445-449.

111. "The Red Triangle," *Missionary Herald* CXIV (November 1918), 483.

112. "Activities in Sivas," *Missionary Herald* CXIV (December 1918), 500.

113. "Turkey," *Missionary Herald* CXIV (November 1918), 515.

114. "Laus Deo!," *Missionary Herald* CXIV (December 1918), 534.

115. "Turkey's Surrender," *Missionary Herald* CXIV (December 1918), 534.

116. Ibid.

117. Turkey still struggles with the question of religious freedom. Nationalist circles in Turkey hounded and assassinated Hrant Dink, the editor of the Armenian *Agos* newspaper, in front of his office in Istanbul in January, 2007. They brutally executed three Protestant Bible workers in Malatya in April, 2007, and murdered an Italian Catholic priest in Trabzon in February, 2006.

Chapter 7

CONCLUSION

In her Pulitzer Prize winning book, Samantha Power called Genocide "a problem from hell," and identified the Armenian massacres of 1915 as the first Genocide of the twentieth century.[1] While the facts of what she calls a "race murder" were known throughout the world, thanks to such publications as the *New York Times* and the *Missionary Herald*, only the British made attempts to punish the perpetrators. Even those feeble steps to try and punish the persons responsible for planning and committing the atrocities were abandoned after Mustafa Kemal, leader of the newly-formed Republic of Turkey, seized twenty-nine British soldiers whom he agreed to release in exchange for all of the Turkish suspects in British custody. The British public was anxious to get its soldiers released and Britain capitulated, ending attempts to hold the officials of the Ottoman Empire liable for the Genocide of the Armenians.[2]

From the beginning of the First World War until its end, the *Times* and *Herald* kept the American people informed about the events occurring in Turkey and the Caucasus. The resulting outpouring of funds given by Americans to save and care for the surviving victims of Turkey's malevolence towards the Armenians demonstrates that the American public cared about these happenings and wanted to help in any way that they could. Nevertheless, the government of the United States refused to support plans to bring the leaders of the Ottoman Empire to justice. American officials objected to the concept of universal principles of justice that would call for punishment of the perpetrators of Genocide. The laws of humanity were a *personal* principle, not a universal standard, urged United States Secretary of State Lansing, and the sovereign of a land is necessarily exempt from responsibility. If tribunals to try the Turks were established, Secretary Lansing proclaimed, the United States would not participate. America's only interest, he said, was in holding accountable those who injured United States citizens or their property.[3] The discourse about these events died down, eventually disappearing altogether.

American foreign policy has not changed much since Lansing was Secretary of State. Although the prosecution of Slobodan Milosevic demonstrated that American governmental officials had begun to articulate the view that state sovereignty does not protect individuals from culpability for Genocide, only feeble efforts have been made to stop mass murder. In 1994, the Hutus of Rwanda executed 8,000 Tutsi *each day* for *one hundred* days without foreign intervention by the United States, the United Nations, or any other body.[4] In a parallel with the Armenian Genocide, four years of attacks on the people of Darfur have led to the deaths of hundreds of thousands of civilians, while two and one-half million people have been driven from their homes, to face starvation, disease, and rape.[5] Despite mouthing concern, Americans, in both public and private life, have for the most part turned a "blind eye" toward these events.

At the end of the twentieth century, however, interest in the Armenian Genocide has resumed, despite ongoing Turkish attempts to recast the events of the First World War. "[A] consensus has emerged that the Armenian Genocide of 1915 is of universal significance," wrote the noted First World War historian, Jay Winter, in the introduction to a book he edited, *America and the Armenian Genocide of 1915*.[6] The Ottoman Empire, stated Winter, fought a war for national survival in which it turned against an element of its own population, actions that cannot be viewed simply as a result of the end of their imperial hegemony. Other empires also lacking democratic foundations, such as Russia, Germany, and Austria-Hungary, suffered from the same threat of destruction, yet did not conduct "mass slaughter, abuse, and starvation of an ethnic group."[7] Moreover, the threat of Armenian subversion inside the Empire cannot be used as an excuse, Winter asserts. The Germans instigated trouble in Ireland, yet the British government did not exterminate the Irish, nor did Austria-Hungary massacre those of its citizens whom Britain and France were trying to subvert. Only in Turkey did the threat of subversion lead to the deaths of hundreds of thousands of men, women, and children.[8]

Samantha Power, responding to the recent blitz of Turkish lobbying over a proposed House of Representatives Resolution that would acknowledge the Armenian Genocide, wrote that suddenly "historical truths – about events carried out in another continent, in another century – are igniting controversy among politicians as if the harms were unsubstantiated, local and recent."[9] Held hostage by the Turks because of the United States' desire to use Turkish bases to ferry military supplies into Iraq, the United States has again "knuckled under" to Turkish demands that the Armenian Genocide not be acknowledged by the government of the United States. Urging the House of Representatives to stand up to the Turks, she argued that honesty is the best policy. The issue will not go away, she stated, because the vehement support of the Armenian diaspora is increasing, not diminishing. Most importantly, "a stable, fruitful, [twenty-first] century relationship between the United States and Turkey cannot be built on a lie."[10]

While the Turks may be hoping that the passage of time will blunt the demand for recognition of the Genocide, those who read these contemporary accounts cannot help but become aware of the power of the story they tell. The stories told by the *New York Times* and the *Missionary Herald* retain a freshness that demands that their readers confront anew the Armenian Genocide of 1915.

End Notes to Conclusion

1. Samantha Power, *"A Problem From Hell:" America and the Age of Genocide* (New York: Perennial, 2003), 14.

2. Ibid., 16.

3. Ibid., 14.

4. Ibid., 503.

5. United States Holocaust Memorial Museum,"Sudan:Darfur Overview," http://www.ushmm.org/conscience/alert/darfur/contents/01-overview/, accessed November 4, 2007.

6. Jay Winter, "Introduction: Witness to Genocide," in *America and the Armenian Genocide of 1915*, ed. Jay Winter (Cambridge: Cambridge University Press, 203), 1.

7. Jay Winter, "Under Cover of War: The Armenian Genocide in the Context of Total War," in *America and the Armenian Genocide of 1915*, ed. Jay Winter (Cambridge: Cambridge University Press, 203), 49.

8. Ibid.

9. Samantha Power, "The U. S. and Turkey: Honesty is the Best Policy," *http://www.time.com/time/printout/0,8816,1672790,00.html*, accessed November 4, 2007.

10. Ibid.

BIBLIOGRAPHY

Primary Sources

The New York Times, vols. LXIV-LXVIII, 1914-1918.

The Missionary Herald, vols. CX-CXIV, 1914-1918.

Secondary Sources

Ahlstrom, Sidney E. *A Religious History of the American People.* New Haven, CT: Yale University Press, 1972.

The Armenian Genocide: News Accounts From the American Press: 1915-1922, comp and ed Richard D. Kloian, 4th ed. Richmond, CA: Heritage Publishing, 2005.

Balfour, John Patrick Douglas, Baron Kinross. *The Ottoman Centuries: The Rise and Fall of the Turkish Empire.* New York: Morrow Quill Paperbacks, 1977.

Barton, James L. *Daybreak in Turkey.* Boston: Pilgrim Press, 1908.

Barton, James L. *The Story of Near East Relief (1915-1930): An Interpretation.* New York: Macmillan, 1930.

Bedrosian, Robert. "Armenia During the Seljuk and Mongol Periods." In *The Armenian People From Ancient to Modern Times.* Vol. 1, *The Dynastic Periods: From Antiquity to the Fourteenth Century.* ed. Richard G. Hovannisian. New York: St. Martin's Press, 1997.

Bliss, Edwin Munsell. *A Concise History of Missions.* New York: Fleming H. Revell, 1897.

Bloxham, Donald. *The Great Game of Genocide: Imperialism, Nationalism, and the Destruction of the Ottoman Armenians.* New York: Oxford University Press, 2005.

Chaillot, Christine. "The Ancient Oriental Churches." In *The Oxford History of Christian Worship.* ed. Geoffrey Wainwright, Karen B. Westerfield Tucker. Oxford, England: Oxford University Press, 2006.

Cleveland, William L. *A History of the Modern Middle East.* Boulder, CO: Westview Press, 2000.

Courbage, Youssef and Philippe Fargues. *Christians amd Jews Under Islam.* Translated by Judy Mabro. London: I.B. Tauris, 1997.

Daniel, Robert L. *American Philanthropy in the Near East 1820-1960*. Athens, OH: Ohio University Press, 1970.

Davison, Roderic H. *Turkey: A Short History*, 3d ed. Updated by Clement H. Dodd. Huntingdon, England: Eothen Press, 1998.

Finnie, David H. *Pioneers East: The Early American Experience in the Middle East*. Cambridge, MA: Harvard University Press, 1967.

Garsoian, Nina. "The Arsakuri Dynasty (A.D. 12-[180?-428)" In *The Armenian People: From Ancient to Modern Times*. Vol. 1, *The Dynastic Period: From Antiquity to the Fourteenth Century*. ed. Richard G. Hovannisian. New York: St. Martin's Press, 1997

Global Ministries of the Christian Church (Disciples of Christ) and United Church of Christ. http://www.globalministries.org/index.php?option=com accessed February 18, 2007.

Grabill, Joseph L. *Protestant Diplomacy and the New East: Missionary Influence on American Policy, 1810-1927*. Minneapolis: University of Minnesota Press, 1971.

Hewsen, Robert H. *Armenian: A Historical Atlas*. Chicago, University of Chicago Press, 2001.

Hovannisian, Richard G. "Introduction." In *The Armenian People: From Ancient to Modern Times*. Vol. 1, *The Dynastic Period: From Antiquity to the Fourteenth Century*, ed. Richard G. Hovannisian. New York: St. Martin's Press, 1997.

Kaiser, Hilmar. *At the Crossroads of Der Zor; Death, Survival, and Humanitarian Resistance in Aleppo, 1915-1917*. In collaboration with Luther and Nancy Eskjian. Princeton, NJ: Gomidas Institute Books, 2001.

Kaiser, Hilmar. "Introduction." In *Eberhard Count Wolffskeel Von Reichenberg, Zeitoun, Mousa Dagh, Ourfa: Letters on the Armenian Genocide*, ed. Hilman Kaiser. Princeton, NJ: Gomidas Institute Books, 2001.

Kloian, Richard D., ed. *The Armenian Genocide: News Accounts From the American Press (1915-1922)*.

Lewy, Guenter. *The Armenian Massacres in Ottoman Turkey: A Disputed Genocide*. Salt Lake City: University of Utah Press, 2005.

Makdisi, Ussama. *The Culture of Sectarianism: Community, History, and Violence in Nineteenth-Century Ottoman Lebanon*. Berkeley: University of California Press, 2000.

Moranian, Suzanne E. "The Armenian Genocide and American Missionary Relief Efforts." In *America and the Armenian Genocide of 1915*. Studies in the

Social and Cultural History of Modern Warfare, ed. Jay Winter. Cambridge: Cambridge University Press, 2003.

Henry Morgenthau, *Ambassador Morgenthau's Story*, Doubleday: New York, 1918; reprint, London and Princeton: Gomidas Institute, 2000.

Nersoyan, Tiran. *Armenian Church Historical Studies: Matters of Doctrine and Administration*. New York: St. Vartan Press, 1996.

Nisan, Mordechai. *Minorities in the Middle East: A History of Struggle and Self-expression*, 2d ed. Jefferson, NC: McFarland, 2002.

Parker, Alan. *The Decline & Fall of the Ottoman Empire*. New York: Barnes & Noble Books, 1992.

Peterson, Merrill D. *"Starving Armenians:" America and the Armenian Genocide, 1915-1930 and After*. Charlottesville, VA: University of Virginia Press, 2004.

Pierce, Leslie. *Moralty Tales: Law and Gender in the Ottoman Court of Aintab*. Berkeley: University of California Press, 2003.

Power, Samantha. *"A Problem From Hell:" America and the Age of Genocide*. New York: Perennial, 2003.

Quataert, Donald. *The Ottoman Empire, 1700-1922*. Cambridge: Cambridge University Press, 2000.

Riggs, Alice Shepard. *Shepard of Aintab*. With a new foreword by Constance Shepard Jolly. Princeton, N.J.: Gomidas Institute Books, n.d.

Thomson, Robert. "Armenian Literary Culture through the Eleventh Century." In *The Armenian People: From Ancient to Modern Times*. Vol. 1. *The Dynastic Period: From Antiquity to the Fourteenth Century*, ed. Richard G. Hovannisian. New York: St. Martin's Press, 1997.

Tootikian, Vahan. *Highlights of Armenian Christendom*. Southfield, MI: Armenian Evangelical World Council, 2002.

Trumpener, Ulrich. *Germany and the Ottoman Empire 1914-1918*. Princeton, NJ: Princeton University Press, 1968.

Walker, Christopher. "World War I and the Armenian Genocide." In *The Armenian People: From Ancient to Modern Times*. Vol. II, *Foreign Dominion to Statehood: The Fifteenth Century to the Twentieth Century*, ed. Richard G. Hovannisian. New York: St. Martin's Press, 1997.

Winter, Jay. "Introduction." In *America and the Armenian Genocide*. Studies in the Social and Cultural History of Modern Warfare, ed. Jay Winter, 1-6. Cambridge: Cambridge University Press, 2003.

Winter, Jay. "Under Cover of War: The Armenian Genocide in the Context of Total War." In *America and the Armenian Genocide.* Studies in the Social and Cultural History of Modern Warfare, ed. Jay Winter, 37-51. Cambridge: Cambridge University Press, 2003.

Zurcher, Erik J. *Turkey: A Modern History.* London: I.B. Tauris, 2004.

INDEX

A
Abdul Hamid II, Sultan 12–14, 181
ACASR (American Committee for Armenian and Syrian Relief) 67, 75–85, 90, 91, 103–106, 108, 112–120, 125–129, 133, 134, 137–139, 143, 145, 157–169, 172, 174, 176, 178, 180, 181, 189–198, 201, 204, 205
Adana 41, 111, 121, 125, 127, 145, 147, 150, 170, 183
Aintab 3–5, 13, 17, 50, 74, 115, 125, 126, 145, 147
Alai Bey 112
Aleppo 5, 10, 21, 102, 103, 117, 125, 130, 136, 142, 145, 147, 168, 170, 174
Alexandropol (Gumri) 167, 179, 197, 210, 212
Allenby, General 199
Antioch 35
Ardahan 12, 190, 203, 216
Assyrians 15, 165, 215
Atkinson, Dr. Henry H. 58, 59, 116, 184
Azerbaijan 210, 215

B
Baghdad 5, 13, 142, 160, 174, 189
Baku 179, 191, 196, 213, 216
Barton, Dr. James L. 22, 23, 41, 67, 68, 74, 79, 85, 90, 111, 139, 148, 158, 199, 215, 217, 219
Batum 190, 203
Bayazid 126, 197

Beirut 158, 174, 180, 189
Bernstorff, Count von 66, 67
Beyazit 12
Bitlis 17, 56, 62, 63, 82, 86, 87, 109, 117, 174, 176, 198, 215
Bonapartian, Dr. 198, 199
Brousa (Bursa) 145, 160, 170
Bryan, William Jennings (US Secretary of State) 54
Bryce, Viscount James 64, 78, 82, 83, 102, 107, 138, 139, 141, 142, 146, 158, 199

C
Caesarea (Kayseri) 66, 130, 142, 160, 168
Cairo 174, 189
Camp, Isaac 209
Cardashian, Vahan 120, 121
Case, Dr. and Mrs. 59
Cecil, Lord Robert 84
Chambers, Rev. Nesbitt 41, 42, 121, 122, 150
Chambers, William N. 191, 214, 218
Charif Pasha, Mehmed (Grand Vizier) 78
Clark, Dr. 51, 58
Cowley, Lord 17
Crane, Charles R. 25, 67, 68, 76, 82, 105, 108, 117, 158, 159
Crawford, Dr. Lyndon S. 58, 71, 134, 135, 182, 183, 205, 214
Crewe, Lord 63
Cushman, Miss 146, 168

D

Damascus 6, 10, 117
Dardanelles 57, 162, 219
Dersoon Effendi (Kurdish sheik) 112
Dilijan 127
Diyarbekir 56, 64, 66, 125, 142
Djevad Eyou 106
Dodd, Dr. W. S. 44
Dodge, Cleveland H. 21, 55, 68, 158, 204
Dodge, D. Stuart 68
dogu 203
Dowling, Justice Victor 216
Dutton, Samuel 67, 68, 84, 158, 216

E

Ebussuud Efendi 6
Echmiadzin 126, 178, 197, 208, 210, 212, 213
Eliot, Charles W. 63
Elisavetpol 85
Elkus, Abram I. (US Ambassador, Constantinople) 131, 145, 172
Ellis, William T. 206, 207
Elmer, Rev. Theodore 212–214
Ely, Miss 86
Enver Pasha (Ottoman Minister of War) 52, 191, 215
Erivan (Yerevan) 85, 117, 125, 128, 166, 167, 171, 172, 177–179, 196–198, 208–213
Erivan Plain 104, 105
Erzerum 13, 17, 35, 36, 44, 51, 54, 58, 60, 66, 74, 107, 113, 117, 118, 123, 142, 149, 171, 179, 182, 183, 195, 197, 199, 206, 207, 211, 212, 214
Erzingan 197, 207

F

Fisk, Pliny 16, 199
Fowle, Mary C. 137, 159, 160, 214

G

Garmaloo 197
Gates, Charles P. 216
Gibbons, James Cardinal 217
Goodsell, Fred Field 202
Gracey, Rev. 129, 134, 166, 167, 176, 177, 196, 201
Gracie, Rev. George 125
Graffam, Mary Louise 51, 58, 59, 86, 137, 159, 160, 168, 218
Greeks 3, 8, 15, 16, 36–39, 62, 67, 80, 85, 88, 135, 141, 149, 159, 160, 165, 172, 181–184, 202, 216, 217
Greer, Bishop 63
Grey, Lord 140

H

Haas, Dr. 125
Hadjin 112, 113, 170
Hagobian Taft, Elise 20
Halil Bey 81, 143, 144
Hamlin, Dr. 130
Harpoot 13, 17, 44, 58, 59, 61, 85, 115, 116, 119, 142, 145–147, 170, 171, 182, 184, 198, 200, 209
Hatch, Harold A. 216
Heald, Mr. 197
Heizer, Oscar (US Consul, Trebizond) 135
Hickson, Mrs. Mary 129
Hill, Richard 117

J

Jackson, Jesse (US Consul, Aleppo) 21, 102
James, Arthur Curtiss 68
Javid Bey 15
Jemal Pasha (Ottoman Minister of Marine) 15
Jerusalem 174
Jews 3–9, 16, 40, 84, 85, 146

K

Kaish, Mr. S. S. 101, 102

Kars 12, 85, 179, 190, 197, 203, 210
Karsagh river 210
Katma 20
Kennedy, Dr. 198
Knapp, Dr. 85
Konia 44, 126, 145, 146, 160
Kung, Mr. 217

L
Leslie, Rev. F. H. 71, 83, 88
Loughbridge, Miss Stella N. 168

M
Macallum, Dr. F. W. 125, 134, 191, 192
MacLaren, Grisell 61, 87, 174, 175
Mahdesian, Arshag 81, 101, 102, 106, 107, 144
Main, John H. T. 216
Mamakhatun 118
Marash 13, 69, 145, 147, 160, 168
Mardin 17, 60, 86, 115, 116, 119, 130
Marsovan 17, 38, 39, 42, 51, 111, 115, 130, 131, 136, 167, 168, 173
Martha, Schwester 61, 87
Maynard, Rev. and Mrs. 136, 174, 176, 180, 198, 201, 205
Mercier, Cardinal 145
Merrill, Mr. 74, 146
Meskene 157
Mezereh (Elazig) 59, 116
Moks (Bahçesaray) 64
Moore, Edward C. 215
Morgenthau, Henry (US Ambassador, Constantinople) 18–21, 54–57, 60, 65, 77, 78, 83, 84, 90, 108, 119–123, 158, 163, 181, 204
Mosul 9, 10, 142
Mott, John R. 68
Moush 56, 57, 82, 109, 142, 171
Mufti of Hadjin 112
Mufty-Zade, Zia 79–81

Munif Bey, Djelal 79
Murray, Professor Gilbert 140

N
Nazim Bey, Dr. 85
Nicholas, Grand Duke 126
North, Frank Mason 68
Nourri Pasha 215

O
O'Connor, T. P. 84
Orvis. Miss 214

P
Parsons, Levi 16, 199
Partridge, Mr. 60, 214, 217, 218
Pears, Sir Edwin 39
Peet, William W. 43, 50, 51, 112, 123, 131, 160, 161, 165, 169, 170, 172, 215
Peters, Mr. (US Consular representative, Samsun) 131
Petrograd (St. Petersburg) 35, 36, 64, 70, 88, 109, 199
Putnam, George Haven 109

R
Racoubian, Roupen 38
Ramsay, Sir William 205
Raynolds, Dr. George C. 75, 86, 136, 162, 171, 176, 196, 197, 201, 209, 211, 214
Revere, Paul 134
Rhinelander, Bishop Philip M. 63
Riggs, Rev. Charles T. 40, 41
Riggs, Rev. Henry 44, 200, 201
Riza Bey, Ahmed 113
Ryan, Rev. Arthur C. 149

S
Samsun 66, 82, 131, 189, 190
Sasun 34, 102, 145, 146, 171
Seligman, Isaac N. 63
Serabian, R. N. 144
Sewney, Dr. and Mrs. 51
Sewny, Dr. and Mrs. 51, 58, 59

Shane, Myrtle 87, 174, 175
Shepard, Dr. Fred Douglas 116
Sidon 174
Sivas 38, 51, 58, 60, 86, 115, 130, 137, 142, 145, 147, 159, 160, 168, 209, 217, 218
Sloane, William 68
Smith, Dr. Floyd 125
Smith, Edward Lincoln 71, 72
Smyrna (Izmir) 16, 19, 22, 111, 125, 145
Stapleton, Rev. and Dr. 59, 74, 118, 119, 123, 124, 149, 150, 182, 195, 196, 206, 214
State Department 21, 22, 50, 55, 56, 61, 67, 74, 76, 77, 79, 106, 116, 129, 131, 133, 145, 158, 162, 208, 213, 214
Storey, Moorfield 140
Straus, Oscar S. (US Ambmassador to Constantinople) 63, 105, 181

T

Tabriz 174
Talaat, Mehmet (Ottoman Minister of Interior) 14, 15, 48, 49, 52
Talas 50, 60, 111, 168, 169
Tarsus 111, 145, 160
Taxim Bey 118
Tchorum (Chorum) 20
Teheran 174, 189
Thom, Dr. Daniel 60, 116
Tiflis 54, 61, 74, 75, 81, 85–87, 112, 117, 125–127, 133, 136, 172, 174, 189, 196, 201, 204, 205, 208, 209, 213, 218
Trebizond (Trabzon) 13, 44, 58, 66, 71, 117, 134, 135, 142, 182, 184, 190, 197, 202, 205, 207, 214

U

Urfa 13, 50, 66, 71, 83, 88, 125, 142, 147
Urmiah 54, 55
Ussher, Dr. Clarence 44, 61, 70, 73–75, 86, 114, 149, 197

V

Van 9, 44, 54–57, 61, 62, 70–74, 77, 82, 86, 87, 109, 114, 117, 126, 127, 130, 134, 136, 142, 149, 171, 197, 207, 209
Varandian, Mikael 204
Vladivostok 124, 196, 201, 213, 218

W

Walsh, Mr. 197
White, George E. 38, 42, 51, 131, 132, 158, 173, 214
Williams, Aneurin 64
Willoughby-Smith, F. (US Consul, Tiflis) 88, 117, 125, 127, 172, 196, 199, 205, 208, 213, 218
Wilson, Rev. 117, 125, 127, 128
Wilson, Woodrow (US President) 21, 37, 54, 55, 68, 83, 91, 105, 106, 119, 128, 133, 146, 162, 181, 199, 216
Wingate, Rev. Henry 60
Wise, Rabbi Stephen S. 68, 216

Y

Yarrow, Rev. and Mrs. 61, 77, 136, 171, 176–179, 196–198, 201, 205, 214

Z

Zbinden, Miss 132
Zeitun 12, 19, 54, 55, 76
Zenger, Miss 51, 58, 59
Zinzirdere 169
Zor (Der Zor) 117, 148, 157, 194

ABOUT THE AUTHOR

Anne Elizabeth Elbrecht is a graduate of Wheaton College, Illinois, where she majored in History. She received her training in librarianship at the University of California Berkeley, following which she served as a Peace Corps librarian in Ghana, West Africa. After she returned home, she began working as a librarian at the State Law Library in Sacramento. It was there that she met her husband, the late Richard Elbrecht. Shortly after her marriage, Anne completed her training in Law, passed the bar, and was licensed as an attorney in California.

Starting in 1987, Anne and her husband spent many summer vacations in Turkey, photographing Armenian ruins in Historic Armenia. After her husband's death, Anne continued her studies in History and was granted the M.A. degree in History by California State University Sacramento.

Anne lives in Davis, California.

also by the same author

Churches of Historic Armenia
A Legacy to the World

An Exhibition of color photographs
by Richard A. Elbrecht and
Anne Elizabeth Elbrecht,
presented to the Armenian Studies Program,
California State University, Fresno

http://armenianstudies2.csufresno.edu/
research/churches/index.shtml

ARMENIAN GENOCIDE DOCUMENTATION FROM THE GOMIDAS INSTITUTE
www.gomidas.org

PRIMARY SOURCES

Ara Sarafian (comp., ed. and intro.), *United States Official Records on the Armenian Genocide 1915-1917*

Henry Morgenthau, *United States Diplomacy on the Bosphorus: The Diaries of Ambassador Morgenthau, 1913-1916*

Henry H. Riggs, *Days of Tragedy in Armenia: Personal Experiences in Harpoot, 1915–1917*

James L. Barton, compiler, *"Turkish Atrocities": Statements of American Missionaries on the Destruction of Christian Communities in Ottoman Turkey, 1915–1917*

Bertha Morley, *Marsovan 1915: The Diaries of Bertha Morley*

Tacy Atkinson, *"The German, the Turk and the Devil Made a Triple Alliance:" Harpoot Diaries, 1908–1917*

Maria Jacobsen, *Diaries of a Danish Missionary: Harpoot, 1907–1919*

Carmelite Christie, *Years of Trial and Trepidation: Tarsus, 1915-1920*

James Bryce and Arnold Toynbee, *The Treatment of Armenians in the Ottoman Empire, 1915–1916: Documents Presented to Viscount Grey of Fallodon by Viscount Bryce [Uncensored Edition]*, edited and with an introduction by Ara Sarafian [also available in Turkish]

Vahram Dadrian, *To the Desert: Pages from My Diary*, trans. Agop Hacikyan; ed and intro by Ara Sarafian

Yervant Odian, *Accursed Years: My Exile and Return from Der Zor*, 1914-1919

Aram Andonian, *Exile, Trauma and Death: On the Road to Chankiri with Komitas Vartabed*, transl., ed. and annot. by Rita Soulahian Kuyumjian

KEY SECONDARY SOURCES

Hilmar Kaiser, *At the Crossroads of Der Zor: Death, Survival, and Humanitarian Resistance in Aleppo, 1915–1917*

Paul Leverkuehn, *A German Officer during the Armenian Genocide: A Biography of Max von Scheubner-Richter*, translated by Alasdair Lean with a preface by Jorge Vartparonian and a historical introduction by Hilmar Kaiser.

Rita Soulahian Kuyumjian, *Teotig: Biography* with translation of Teotig's "Monument to April 11" by Ara Stepan Melkonian

www.ingramcontent.com/pod-product-compliance
Lightning Source LLC
Chambersburg PA
CBHW021807220426
43662CB00006B/216